English Language Teachers on the Discursive Faultlines

D1571264

MIX
Paper from
responsible sources

FSC
www.fsc.org

FSC® C014540

NEW PERSPECTIVES ON LANGUAGE AND EDUCATION

Series Editor: Professor Viv Edwards, *University of Reading, Reading, Great Britain*
Series Advisor: Professor Allan Luke, *Queensland University of Technology, Brisbane, Australia*

Two decades of research and development in language and literacy education have yielded a broad, multidisciplinary focus. Yet education systems face constant economic and technological change, with attendant issues of identity and power, community and culture. This series will feature critical and interpretive, disciplinary and multidisciplinary perspectives on teaching and learning, language and literacy in new times.

Full details of all the books in this series and of all our other publications can be found on http://www.multilingual-matters.com, or by writing to Multilingual Matters, St Nicholas House, 31–34 High Street, Bristol BS1 2AW, UK.

English Language Teachers on the Discursive Faultlines

Identities, Ideologies and Pedagogies

Julia Menard-Warwick

MULTILINGUAL MATTERS
Bristol • Buffalo • Toronto

Library of Congress Cataloging in Publication Data
Menard-Warwick, Julia, author.
English Language Teachers on the Discursive Faultlines: Identities, Ideologies and Pedagogies/
Julia Menard-Warwick.
New Perspectives on Language and Education: 35
Includes bibliographical references and index.
1. English language—Study and teaching—Foreign speakers. 2. English language—
Study and teaching—Chile—Foreign speakers—Case studies. 3. English language—
Study and teaching—California—Foreign speakers—Case studies. I. Title. II. Series:
New Perspectives on Language and Education: 35.
PE1128.A2M4275 2014
428.2'4–dc23 2013039326

British Library Cataloguing in Publication Data
A catalogue entry for this book is available from the British Library.

ISBN-13: 978-1-78309-110-2 (hbk)
ISBN-13: 978-1-78309-109-6 (pbk)

Multilingual Matters
UK: St Nicholas House, 31–34 High Street, Bristol BS1 2AW, UK.
USA: UTP, 2250 Military Road, Tonawanda, NY 14150, USA.
Canada: UTP, 5201 Dufferin Street, North York, Ontario M3H 5T8, Canada.

The policy of Multilingual Matters/Channel View Publications is to use papers that are
natural, renewable and recyclable products, made from wood grown in sustainable for-
ests. In the manufacturing process of our books, and to further support our policy, preference is given to printers that have FSC and PEFC Chain of Custody certification. The FSC
and/or PEFC logos will appear on those books where full certification has been granted
to the printer concerned.

Typeset by Techset Composition India (P) Ltd., Bangalore and Chennai, India.
Printed and bound in Great Britain by Short Run Press Ltd.

Contents

Acknowledgments

Thanks to my husband Peter for taking the cover photo, and for journeying with me over the last 30 years, also to him and my children Celsiana and Dashiell for appreciating Chile when we all went there together in 2005. Thanks to Celsiana for helping me understand Bakhtin as a classical scholar. Thanks to Claire for introducing me to the literature on the politics of English language teaching and encouraging me to apply to Fulbright; thanks to Ali for testing my oral proficiency in Spanish (and rating me as 'advanced') when I was in the process of applying; thanks to Claire and Glynda for introducing me to Bakhtin. Thanks to Duane for letting me use his email, and to Kerry for face-to-face and electronic conversations about cultural pedagogy in teacher education. Thanks to Vai for many, many things that led to this book, but specifically for conversations about language ideologies that shaped Chapter 3. Thanks to Aneta for answering a compli-cated Bakhtin question on short notice over email. Thanks to Suresh and his anonymous reviewers from *TESOL Quarterly* for all the thought you put into what became the first half of Chapter 5 as well as bits of Chapter 7. Thanks to my students both in California and Chile whose questions have made me think ever more deeply about these issues, especially my MA students whom I cite in Chapter 7 (Whitney, Kate, Dennis), and my PhD students who have participated in my ongoing dialogue with Bakhtin (Li-fen, Serena, Miki, Anna). Thanks to Sophia, Taylor, Dionne, Cecilia, Katie and Emily for research assistance at various points in the project. Thanks to my Chilean friends and colleagues, some of whom appear in this book under other names, and all of whom have helped me understand the social and educa-tional context of contemporary Chile: Gladys, Jaime, Hildegard, Ana, Justo, Aurora, Daniel, Claudia and Daniela. Thanks to colleagues who shared their thoughts with me at conferences where I presented parts of this research, including AAAL 2007, PacSLRF 2008, TESOL 2011 and LISO 2011. Thanks to all the teachers and prospective teachers in both Chile and California who let me observe their classrooms and answered my interview questions so thoughtfully. This book was made possible by them, and also by funding from the US/Chile Binational Fulbright Commission and from UC Davis. *Gracias a todos, gracias a Dios.* Any errors are my own.

1 English Language Teachers in Sociohistorical Context[1]

English language teaching (ELT) worldwide is increasingly seen as a 'vector' (Markee, 2000) for a suite of cultural practices, ideologies and commodities ranging from free-market capitalism and neoliberal democracy to fast food and rap videos. The consequences of ELT's proliferation have been long debated (Block & Cameron, 2002; Pennycook, 2010; Phillipson, 1992). Almost absent from these debates, strangely, have been the voices of teachers, those directly responsible for mediating the cultural messages of English in specific classroom contexts (but see Phan, 2008). Moreover, few studies compare the tensions around English instruction in international contexts with the similar linguistic and cultural tensions that surface in educational programs serving immigrants in English-dominant countries (Auerbach, 1992; Duff, 2002).

What is a discursive faultline (Kramsch, 1993; Katz, 1999)? On 13 June 2005, the edge of the Nazca plate slid under the South American plate, triggering an earthquake that killed 11 people in the Andes of northern Chile. A day later, and about 10,000 kilometers northwest, off the coast of California, the Gorda plate skidded along the Juan de Fuca plate, triggering tsunami warnings. Although I was in California, packing to leave for Chile, I heard nothing about the Chilean earthquake and little about potential tsunamis, because the news was dominated by the acquittal of pop singer Michael Jackson on child molestation charges. Two weeks later, I was observing an English class at the University of Las Peñas[2] (ULP) in the north of Chile, where a struggling older student gave a brief oral presentation on the Michael Jackson case. His professor, Paloma,[3] responded, 'This was quite the news the day of the earthquake! I think a lot has been said about this. Was it really a fair trial? And you start getting into "was it money?" etc.'

Thus, there are literal faultlines in Chile and California where tectonic plates slide along the Pacific Rim – and other metaphoric faultlines, where tensions, stresses and collisions occur between discourses, which can be defined as competing ways of referring to and evaluating particular topics, such as sexuality, celebrity and the legal system – or ELT, the topic of this book. Almost always these are realized through language, for example, through the use of typical vocabulary, but they often involve visual imagery as well, especially in the news media. Discourses easily cross language boundaries (Risager, 2007) – but also get associated with particular languages, so that language acquisition generally involves the simultaneous encounter with unfamiliar or unsettling discourses, which may be appropriated or resisted.

Theorizing connections between language and power, the great post-structuralist Foucault famously stated, 'Discourse is not simply that which translates struggles or systems of domination, but is the thing for which and by which there is struggle, discourse is the power which is to be seized' (Foucault, 1984: 110). However, in examining encounters between actual speakers in particular historical contexts, it often turns out that discourse(s) are hard to seize, or at least hard to hold onto. They tend to be slippery, constantly in motion and subject to the vagaries of human agency. For this reason, I find the theoretical perspectives of Russian linguistic philosopher and literary scholar Mikhail Bakhtin more useful than French post-structuralism for analyzing language(s) and discourse(s) in my context of research, as I shall explain in Chapter 2. Here I should also mention that along with 'language(s)' and 'discourse(s)', I will often have occasion to use the term 'ideolog(ies)' (as does Bakhtin). Influenced by van Dijk (1998), Fairclough (1992) and contemporary linguistic anthropology as well as Bakhtin, I use *ideology* to refer to beliefs and perceptions linked to power relations between social groups – which may or may not be expressed explicitly as discourses, but often become apparent in taken-for-granted practices (I discuss this in most depth in Chapter 3).

This book is based on interviews with English language teachers and observations of some of their classrooms at a small university in northern Chile and at several community colleges and adult schools in northern California, primarily in 2005 and 2006 (more on this later in the chapter). A central premise of my research is that every instance of language use, and thus language teaching, is 'intrinsically historical' (Blommaert, 2005: 18), and thus must be seen in a historical context (Bakhtin, 1981, 1984, 1986b). In this chapter, I contextualize the place of ELT in Chile and California by discussing the recent histories of both contexts, with special reference to 'discursive faultlines': Chile's transitions between dictatorship and democracy, and California's politics of immigration and ethnicity.

In order to connect history to teacher identity development, I illustrate recent Chilean and Californian history through life history narratives of one Chilean and one Californian English teacher, Diego and Veronica, respectively. I begin the book with the stories of these two teachers, Diego and Veronica, because their life history narratives intersect most explicitly with the historical currents that shaped the identities of all the teachers in this study. Rather than trying to cover each teacher's entire life history, I focus on narratives that illustrate how the sociohistorical contexts of Chile and California in recent decades have influenced the linguistic and cultural identities of English teachers. Having thus situated my research in its sociohistorical context, I will explain how I came to conduct this study, detail its aims and focus and give an overview of the contents of each chapter.

My analysis of the narratives in this chapter is primarily thematic rather than discursive (Riessman, 2008). Nevertheless, while looking more at content than linguistic resources, I try to never lose sight of the fact that 'stories (are) co-constructed...discursive constructions that are situated in a specific place in history' (Vitanova, 2010: 31, citing Pavlenko). Specifically, I examine teacher identity construction in the narratives, defining identity as a negotiation over time between the social positions that individuals claim for themselves and those they are assigned by their interlocutors (Blackledge & Pavlenko, 2001). Seeing identity as *negotiated* entails the recognition that language teacher identities develop in connection with the social contexts where they have learned, used and taught languages (Varghese *et al.*, 2005).

In sharing Diego's narratives of Chile and Veronica's of California, I leave out most back-channeling, false starts and repetitions (this is my practice throughout the book). I use pseudonyms to talk about the regions of Chile and California where I conducted my study: Las Peñas for the city and university where I have worked in northern Chile, and Farmington for the urban–suburban–rural region of northern California where I live and teach, and which contains several cities and numerous educational institutions.

Chilean History: Diego

Diego was born in 1959 in northern Chile; when I interviewed him on 13 July 2006, he had lived in that region all his life. His parents were from northern Chile, but both his grandfathers were *guasos* (cowboys) from southern Chile, while one grandmother came from an indigenous community in Bolivia. At that time, he had three positions teaching English in the city of Las Peñas, at a private high school, a public adult school and as a university adjunct. He was also working on his Masters in English Teaching at the ULP. In 2005, he had been my student in an intensive Masters class on Second Language Acquisition, and at the time of the interview, he was about to become my student again, in a class entitled Language and Cultural Identity.

When I first got to know Diego in 2005, he told me he had traveled to Russia as a child, and also gone on a teacher exchange to Iowa in 2004. He had spoken at length about the Iowa trip, and now a year later, I wanted him to articulate its influence on his English teacher identity:

Julia: Umm, any other kinds of experiences you've had, with English, or with other cultures... uhh, you went to Iowa, right?
Diego: Oh yes, yes.
Julia ((overlapping)): Could you tell me about that experience?
Diego: When I was 13 years old? In July, August, I don't remember, I was chosen as the best student in my primary school. And I receive a grant from...you know at that time? The president was Salvador Allende?
Julia: Yeah.
Diego: Mmhmm ((pause)). So my school received a grant from Russia. A trip. To visit Russia. So I travelled. I travelled to Russia. At that time I was there for 30 days. Visiting several communities in Russia.

Before he could describe his trip to Iowa as a middle-aged school-teacher, Diego needed to tell me about his first experience with 'English or with other cultures'. He had already mentioned that he was born in 1959, so when he said he was 13 and the month was July or August, he was perhaps expecting me to do the math like a Chilean, to realize that he was talking about 1973, in the last month or two before the military coup in September. To make sure I was following him, he mentioned the name of the president at that time, Salvador Allende, the socialist who was democratically elected in 1970 and then overthrown by his own military, under General Augusto Pinochet. Diego did not know, and was too polite to ask, where I stood on the question of Allende, or even how much I knew about Chilean history. My presence in Chile was partly funded by the US government via the Fulbright Commission; I was in Chile on a US passport, and thus as an 'American'[4]; the US government under Richard Nixon had been complicit in the coup that put Pinochet in power for the next 17 years (Loveman, 2001; Qureshi, 2009). Diego was clarifying why he went to Russia: Chile had briefly been part of the socialist world. It went unstated that his government and mine had been temporarily on opposite sides of the Cold War.

Having introduced this story, Diego went on to recount memories of Soviet Communism:

Diego: And I remember I visited the Red Square? Plaza Roja? That's nice in English, Red Square?
Julia: Yeah. Red Square, uh huh.
Diego: And I didn't know what was going on there. And then we stood in line? And there was a building, mausoleum I think, and we toured, we make a tour around, and there was the body, the corpse?
Julia: Yeah, the body, yeah, yeah.
Diego: The body of Lenin there. Frozen ((laughs)). Wow! ((laughing)) Like that ((gestures)). He was with his left hand...
Julia: Ah, in a fist.
Diego: In a fist.
Julia: Uh huh ((laughing)).
Diego: Very interesting. Something's going on here, something's going to happen here. Well, that was the experience when I was a kid.

In telling me this story, Diego is not confident of the English words for certain things: Red Square, the body of Lenin, Lenin's fist, so I co-construct this narrative with him, during which he embodies the frozen corpse of Lenin by clenching his own fist. We both laugh. His evaluation is briefly serious, 'very interesting...something's going to happen here', but he dismisses this reaction as a child's view. Then I had another question:

Julia: How did you communicate with people?
Diego: English.
Julia: English? So you took what little bit of English you knew then...
Diego: Yes, I...we had time for about three months to prepare in English, I was in primary school. I had a teacher, a teacher of English, I didn't learn a lot with the teacher, but I learnt a lot when I was there...
Julia ((overlapping)): Because you had to use it...
Diego ((overlapping)): When I was...I had to. Communicate things.
Julia: Yeah.
Diego: So 'how do you say that, how do I say that? OK.' So I started, you know, it was communicative.
Julia: Oh, yeah!
Diego: Really communicative. So I think those influenced, when I was in...when I arrived in university.

This is where Diego's trip to Soviet Russia in 1973 connects to his identity as an English teacher. Even at the height of Soviet power, in the heart of the Soviet empire, English was the lingua franca in which socialist children from around the world were expected to communicate. As contemporary language teachers, Diego and I share our evaluation of the importance of communication for language acquisition: 'it was communicative.' 'oh yeah!' 'really communicative' (Savignon, 1983). Then he remembered the museums:

Diego: Lots of museums, because I…we went to a museum of astronomy. It was the first time, it was in 1973, and we were in the museum, we got together in groups of ten and they say, 'OK, this ten, go inside this room.' Completely dark. And then the lights turned on, it was like uhh, you are in space.
Julia: Yeah. Like a planetarium.
Diego: It was a planetarium. And I didn't know that. Beautiful. Amazing. Very nice. Good technology. At that time, 1973, we didn't have that kind of technology in Chile. […] So, many, many things that I never imagined I could, you know, experience.
Julia: Yeah. Do you think that inspired you to keep learning more about languages and experiencing other cultures?
Diego ((overlapping)): Yeah, absolutely, absolutely. I was very lucky ((laughs)).

Chileans often draw discursive connections between English and advanced technologies, so this incited my question on whether the planetarium had led him to language learning. He told me about traveling home via Cuba, and then he began to talk about Iowa:

Diego: Well, then I took the chance when I was forty three years old. Yeah, I was very old when I took the chance to go to the United States.
Julia: So between the time you went on this trip to the Soviet Union and Cuba…you were in Chile straight through till you were 43 pretty much…
Diego: ((overlapping, laughing)) I couldn't…because when I travelled to Russia, we arrived here in August ((pause)). And in September we had the…political trauma.

I simply wished to clarify whether Diego had other foreign travel experiences, but my comment triggered the memory of the coup, 'in September we had the …political trauma'. Although the dictatorship did not prohibit foreign travel, nevertheless, Diego subjectively experienced this as a time of closed borders, an era when Chile was separated from the world. To answer my question, he recounts the erasure of his nascent global citizenship:

Diego: So all the stuff that I brought from Russia, lots of books. . .They disappeared.
Julia: Your parents had to get rid of them, or?
Diego: ((overlapping)) It was very dangerous!
Julia: Yeah.
Diego: Very dangerous. One of my teachers, the art teacher, Valenzuela, I remember his surname, he said, 'Diego. . .' I was in eighth grade. He said, 'Diego, I want to talk to you. It's urgent ((pause)). So you can go to my house?' And when I was there he say, 'Diego? Everything that you brought from Russia? Burn it. Don't even hide it. Burn it.'
Julia: Wow.
Diego: And I did.

Similarly, Diego told me that the school principal made all the records disappear. His parents were anxious, but never actually found themselves in political trouble. There was a local conspiracy of silence and forgetting, which protected Diego's family from problems with the military. As Gómez-Barris writes, 'historical processes of memory making and forgetting. . .are often symbolic strategies that assist in the process of smoothing over painful memories on the path toward national unity' (Gómez-Barris, 2009: 4–5; cf Moulián, 1997); Diego's story perhaps shows how these processes start as pragmatic strategies for survival under oppression. In Diego's case, the operation of the national process of forgetting was what allowed him to take on the identity of an English teacher for the Chilean military years later:

Diego: Well my mom was absolutely very worried about what was happening with us because she, 'You travelled to ( ) Russia.' Fortunately, it was nice. Well, I have nothing against the military people. Because I never had problems. When I finished my studies in the university, I started working for the military people.
Julia: Ahh. Teaching English?
Diego: Teaching English. Uh huh. I still do [at the adult school].

When we finally started talking about Diego's Iowa trip, he explained it as a project in the *Diplomado* (diploma) *de Emprendimiento* in the university. I asked what Emprendimiento meant, and he replied, 'To be a businessman, you know, to have business, to be alert about how you can get more, how you can make more money.' When I looked this up on the internet, I found that English speakers in online forums had been asking the same question, and receiving as an answer 'enterprise' or 'entrepreneurship'. This brings us to Chile in the 1990s, the conditions under which the country returned to democracy, and how 'enterprise' connects not only to English teaching but also to a more globalized English teacher identity, now claimed by Diego.

As Chile's Minister of Education told the New York Times, 'We know that our lives are linked more than ever to an international presence, and if you can't speak English, you can't sell, and you can't learn' (Rohter, 2004). This is a good example of the worldwide discourse that links the English teaching profession to global capitalism; at the same time, as Holborow points out (2012a), there are material causes and consequences connected to this discourse. In 2006, the year of my interview with Diego, Chile exported a total of 5220 products, worth nearly 56 billion in US dollars to 185 countries, its main trading partners being the United States, Japan and China (PROChile, 2007). This participation in the global marketplace is taken for granted by many Chileans. Nevertheless, social critics note that the current economic model was imposed on Chile by disciples of US economist Milton Friedman, referred to (in English) as the 'Chicago boys' (Hojman, 1993) during the dictatorship. Economic policy since Pinochet has prioritized favorable conditions for international business through 'privatization of public activity, deregulation of private activity, and production primarily for export and fiscal austerity' (Hershberg & Rosen, 2006: 7). These policies are based on neoliberal ideology, which 'begins with the premise that freedom of choice and the rational calculation of economic actors...is the principle underlying human behaviour' (Bell Lara & López, 2007: 18).

Although this economic model was imposed by a dictatorship which did not otherwise value 'freedom of choice', Chile's transition from dictatorship to democracy in 1990 came as the result of a national 'consensus' forged between diverse political parties who were willing to keep in place Pinochet's economic policies in return for democratization (Drake & Jaksic, 1999; Arrate & Rojas, 2003). The Chilean economy is generally considered 'successful'; in their critique of neoliberalism in Latin America, Hershberg and Rosen write, 'economic performance has been disappointing almost everywhere except, perhaps, Chile' (Hershberg & Rosen, 2006: 3), but then add that Chile continues to suffer social stratification. While economic inequity has eased slightly over the last two decades, in 2010, the elite upper quintile of the Chilean population enjoyed 58% of the income (compared with 60% in 1990 at the end of the dictatorship), while the bottom quintile of the population survived on 4% of the income (up from 3% in 1990).[5] According to Chilean social critic Tomás Moulián, writing in the early years of democracy (1997), the 'inevitability' of the neoliberal model under democracy suppressed public debate on national goals, with Chile becoming a nation of consumers rather than citizens.

In neoliberal society, where individuals are considered responsible for their own destinies without support or coercion from the state (Hershberg & Rosen, 2006), social entrepreneurship (i.e. emprendimiento) becomes key to positive lifestyle changes (Holborow, 2012b). The teacher exchange project in which Diego participated received grant funding because it exemplified ideas current in Chile about the importance of learning English to become part of the globalized world. He spent January 2004 in rural Iowa:

> **Diego**: You know, for me, Julia, being 43 years old, it was really a dream, because we didn't have such opportunities when I studied in university. [...] So I was like a kid, enjoying every every every meter of the United States! Absolutely! It was summertime in Las Peñas, and it was wintertime in the United States, you see that? The only time when [we] can see snow is in a Christmas card.
>
> **Julia**: Ahh.
>
> **Diego**: You see that? But when we were arriving into Cedarville[6] it was cloudy, and then we saw that everything was covered with snow. Pine trees covered with snow the same as Christmas cards? It was beautiful. Really beautiful. They have decorations, Christmas decorations, some of the houses, because it was January, January the 10th. There were many beautiful decorations. It was nice. I mean, the freezing air, there's nothing compared with that, thirty, minus thirty degrees.

In the excerpt above, I have omitted a lengthy account of all the airports the teachers passed through. For me, flying between Farmington, California and Las Peñas, Chile is a taken-for-granted ordeal of little sleep, bad food and cramped seats. For Diego, this was a wonderful experience of gradually being surrounded by English, and finally ending up in a town that looked like a 'Christmas card' – given that everywhere in the globalized world, Christmas looks like a snowy New England village. Diego found the Iowans to be kind and friendly. In an essay he wrote for my 2006 seminar, he happily remembered ice-fishing:

> I learned several names of strange fishes, and lots of words connected to this activity, and this saying: 'A bad day of fishing is still better than a good day at the office!' All the friends there played jokes on me about the

guy who came from the driest desert in the world and was now dying from cold there in the middle of the frozen river.

However, he was really there to help in Spanish classes, and to share with these small-town Midwesterners an experience of a different world:

> **Diego**: We were kind of an assistant to the ( ) teacher [...] And I interacted...I made presentations in primary school, and in high school. Primary school was nicest for me, because I made a presentation to a second grade, very small kids. And I talked about Las Peñas, I talked about the valley of Las Peñas, about the fruit that grow here, about the weather, that it never rains here, we don't have snow. So at the end of the class, the teacher gave every student a piece of paper, and say, 'Now you're going to draw what Teacher Diego talked about.' So they draw tomatoes, olives, beaches, and they stuck it, you know, on the wall, because it was beautiful. Very nice.

For Diego, the Iowans' interest in him was gratifying, affirming his identity as a globalized language teaching professional valued across national contexts, as well as reinforcing his Chilean national identity and specifically his local Las Peñas identity. However, he valued more the things he could learn from them:

> **Diego**: And well, the technology is amazing in the United States, I love that. The way I say that...when I came back from the United States, I was speeding at 200 kilometers an hour. Because I wanted to change things, I wanted to do things.
> **Julia**: For example?
> **Diego**: ((overlapping)) And my colleagues say, 'hey, Teacher Diego, relax, take it easy, this is Chile, what are you talking about? You can't change everything.' Because we waste time here. In my class ( ) I say, 'We don't waste time, let's go into the class immediately, why waste time? What are we doing, waiting in line for ten or fifteen minutes??'
> **Julia**: ((overlapping)) Oh, waiting in line. Wow.
> **Diego**: 'Why is that?' I have with my fourth [year class in] high school, I have only three periods of English, and one of the periods, when I have 45 minutes, 15 minutes and I am waiting in line. And why is that? Let's go and meet in my room. OK. But I am not going to say that any more because I was about to be kicked out.
> **Julia**: Wow.
> **Diego**: You see that? 'OK, don't worry. No more ideas from Teacher Diego. That's fine. Let's go on moving the same way.' ((pause)) I wanted to do many things.

Having students line up, with good order and discipline, before the beginning of each class period, is a traditional practice in Chilean schools. As Diego notes, it can take 15 minutes for unruly adolescents to get into a straight line. While this practice undoubtedly pre-dates the Pinochet dictatorship, it also exemplifies its values. As Diego points out, lining up steals time from academic activities. This is precisely the kind of lesson that the funders of the teacher exchange project were hoping to inculcate: there are educational practices in English-speaking countries that Chilean teachers can borrow as the nation competes in the globalized world. From this neoliberal ideological perspective, teachers need to take on the identity of 'change agents'. From the perspective of Diego's old-fashioned administrators, such change is unacceptable; for Diego, it is not worth losing his job.

Thus, under Chilean democracy, it is possible to have foreign travel experiences and unorthodox opinions and to share them, but it still remains difficult to be an 'agent of change' within institutions that are still imbued with the practices of dictatorship, practices that embody the ideology that discipline and order are more valuable than actual learning. Both English teaching and *emprendimiento* support the neoliberal push to embrace global values of individualism and efficiency. However, on these particular faultlines, where pedagogical efficiency collides with traditional ideologies of good order, neoliberalism loses out and Diego is not able to fully claim an identity as a globalized English-teaching professional.

Nevertheless, since media censorship ended in 1990 with the dictatorship, and especially since the advent of the internet, the global free market has flooded the country with a vast array of cultural products promoting lifestyles and values that would have been unthinkable to most Chileans in the 1980s. Rapid cultural change has erased any clear sense of continuity with the Pinochet era. At the same time, just as standing in line to enter class continues to embody conservative ideologies, global popular culture consumption pre-dates the current era. Even more than his trip to Russia, Diego credits his interest in English to The Beatles:

> **Diego**: I remember that I was influenced when I was in high school for all the music coming from Great Britain, in English, so I wanted to learn about the lyrics. [...] And you know, it was very hard to get lyrics at that time. You know, those people who were able to get the lyrics, they were, like you know, gods.
> **Julia**: Uh huh ((laughing)).
> **Diego ((imitating teenagers))**: 'You got the lyrics? The lyrics? *Strawberry Fields Forever?* Ohh, what is this? Forever and ever. Ohh, that's...Ohh, you're tremendous. How did you get it?' 'You know,

I got it because my brother lived in London, and he sent me a letter.'
'Ohh, that's amazing!' [...] So everything started because of the
music. [...] Well in the first place the Beatles played popular things,
you know? But then I realized that John Lennon? He was very...
like...he was very sharp, with good lyrics. So he was...you know, I
was entering in a new world, about poetry, things like that.

Diego uses reported speech to reconstruct the youthful identities of himself and his friends, and the blissful tone of these adolescent voices indicates
the prestige of English-language popular music in his subculture. This sets
the context for explaining how 'everything' (his career, his life up to now)
'started because of the music'. In this way, he connects his developing identity as an English learner and teacher to what might be considered the identity of a thoughtful global citizen, who appreciates John Lennon not only for
his music but also for his artistic use of language ('poetry') and for the intelligence of his lyrics ('he was very sharp'). Diego does not mention the leftist
political content of those 'sharp' lyrics, but I think I can assume that he
would assume my awareness of Lennon's politics.

The Beatles were mentioned to me as influential by a number of Chilean
English teachers over 40; another British rock group popular with both
older and younger teachers (including Diego) was Pink Floyd. While the
dictatorship apparently allowed Beatles music (at least no one complained
to me that they didn't), Pink Floyd's 1982 film *The Wall* suffered censorship,
as Diego explains:

Diego: Uhh, [in *The Wall*] there is about 20 minutes, they are referring
to military people. You seen that? So it was not allowed, the movie to be
seen in Chile. OK. But you know what happened? I was in high school.
You know what happened? The movie...we could see the movie in
[Peru]. ((laughing)): So we travelled to [Peru]. And we saw the movie
there. No problem!

Thus, despite the restrictions of the dictatorship, Diego depicts himself
participating in global popular culture, 'no problem!' He is not overtly resisting, or even making a political critique, merely claiming the right to consume
Pink Floyd's music by circumventing rather than opposing the Pinochet regime.
Thus, to some extent, Diego constructs himself as an apolitical and pragmatic
global citizen, as ELT professionals have been wont to do (Pennycook, 1994) –
while at the same time *ambiguating* this construction by highlighting the leftist
political content of the media product that he went to some trouble to enjoy.
In any case, Pinochet's media censorship is clearly contrary to contemporary

ideologies of consumer empowerment through globalization. As one teacher described the Chilean media under dictatorship: 'Movies were cut, the news were like filtered and selected, and all the programs, the language that they used on television was very careful, very formal, there wasn't much space for improvisation' (Alán interview). Thus, the end of censorship, along with the advent of the internet and cable television, facilitated Chileans' consumption of global media and their construction of global citizen identities.

Over decades, Diego has constructed his English teacher identity through positioning himself as an active participant in the globalized world, a position that was restricted under Pinochet, but which he has nonetheless maintained throughout his life. Although research into teacher identity in TESOL has often highlighted the way non-native English-speaking teachers are marginalized in the profession (Morgan, 2004), Diego's complex relationship with English cannot be reduced to the fact that he first encountered the language in adolescence. His English-language identity has been shaped by encounters with world socialism in 1973 and global *emprendimiento* in 2004 – both of which were facilitated by the use of English, and both of which reinforced his attraction to the language and to international participation.

As Varghese *et al.* wrote, Diego's teacher identity is 'not context-free but (rather)...related to social, cultural, and political context(s)' (Varghese *et al.*, 2005: 23) in which he has learned and taught English. Chilean history, as it flirted with socialism and then embraced free-market capitalism, propelled him on these journeys to Moscow and Cedarville. Ideologies of individual empowerment that connect the global marketplace with English teaching have shaped his thinking, despite his fairly conventional lifestyle as a small-town schoolteacher. Moreover, Diego's identity, my own identity and our relationship to each other have been shaped by our participation in the imagined global community (Kanno & Norton, 2003) of English language teachers, who share practices and discourses, such as the value of 'communication' in language learning (Savignon, 1983).

California History: Veronica

Veronica was born in the late 1950s in San Francisco to an Anglo-American mother and German-American father. An adult convert to Judaism, she claims a Jewish as well as an Anglo identity. When I interviewed her, 6 January 2006, she was teaching high school English in the Farmington area. I had met her the previous fall at an adult-school Spanish class; I decided to interview her because of her efforts to learn the language of her Latino

English as a Second Language (ESL) students (data from this interview also appears in Menard-Warwick, 2011b). In the interview, I first asked about her family background, and learned that she was raised in poverty by a single mother, who was a Scientologist – one of many stereotypically Californian alternative religious groups (Starr, 2004). The family moved frequently in her childhood, including sojourns in England, the South and the Midwest. Having established that Veronica knew only English in her childhood, I asked her my standard question, 'could you tell me about your experiences learning second languages?'

Veronica: Well, what happened, ((pause)) we left L-, we ended up in Los Angeles in the seventies, in 1970, 69, and I went to school, and all of a sudden that was my first experience meeting Latinos, and in the part of Los Angeles we lived in was a huge section Central American community, El Salvadoran community, and lots of good food and neighbors speaking Spanish and English, so that was really fascinating to me, that all, and my classroom, it was the most integrated, beautiful classroom in 69 and 70.
Julia: Mmhmm.
Veronica: My sixth grade classroom, people, Asian, Latino, white, just a huge mix, and no one kind of outweighing anyone, we were all really pretty well even, and we got along really well, in terms of that, and then (there were) kids (that) spoke Spanish, and there was a boy from Germany oddly enough, (Wolfy) we called him, and then a boy brand new from Korea who didn't speak any English, so a very interesting community, and a really good teacher, who made everyone feel safe and comfortable in (this) public school...
Julia ((overlapping)): Mmhmm, Mmhmm.
Veronica: ... hodgepodge, we lived near um Macarthur Park, and um, it's a really run-down scary place now, but in 69 and 70, it was still very nice, you know, (average) working class families...Things were cheap, but um...((pause)) So my first experience of, a direct experience with Spanish, actually was a boy who had a crush on me, named Jesús [Spanish pronunciation], [...] and he'd come to my house, and he'd go 'Verónicaaaaa' [Spanish pronunciation] and I'd look out the window and he and three of his buddies would be on their little Stingrays [bicycle model], 'Verónicaaaaa' [Spanish pronunciation] [...]. So it didn't, I didn't have a compulsion to really learn those languages, but I loved the sound and the experience of those languages around me.

California became a majority minority state in the year 2000, when the 'non-Hispanic white' population dipped below 50%. In 1970, when Veronica finished sixth grade, the 'non-Hispanic white' population was still a large majority statewide, about 15.5 million out of 20 million Californians, roughly 78% (California Department of Finance Demographic Research Unit, 2007). However, Veronica's description of the Los Angeles neighborhood where she arrived in late elementary school suggests that it was a harbinger of the diversity to come. On the 2010 census, out of a total state population which had risen to 37 million, white Californians (non-Hispanic) had dropped numerically to just under 15 million, or about 40% of all Californians. These changes and more are chronicled in the following table (California Department of Finance Demographic Research Unit, 2011):

Race/ethnicity[7]	1970 percent of California population (approximate)	2010 percent of California population (approximate)
(Non-Hispanic) White	78	40
Black	7	6
Hispanic	12.5	38
Asian	3	13
Native American	1	0.5

In answering my question, Veronica's first thought is to talk about her first experience of studying Spanish, which happened after her family left Los Angeles. However, to explain why she chose Spanish, she first has to explain Los Angeles in 1970, where she experienced a utopia of diversity in her sixth grade classroom: 'Asian, Latino, white, just a huge mix, and no one kind of outweighing anyone, we were all really pretty well even....' For Veronica, in memory, this was a 'very interesting community', presided over by 'a really good teacher, who made everyone feel safe and comfortable in this public school' – and where her first boyfriend pronounced her name in Spanish, courting her from atop his Stingray bicycle. Veronica's description of her happy Los Angeles experience constitutes her initial claim to a multicultural California identity. Meanwhile, my 'mmmhmms' ratify this claim, and reassure her that she is 'on track' in answering my question about why she decided to learn Spanish.

Veronica's depiction of her sixth grade classroom also represents the promise of California, where people from all over the world seek a place to live in harmony and find opportunity, believing that:

In the tolerant atmosphere of a new frontier, where there (is) enough land and opportunity to go around, virtually everyone (is) welcomed, and different ethnic groups (relate) to one another harmoniously. (Rice et al., 2002: 3–4)

However, as these authors entitle their history, California is an *'elusive Eden'* (italics mine), as represented in Veronica's narrative by the fate of this Los Angeles neighborhood, 'it's a really run-down scary place now'. In the 1980s and 1990s, Los Angeles became famous for drug crime, gang wars and riots. As Rice *et al.* go on to describe California's heritage of diversity over 150 years of state history, 'Persistent inequality, attempts by groups to subordinate others, and intergroup tension...have been major themes' (Rice *et al.*, 2002: 7). ·

California's dominant libertarian ideology, similar to the neoliberal beliefs current in Chile, asserts that 'people (succeed) through diligence and intelligence...and (fail) because of their own weakness' (Rice *et al.*, 2002: 3) – and moreover, that government regulation or taxation limits opportunity. Thus, it has been common in California over the last several decades for 'celebrations of rights, freedom, opportunity and equality (to sustain)...patterns of racial domination' (HoSang, 2009: 2), such as persistent inequality of resources in public schooling. California is a state where much public policy comes in the form of voter initiatives, a process by which any group with sufficient passion and funding can place measures on the ballot for voter consideration (Allswang, 2000; HoSang, 2009). HoSang as well as Jacobson (2008) argue that voter initiatives on racially charged issues construct (not merely reflect) racial attitudes in California: 'generating racial meanings and forging racialized political communities' (HoSang, 2009: 4).

In a trend that perhaps began in the 1950s but accelerated in the 1970s, many white families moved their children out of Los Angeles schools (HoSang, 2009), citing racially charged issues such as crime and declining public education. In her interview, Veronica mentioned the rising crime rate ('it was getting scarier, and we'd been robbed') as the reason why her mother decided to move out of the city into Orange County, the vast suburban area to the south, around the time she started Spanish in high school:

> **Veronica**: I struggled academically, and I struggled socially, because we were raised as Scientologists, we were kind of outsiders, and then we moved at that time, to Orange County, and that was hell for me. It was so startling to be in this pure white land, kind of ((pause)) [...] where I was teased for being completely different from everyone else, even though I looked like everyone else, and we had a different religion than everyone else, it just was horrible, you know, and by the time I got to ninth grade, I signed up for my Spanish class, and I ended up dropping out of high school.

In Veronica's experience, the lack of ethnic diversity in Orange County in the 1970s translated into suburban residents' lack of appreciation for all types of diversity, including religious diversity. She came to associate whiteness ('the pure white land') with bigotry. Her first experience of learning Spanish ended quickly when she dropped out of high school. In the next two years, she 'hung out' with adults in Scientology communities, studied on her own, worked and saved money to fulfil a dream of traveling to France. She eventually spent a year in Paris, studying French, living with a French boyfriend and constructing a personally satisfying cosmopolitan identity. Her French teacher's pedagogy made a strong impression, and continues to influence her ideas about effective language learning:

Veronica: I had this wonderful, wonderful great teacher, so it was a beautiful, beautiful experience.
Julia: What happened in class? What kinds of things did you do?
Veronica: He, um, well I just remember the first he said, ( ), my French is, I've lost a bit, '*C'est une plume,*' you know, '*Ahh, une plume!*' you know, '*Une chaise, une chaise,*'[8] so we started out like that, but he never dared speak, he didn't speak a word of English ever, so it was a complete immersion, and we started with just the basic vocabulary, and [...] we learned really quickly, and he did some writing with us, and some grammar [...] You know, [the teacher] was like the master controller, he was such a sweet man, though, so it was a beautiful, beautiful supportive experience.

Thus, Veronica's first successful language learning occurred with a teacher who spoke only French in class, who 'never dared speak, didn't speak a word of English ever', and who made himself understood by using classroom objects like chairs and pens. She evaluates this French immersion very highly as a 'beautiful supportive experience'.
Meanwhile, she was also using French outside the classroom, getting to know French people, and thinking about her own identity as an American:

Veronica: This is what people said, now I remember, they said, 'You know, you don't seem American to us' [...] so at first they would always assume actually that I was Canadian or British [...] ((pause)) but um, so there was that, 'You're not like a typical' and I also, that made me feel good, that I didn't stick out like a sore thumb like (gross) typical Americans, but in a certain way, I always felt separate from America, or separate from white America, or separate from mainstream America, because I grew up outside of it. [...] But people were open, people were really open to me, because they were curious why I'd be there by myself, they were impressed that I was taking the time to learn the language.

Using her minimal French to interact with French people, seeing herself through their eyes, Veronica's national identity as an 'American' became salient to her, but it also became important not to embody French stereo-types of 'gross typical Americans'. She realized she had always felt 'sepa-rate from America' because of her non-traditional upbringing – she first specifies this sense of alienation in terms of race ('separate from white America'), but then clarifies this more as 'separate from mainstream America'. From her perspective, this separation led to the acceptance she felt from French people, as an atypical American girl who was taking time to get to know their language and culture. Although she does not explicitly compare this to her Orange County alienation, the contrast is clear. After discussing further travel experiences, I finally brought the topic back to Spanish:

Julia: So how did you learn Spanish?
Veronica: Well what happened, I was going to school, getting my B.A., and then I stayed in L.A. [Los Angeles] and got my credential. David [Veronica's partner] lives up here, so at the end of my credential, I moved up here and started applying for jobs to be an English literature teacher, regular English literature teacher, and Farmington was the first to respond, and the person, hiring person, said, 'Would you be interested in teaching ELD?? (because) we need ELD teachers,' and I went 'Yeah!' without hesitation, because that went 'click' for me, and (then) it's like my whole life was preparing me to do that.

Although Veronica had trained to be a 'regular' English teacher, she depicts the suggestion that she teach ELD as a vocational epiphany: a career option that connects not only to her interest in languages but also to her identification with immigrant communities, sophisticated Europeans and indeed almost anyone outside the US mainstream.

Since the 1970s, as the California populace has diversified, the state's policy context has increasingly come to enforce 'the mainstream' as the legal norm – with standardized English as the linguistic norm. Woolard (1989) chronicles this process in (famously 'liberal' and 'progressive') San Francisco in 1983 when a citywide voter initiative banned multilingual ballots. Proponents convinced a majority of voters that requiring all citizens to use English-Only ballots would 'free language minorities from the "illusion" that they could become fully empowered citizens without learning English' (HoSang, 2009: 136). A similar measure was passed statewide in 1984, based partly on the argument that multilingual ballots are unfair to taxpayers (HoSang, 2009: 141).

A 1986 initiative proclaimed English the state's official language. This had little direct effect, and a 2009 US census estimate found that 43.1% of Californians spoke a language besides English at home (Statistical Abstract of the United States, 2012). However, many monolingual Californians continue to find societal multilingualism disturbing. In Jacobson's analysis, proponents of English-Only initiatives in California saw 'linguistic, moral, and cultural homogeneity' as essential 'to maintaining a functioning democracy' (Jacobson, 2008: 90). The English-Only initiatives helped to build an anti-immigrant political movement, which was able to pass more stringent ballot measures in the 1990s.

In 1994, Proposition 187 prohibited undocumented immigrants from accessing state services, including education, and required teachers and medical personnel to report suspected 'illegal aliens' to law enforcement. Proponents again stressed 'fairness' to taxpayers (Jacobson, 2008: 267), but the initiative was widely seen as targeting Latinos. After a contentious campaign centered in Orange County (Jacobson, 2008), it passed by strong margins, but much of it was overturned in court. Then in 1998, Proposition 227 severely restricted bilingual education, requiring students (with few exceptions) to be educated entirely in English. Thus, ELD programs for 'newcomers', such as the one that hired Veronica, became increasingly widespread in California around the turn of the millennium. Without training in either ELD or bilingual education, and in a policy context that encouraged English-Only teaching, Veronica was initially unconcerned about her lack of Spanish:

> **Veronica**: I was this brand new teacher, and I had newcomers, and I was very excited about that, because I remember (that) in France, you didn't need to have English to teach, you know, I figured I'd just teach, speak in English, I didn't need Spanish.

Thus, Veronica drew on memories of her French-only class in Paris in the 1970s to formulate her ideas about effective second language (L2) pedagogies for newcomer high school students in California in the 2000s. Unlike many California teachers, however, she soon had second thoughts about an English monolingual approach to ELD:

> **Veronica**: I thought, 'Oh well, I maybe should know how to speak Spanish, so I could speak to people, parents at least.' So at the time that I started teaching, I enrolled at Farmington Community College. […]

and then went to Ensenada that summer for an immersion experience for two weeks, and I picked up enough Spanish very quickly to be able to communicate with parents, by the end of my first year, I could pick up the phone and call a parent.

She explained that she still finds Spanish helpful although she is no longer teaching newcomers, instead a mixed class of advanced language learners and native English speakers:

> **Veronica**: Yeah, and some of them, I have one class where I have some more recently arrived students who are really accelerated, so they're fun to work with [. . .]. And what's cool is when they figure out that I understand (them) when they're speaking Spanish, it's kind of this instant trust in me, and then I call their parents, and then they're like, 'Ah, damn' ((laughing)).

Thus, for Veronica, having an identity as a Spanish-speaking teacher helps her to affiliate with Latino students, who trust her more when they know she speaks Spanish, even though they could communicate with her in English. However, this affiliation with students is in tension with her original goal for learning Spanish, to communicate better with her students' parents (because the students fear that she will use the language to report their bad behavior). Moreover, despite Veronica's efforts to learn and use Spanish, she still values English-Only pedagogy:

> **Veronica**: What's interesting is I felt like I become a, became a less effective ELD teacher as my Spanish got better, so I really had to make myself not speak Spanish,
> **Julia**: Mmhmm, Mmhmm.
> **Veronica**: in the classroom, ultimately, once it was there, and not respond to kids who were speaking Spanish to me.

From this perspective, bilingualism is useful for building trust with students and talking to parents, but gets in the way of effective ELD pedagogy, which in Veronica's understanding depends on L2 communication. This is similar to the perspective that Diego and I co-constructed above about the communicative approach (Savignon, 1983). When I asked Veronica to elaborate on her support for English-Only pedagogy, however, she continued speaking about her recent assignment to teach classes that mix advanced English learners with monolingual English speakers. Although using her third language in English-Only California gives her a sense of rapport with Spanish-speaking Latino students, she has no means of building similar connections with students from her own ethnic background:

> **Veronica**: I have a class where I have five girls, one's like Kirsten, Karly, Kelly, five K-names, ((Julia laughing)) and then they're kind of blonde (blue-eyed) girls. [...] These girls, I kept calling (one of them), 'Come on Kirsten, wake up,' and she says, 'I'm not Kirsten, I'm Karly!'
> **Julia**: Uh-huh ((laughing))
> **Veronica**: and finally one day, because I just had had it, because they're so kind of (snippy), I went, 'I'm sorry, but all you white girls look alike!' ((Julia and Veronica laughing)) [...] I couldn't find the way past what seemed all the same to me in them, and I think that's linked to my feeling growing up as a complete outsider.

Thus, just as teaching immigrants connects to pleasant childhood memories of multiethnic Los Angeles, Veronica links her sense of alienation from the 'white girls' to her adolescent identity as an outsider in all-white Orange County, a disconnect that she refers to as 'cultural shock'. Discomforted by the assumption of cultural sameness, she constructs for herself an imaginary community (Kanno & Norton, 2003) of California multiculturalism in her spare time:

> **Veronica**: I've been finding like detective novels written by Icelandic writers and things [....] We see a lot of foreign films. [...] I keep looking at these Israeli films that look interesting, I've gone to see a few at [theatre], but there's some that are now starting to show up on video that we can look into renting... Germany, Iceland, Israeli, [...] and then food, which is the best, you know, ((laughing)) food from different places...
> **Julia**: Do you cook food from different places, or?
> **Veronica**: We cook with, we do a lot of Mexican kind of stuff, we eat beans, tortillas, and we always have salsa, and we also use a lot of Asian things.

This account is abridged from two and a half pages of single-spaced interview transcript, in which Veronica also talked about her love for French and Chinese movies, Japanese young-adult novels, African and Balinese music, Indian spices, Salvadoran restaurants and Korean sushi. From my point of view as a Californian, Veronica's multicultural enthusiasms are on the extreme end of normal. Nevertheless, I recognize them as somehow prototypical in this self-consciously diverse state of California (see Chapter 3), where eating food, listening to music and watching movies from around the world has become a status symbol.

In her work life, however, Veronica situates herself on the border between the two largest cultural groups in California, Anglo and Latino. It is this border that she references repeatedly in her narratives, comparing her sense of comfort in Latino communities with her unease around Anglos:

> **Veronica**: I once had a student say to me, that, she said, just 'Well, you know, we're all Mexicans here,' and I said, 'I'm not Mexican,' and she said, 'No, you're an honorary Mexican' [...]
> **Julia**: Mmhmm. And do you also feel like an honorary Mexican from your relationship with (your) students?
> **Veronica**: I do, you know, [...] I do feel, and that affinity for, especially, I think Mexican women, I really, really enjoy. (They're) the professional Mexican women I've worked with, they're tough, and they're smart, and they're funny, and bawdy, and I love them. I feel a little safer with them than my Anglo teachers at my school.

This, of course, is similar to her narrative in which she quotes herself telling 'the white girls' that they all look alike, as a way of illustrating her alienation from people who share her ethnicity but not her values. 'Honorary Mexican' is an identity that she is happy to be assigned. She claims (but clarifies) that identity again at the end of a narrative about a teacher's meeting:

> **Veronica**: I once said something, we were in hiring for a new principal this year, so we had a Latino principal for two years, he was wonderful, and then he went back (as) a [university] professor, and then [...] my colleague, who's Latina, was on the hiring committee, and I happened to run into her when I was at some kind of district meeting with a bunch of other teachers, people I didn't know that well, and we all were sitting around, and [...] 'Tell me, what's the scoop? Who's the new principal gonna be?' and she went, 'Well, there's some good, someone really interesting,' and I said, 'That person better not be white.' ((Julia laughing)) [...] And it turns out we have a Latina as our principal, I was like, 'Yeah!' ((laughing)) I told her that too, I said, 'I'm so glad you're Mexican.' ((laughing)) You know, because someone needs to be there for our Mexican students, and you can have pretty open and empathetic white folks who still don't know what the hell they're doing, (you know), anyway, yeah, [...] I'm Jewish-honorary-Mexican. ((laughing))

Veronica's identity negotiations over time brought her to this moment in 2006, when she could define herself to a sympathetic interviewer as 'Jewish honorary-Mexican'. In claiming this identity, she draws on memories of Jewish adults who were kind to her when she was a lonely child, as well as narratives of Mexican students and teachers who accept her on their side of the Anglo-Latino border. Born neither Jewish nor Mexican, her identity can easily be seen as 'complex, often contradictory, and subject to change across time and place' (Morgan, 2004: 172). Assigned a non-negotiable 'white' identity by society, she is critical of 'open and empathetic white folks who still don't know what the hell they're doing. . .' and insists on the importance of a school principal who is actually rather than honorarily Mexican, 'because someone needs to be there for our Mexican students'.

Veronica's identities are 'not context-free but (rather). . .related to (the) social, cultural, and political context(s)' (Varghese *et al.*, 2005: 23) of California over the course of her lifetime, as white people have gone from majority to minority status. This is a change that Veronica has embraced: she saw the future in multicultural Los Angeles in the early 1970s, and even then she felt more comfortable surrounded by ethnic diversity than immersed in the 'pure whiteness' of Orange County, where she 'was teased for being completely different from everyone else, even though (she) looked like everyone else'. In becoming a teacher of Latino English learners and monolingual Anglo students, she has constructed for herself an imagined multicultural community (Kanno & Norton, 2003).

Constructing This Research

Having introduced the sociohistorical contexts of my research through narrative, I must now talk more about my research itself and how I came to conduct it. A central assumption of my research is that narratives (and other extended texts) are co-constructed in dialogue, with the relationship between interlocutors crucial to the interpretation of the text (Vitanova, 2010, citing Bakhtin; cf Riessman, 2008). Moreover, it is important to remember that reports of research are themselves a kind of narrative (Vitanova, 2010), constructed by researchers and addressed to the expectations of an envisioned academic audience. Above, I (researcher) have introduced to you (academic audience) two English teachers, Diego and Veronica, by means of life history narratives, initially co-constructed in dialogue with me in 2006, and now re-constructed by me in 2011–2012 with you in mind, as a new partner in the dialogue.

In order to continue this dialogue, I now need to introduce myself, so that you can better interpret the research narrative that I am constructing. The process of inquiry to which I aspire has been described by Vitanova (2010, citing Bakhtin) as *participatory thinking*: this involves entering into another person's perspective, and then returning to one's own. I invite you to share this process with me, keeping in mind that 'strictly speaking, I cannot "analyze" the content of another consciousness at all. I can only address it – that is offer to change it a little, and to change myself a little as well, by asking a question of it' (Emerson, cited in Vitanova, 2010: 79). Thus, my research has involved asking questions of teachers in Chile and California, changing them a little, and myself a little, in the process. In ethnographic traditions (Erickson, 1986; Watson-Gegeo, 1988), it is likewise important to foreground the researcher's positionality, attending to precisely these issues. Therefore, in this section, I offer more details of my own life history, especially highlighting my language learning and teaching experiences within the historical context of the last few decades.

I was born in California in 1960, to an Anglo-American monolingual English-speaking family, with no recent history of immigration. I began pursuing multilingualism in adolescence, in the small Canadian town where my wandering parents had temporarily settled, and where, like Veronica in Orange County, I felt myself to be 'a pure outsider'. It was in that mountain village where I began studying French, and where I was horrified at age 12 by graphic news of the coup in Chile on CBC radio in our kitchen. I studied French throughout high school, Russian in my second attempt at college and began taking Spanish and Japanese at age 22 when I started university for the third time as a first year student. By then I was married and living in Seattle, where, like Veronica, I discovered that I felt most comfortable in multicultural settings. The previous spring I had worked in a job-training program for Laotian refugees, and decided to become an ESL teacher. As an undergraduate, I tutored in the university writing center, and continued volunteering with Central American as well as Southeast Asian refugees. I graduated in 1986 with a major in Japanese but no proficiency in that language – by talking to Central Americans, I had grown far more fluent in Spanish. Starting a MATESL program that fall, I was easily convinced that the 'communicative approach' (Savignon, 1983) to language teaching was best.

Meanwhile, throughout the 1980s, the United States was supporting right-wing governments in Latin America. The stories that Salvadorans told me about death squads in Spanish were not too different from the stories about Communists that Mien and Khmu people struggled to convey in English. My husband and I traveled through Central America in 1985, volunteered briefly with a human rights group in Guatemala, then spent

1988 in revolutionary Nicaragua. Teaching English at a Nicaraguan university, I found tremendous variation in my students' politics and ambitions: while some dreamed of emigrating to Miami, others saw themselves interpreting for delegations of socialist Swedes touring cooperative coffee farms. In class, students from across the political spectrum worked collaboratively, and would even team up against me if they thought I was assigning too much homework.

Back in Washington State, I got a job teaching English to immigrants and refugees at a small-town community college. I was three months pregnant when the revolutionary Nicaraguan government was voted out of office in February of 1990; I remember lying on the couch faintly nauseated as the news came over the radio. The Pinochet dictatorship ended in Chile the same year, but that did not catch my attention. I weaned my daughter in early 1992 so I could fly to El Salvador right after the Peace Accords were signed, but that was the last time I thought much about Latin American politics during the 1990s. In the 10 years I worked at the community college, I became increasingly aware of language loss and cultural conflicts in immigrant families, and gradually moved away from English-Only pedagogy.

I moved my family to California in 1999 so I could start my doctorate in Education at Berkeley. As I had hoped when entering the program, I conducted an ethnographic dissertation study on immigrant language learning at a family literacy program (Menard-Warwick, 2004, 2009a). In 2003, while finishing my dissertation and starting the academic job search, I applied for a Fulbright fellowship to research TESOL in Chile. Despite my focus on immigrant language learning, I had begun reading the literature on English in post-colonial Asia (Canagarajah, 1993, 1999; Lin, 1999), and for the first time, I saw that the English language itself could be a problem not easily resolved by pedagogy. I had also begun considering questions of teacher identity, in order to account for the difficulties I faced as a bilingual researcher in an ESL program where teachers were enforcing English-Only classroom practices. I knew almost nothing about contemporary Chile, but the Fulbright Commission was offering multiple TESOL research fellowships there. Putting it all together, I proposed to Fulbright a study titled 'Linguistic and Cultural Identities of English Language Teachers'.

As part of my application process, I started emailing directors of foreign language departments at Chilean universities, and soon got a response from Norma at the ULP (for more about Norma, see Chapters 3 and 4). Yes, they were interested in my ideas and would support my application. Fulbright accepted me in February 2004, the same month I filed my dissertation and received the offer for my current job at University of California Davis. Since Davis would not defer my position, Fulbright said I should come when

I could. I spent two weeks in Las Peñas in September 2004, then 10 weeks from June to August 2005 and 3 weeks in July 2006. Because that meant less time in Chile than planned, I conducted parallel research with English teachers in California, primarily between April 2005 and March 2006.

All of this personal history has affected the research that appears in this book, where the accounts I construct are inevitably based on my own academic training, but especially on my perspectives about what is relevant – perspectives that I have developed both in and outside of the academy. Moreover, the data that I present should not be seen as transparently factual information, but rather as speakers' representations of their own perspectives in research interviews, where my presence necessarily shapes interviewee responses (Bakhtin, 1986b). In Chile, I am seen as a native English-speaking teacher and researcher, a foreign expert, an advanced Spanish learner; in California, I am an Anglo-American former community-college ESL instructor who became a university professor. In both contexts, my voice could be seen as representing a social group with which participants are in dialogue. Based on this dialogue, I construct interpretive conclusions about participants' perspectives on how their own experiences with language and culture learning have affected their teaching.

Data collection

Between April 2005 and March 2006, I observed the classes of three ULP English instructors in northern Chile (Paloma, Alán, Genaro), and five adult ESL instructors at educational institutions in northern California (two adult school instructors, Cherie and Ruby, and three community college instructors, Susanna, Melinda and Eric), spending eight hours in each classroom over a period of several weeks. I audiorecorded these observations, and also typed notes on my laptop; after observing every day, I refined my field notes by rewriting them while listening to the audiotapes. For more about the classroom observations and how I chose these participants, see Chapter 6. Additionally, I team-taught and videotaped a class on Language and Cultural Identity in the Masters in English Teaching program at the ULP for 25 hours during July 2006[10]; some data from that appears in Chapters 3 and 7.

I conducted audiotaped interviews with the eight observed instructors; I also interviewed, but did not observe, 13 other practicing or prospective Chilean English teachers (including Diego), and 6 other practicing or prospective Californian English teachers (including Veronica). The teachers that I interviewed but did not observe in Chile were either key members of the foreign languages department at ULP (Norma, Javier, Azucena), students in my MA-level workshops who had told me interesting stories about themselves (Diego, Alicia), or students in the classes that I was observing. To choose members of the latter group, I surveyed the classes about their backgrounds with English learning, and their use of English outside class. The survey was anonymous, but included space to leave name and contact information if students were willing to be interviewed. Of the students who were willing, I chose participants who represented a diverse range of involvements with English in and outside the classroom (Renate, Sofía, Francesca, Maritza, Edith, Tomás, Lydia, Reuel). Interviews with prospective teachers in California were conducted in early 2010 with new teachers who were my students in the MATESOL program at my home university: I was concerned to balance the data I had on prospective teachers in Chile with their Californian counterparts. To select these participants, I simply interviewed all willing MA students who had grown up in California (Molly, Charles, Martin, Linnea, Jokwon).

All participants were interviewed regarding their history of foreign language study and use, their experiences as English teachers, their cross-cultural experiences, their views on the role of English in society and their perspectives on culture in language teaching. Interviews lasted from 1–2 hours, and were conducted in English, with some instances of code-switching. I used interview protocols that varied somewhat between groups of teachers (see Appendix 3), but did not follow them strictly, allowing the conversation to develop in unexpected directions (as illustrated in the interviews with Diego and Veronica above). In bringing together (i.e. triangulating) interview and classroom data (Watson-Gegeo, 1988), I found enough congruence between different types of data to feel that I could responsibly draw interpretive conclusions about participants' perspectives on their own intercultural experiences and identities – and on how these affect their teaching. I will talk more about processes of data analysis in subsequent chapters. For dates of all interviews and classroom observations, see Appendix 2, which also has basic demographic information on all the teachers who were observed or interviewed.

Structure of this book

This book brings the perspectives of teachers into a comparative discussion, through an exploration of the language ideologies, linguistic and cultural identities and cultural pedagogies of English language educators in the far north of Chile and an urban–suburban–rural area of northern California. In both educational contexts, there are discursive conflicts around English instruction and the role of English in a changing society; since both geographical contexts are seismically active and located around tectonic faults, I use the metaphor of discursive faultlines to index the increasing stresses. Driving this research is the conviction that as teachers increase their own awareness of the interconnections between language, ideology, culture and identity, they will be better able to make informed decisions about locally appropriate English language pedagogies (Ramanathan, 2005).

Within the structure of this book, I inevitably end up comparing and contrasting 'non-native-English-speaking teachers' with 'native-English-speaking teachers' (Braine, 1999), as I contrasted Diego's and Veronica's experiences in this chapter. Aware that the field of TESOL has often been polarized by the dichotomy between 'native' and 'non-native' teachers of English, I use quotation marks around these terms in order to cast 'a sideways glance' at them (Bakhtin, 1981: 61) and call this dichotomy into question. However, rather than mounting a frontal assault against the (still all too common) idea that encountering a language in adolescence rather than infancy forever delegitimizes a speaker of that language, I instead emphasize teachers' views of their own relationships with English and other languages.

Having discussed connections between teacher identities and sociohistorical context in Chapter 1, I turn to a theoretical framework in the second chapter, based primarily on the work of Mikhail Bakhtin (1981, 1984, 1986b). In Chapter 3, I look more closely at language ideologies connected to ELT in both Chile and California, while in Chapter 4, I discuss how teachers represented their own cultural identities.

I further illustrate intercultural identity development in Chapter 5 through life histories of two transnational English teachers, as well as through an analysis of an internet chat exchange between prospective educators in Chile and California. Chapter 6 examines the approaches to teaching culture that teachers mentioned in interviews and that I observed in Chilean and Californian classrooms. I begin Chapter 7 by bringing the historical context of this research up to date, as of 2012. I go on to draw connections between teachers' life histories and their cultural and linguistic pedagogies, and then explore the implications of these results for cultural pedagogy in teacher education.

Notes

(1) This chapter draws upon some data and analysis that first appeared in Menard-Warwick (2011a, 2011b).
(2) All names of people, institutions and places (aside from major cities) are pseudonyms, unless stated otherwise.
(3) Paloma is the subject of a case study in Chapter 5.

(4)   Although English-speaking Chileans often refer to me as 'American', many Latin Americans critique the common use of this term to signify United States nationality, since 'American' potentially refers to all inhabitants of the Americas. I agree with this critique. When speaking English, I say that I am from the United States or that I am North American; when speaking Spanish, I refer to myself as *norteamericana* (North American) or *estadounidense* (United Statesian). However, the problem with the term 'North American' is that it does not distinguish between US and Canadian nationalities. In terms of historical relations with Chile, having a US or a Canadian nationality positions an individual differently. As a dual citizen, US/Canadian, having spent my adolescence in Canada but most of my adult life in the United States, I am very aware of these different positionings.

(5)   These are World Bank figures, found on http://www.tradingeconomics.com/chile/gini-index-wb-data.html. The US census calculates that in 2010, the top quintile of the US population earned 47.8% of the income whereas the bottom quintile earned 3.8%. California's figures are similar to the national average. http://www.census.gov/hhes/www/income/data/historical/families/

(6)   Throughout this book, I will use 'Cedarville', Iowa, just as I use 'Farmington', California, to conflate several cities and institutions in the interests of simplicity and pseudonymity. I likewise use 'Las Peñas' for the names of a Chilean city, its university and the surrounding region, which have distinct names in actuality.

(7)   The US census counts race and Hispanic ethnicity separately, but these California figures count Hispanic as if it were an exclusive racial group. The 2010 figures do not add up to 100% because I have left out several groups that did not appear at all in 1970, such as Pacific Islander. Although 'Hispanic' is the term used by the census, 'Latino' is a more common term for people of Latin American descent in California, in both English and Spanish.

(8)   In this excerpt, Veronica quotes the French teacher saying, 'This is a pen. Ahh, a pen! A chair, a chair.'

(9)   English Language Development (ELD) is the current acronym in California public schools for what used to be called ESL (English as a Second Language). There is some feeling in California that ESL has become a stigmatizing label, and that the way to remove the stigma is to change the label.

(10) I also taught an intensive Second Language Acquisition class in this program during July 2005, but did not collect data during this experience, aside from keeping a journal. However, it was through teaching this class that I met Diego, as well as Alicia, who appears in later chapters.

2 In Dialogue with Bakhtin[1]

The living utterance, having taken meaning and shape at a particular historical moment in a socially specific environment, cannot fail to brush up against thousands of living dialogic threads, woven by socio-ideological consciousness around the given object of an utterance; it cannot fail to become an active participant in social dialogue. After all, the utterance arises out of this dialogue as a continuation of it and as a rejoinder to it.
Bakhtin, 1981: 277

This chapter follows up on insights from the last chapter: that every instance of language use, and thus language teaching, must be seen in a historical context (Blommaert, 2005). This may be described as attention to historicity: the 'notion that all social acts including language occur in a particular time and place and consciously or unconsciously link to previous times and places' (Williams, 2012: 23). In looking at history as important for understanding the language ideologies, cultural identities, and pedagogical practices of teachers, I find Bakhtin's theories of language and identity development to be helpful. From his perspective, social individuals, including teachers, are constantly in the process of 'ideological becoming', that is, 'assimilating our consciousness to the ideological world' (Bakhtin, 1981: 341), as we position ourselves between the 'authoritative discourses' dominant in society, and the 'internally persuasive discourses' by which we interpret our own experiences (Bakhtin, 1981: 342). In this endeavor, 'our ideological development' is an 'intense struggle within us for hegemony between various available verbal and ideological points of view, approaches, directions, and values' (Bakhtin, 1981: 346).

However, before I connect those ideas to my research, I offer a bit of history.

In the 1920s, in what had recently become the Soviet Union, there were three young scholars, named Bakhtin, Voloshinov and Medvedev. Insofar as this history can be reconstructed, they probably worked in collaboration, that is, in dialogue. Three books were published in the last few moments before the Stalinist terror-imposed monologue: *Marxism and the Philosophy of Language* (under the name of Voloshinov), *The Formal Method in Literary Scholarship* (under the name of Medvedev) and *Problems of Dostoevsky's Poetics* (under the name of Bakhtin).

Three decades later, a new generation of young Russian intellectuals was amazed to find that one of the three men had survived Stalin in quiet exile, was teaching literature at a provincial university and had apparently managed to continue writing (Emerson, 1984). That was Mikhail Bakhtin. He died in 1975. I first read his work in graduate school in 1999, have consistently found 'his' ideas illuminating and spent much of the summer of 2011 attempting to read everything in print in English under his name (and I also read Voloshinov for the first time). Around the end of that summer, I received an email from my former student Duane Leonard (not a pseudonym), forwarding a listserve message from a prominent linguist regarding some recent controversies in Bakhtin scholarship. The email detailed Bronckart and Bota's (2011) rejection of Bakhtin's purported claim to be the real author of Medvedev's and Voloshinov's books,[2] as well as these authors' further contention that many of Bakhtin's published works were plagiarized from Voloshinov. I quote here the email dialogue between Duane and me:

> **Julia**: Bakhtin never claimed to be Voloshinov or Medvedev. Other people claimed that he was. Also, Problems in Dostoevsky's Poetics is very similar to Dialogue in the Novel, and very different from Voloshinov.
> **Duane**: I was interested to see that [prominent linguist] spoke out about this. Doubly interested now that you seem to disagree. I've been instructed to (really) stress the importance of plagiarism with our students... so I'm just intrigued.
> **Julia**: Have you seen the cartoon in Ivanic 'I was charged with plagiarism but I am pleading intertextuality'? I guess I would have to see the arguments about the Dostoevsky book, but it really seems to be written by the same person as Dialogue in the Novel which is apparently not in doubt. People asked Bakhtin point blank toward the end of his life about the authorship of the Voloshinov & Medvedev books and he refused to answer one way or another. I haven't read Medvedev. I would believe that the Voloshinov book was written by .... Voloshinov.
> **Duane**: I do remember the Ivanic cartoon; very drole:). if any of my students plead intertextuality; they will be set free.

I have not read Bronckart and Bota (2011), so will not attempt a refutation of their claims about authorship. I am going to draw freely in this chapter on books and articles published under the name of Mikhail Bakhtin in English during the 1980s, about a decade after the death of the historical Bakhtin, and five decades after the disappearance and presumed death of Voloshinov (and Medvedev). Perhaps the central message in this oeuvre is that 'the word in language is half someone else's' (Bakhtin, 1981: 293): we get our words, our ideas, our ideologies from other people, who are responding at a particular historical moment to previous utterances, and who anticipate a response from subsequent speakers, subsequent writers. In Bakhtin's best-known essay, 'The Problem of Speech Genres', he writes:

> Any speaker is himself a respondent to a greater or less degree. He is not, after all, the first speaker, the one who disturbs the eternal silence of the universe. And he presupposes not only the existence of the language system he is using, but also the existence of preceding utterances – his own and others' – with which his given utterance enters into one kind of relation or another (builds on them, polemicizes with them, or simply presumes that they are already known to the listener). Any utterance is a link in a very complexly organized chain of other utterances. (Bakhtin, 1986b: 69)

This essay, which theorizes addressivity, is one of the works that Bronckart and Bota claim to be really Voloshinov's. The prominent linguist who started the email chain to which Duane and I are responding confesses in his email to often quoting this essay, and vows to credit Voloshinov in future. In another work published under Bakhtin's name but argued by Bronckart and Bota (and now their supporters) to be probably Voloshinov's, it is written:

> The life of the word is contained in its transfer from one mouth to another, from one context to another context, from one social collective to another, from one generation to another generation. In this process the word does not forget its own path and cannot completely free itself from the power of these concrete contexts into which it has entered. (Bakhtin, 1984: 202)

From this perspective, Voloshinov's book (Voloshinov, 1986), written in the 'concrete context' of the late 1920s in the Soviet Union was an utterance in a particular dialogue about the social nature of language; another utterance in the same dialogue is Bakhtin's essay on speech genres (Bakhtin, 1986b). This essay, published in English in 1986, is believed to have been written in the 1950s[3] near the end of Stalin's life, but long before genuine dialogue was actually safe in Bakhtin's homeland. As 21st-century applied linguists, we can use his words, but we should never think we can liberate them from the concrete contexts in which he worked. All language is borrowed from previous speakers. If some of 'his' ideas are half Voloshinov's, I am happy to let him 'plead intertextuality' (Ivanic, 1998). Rather than definitively assigning ownership to words and ideas that were apparently crafted in dialogue during the early days of the Soviet Union, I simply wish to express my gratitude that they survived the decades of Stalin's enforced monologue.

In this book, I am grateful to be able to join in that dialogue – from within my own historical moment, in which it is considered vitally important to establish ownership of words and ideas. In this historical moment, Bronckart and Bota's charge that Bakhtin 'stole' ideas from his deceased colleagues (who may have never existed, but who were probably murdered by Stalin) is seen as heinous enough to invalidate Bakhtin's own scholarship. This is the same historical moment in which Duane as a young ESL instructor is told by his institution 'to (really) stress the importance of plagiarism with our students'.

However, we are also living in an historical moment during which, as Duane and I both recognize, alternative voices are questioning whether words can be truly owned. The term 'intertextuality' was coined by Julia Kristeva as she brought Bakhtin's words into dialogue with French post-structuralism (Kristeva, 1986), but it had by 1998 become so much a part of the working vocabulary of literacy theorists like Roz Ivanic that she did not feel the need to cite Kristeva when she included the cartoon about plagiarism in her book, *Writing and Identity*. Instead she cites the cartoon, where it appears on page 87, as 'the Biff cartoon about plagiarism, from *Biff* September 1993'. In her bibliography, we find that it first appeared in *The Guardian*. I misquoted it slightly in my email to Duane; the actual words are 'they say I plagiarized someone else's work, but I'm pleading intertextuality'. Ivanic cites Kristeva when first introducing the term 'intertextuality' on page 47. In turn, Duane and I are able to align our mutual identities as theory-savvy applied linguists through reference to Ivanic's cartoon as we discuss the charges of Bronckart and Bota against Bakhtin. Kristeva's word is half Bakhtin's; Ivanic's cartoon (which is really Biff's) is half Kristeva's. Duane has ownership of his final joke about students pleading intertextuality (in writing this, I feel called to cite him on that), but he shares that ownership with me (since I reminded him of Ivanic) as well as with Ivanic, Biff, Kristeva and Bakhtin himself (who perhaps was really Voloshinov, or maybe Medvedev). There is a Communism to language that has nothing to do with Stalinism, and it is through this Communism that we construct our identities within the historical moment we inhabit.

In Dialogue with Communist Students, the TESOL Website and Critical Applied Linguistics

In 2005, while conducting research on English teaching in Chile, I was twice told a narrative about Communism and about language that came out of a historical moment very different from Bakhtin's. In this story, a high school student informs his teacher that he refuses to learn English because doing so conflicts with his political beliefs (Menard-Warwick, 2009d). Here is the version that I caught on audiotape, 14 July 2005, during an interview with a highly experienced public high school teacher:

> **Renate**: One colleague told us the other day that she had problems with one student, 'I don't like English, and I'm not going to learn English because I don't like America, I'm a Communist.' 'Oh god,' said the teacher, 'Well please I need your father here, I need to speak to your father.' And ((laughing)) when the father came he came with a T-shirt with a Che Guevara (on it), ((laughing)) 'Well, I don't want my pupil to learn English and that's my decision and you cannot override him to do it.' 'Well,' she says, 'Oh, come on, what shall I do?' And that's it. But those are extreme cases, you know.

In July 2006, I was told the story a third time, by a third Chilean English teacher, Alicia (all names of teachers and students remain pseudonyms unless otherwise specified), whom I will quote more extensively below.

'The Dad in the Che Guevara T-shirt' is a story about clashing language ideologies in English language teaching, and about historicity. The Che Guevara T-shirt invokes a history of Latin American resistance to US imperialism, through reference to the personal history of Ernesto 'Che' Guevara himself: born in Argentina in 1928, an influential figure in the 1959 Cuban revolution, killed (martyred?) when attempting to carry the revolution to Bolivia in 1967. His face on a T-shirt brings that history to bear on a 21st-century conflict about the role of English language teaching in the globalization of the Chilean economy.

Looking beyond the Chilean context to the worldwide ELT profession, we find it described in the introduction to a 2006 edited volume as, paradoxically, 'helping one's students achieve their aspirations (while) supporting the linguistic, cultural, commercial and increasingly military dominance of the USA and its allies' (Edge, 2006: xiii). For Edge, this is a clear example of hegemony, which he defines as 'a type of power that maintains its dominance by inviting those who fall under its sway to support the status quo because to do so is to serve their own interests' (Edge, 2006: xiii). The rest of Edge's introduction clarifies the historicity of his remarks: he is writing at the height of the US war in Iraq, and he starts the edited volume with the story of a long-time English teacher in that country who was murdered by Islamist insurgents. Indeed, as shown by the Chilean teachers' story about the Communist student and his father, not all learners of English see the status quo as 'serving their own interests', and many reject the aspirations connected to learning English in this age of global capitalism.

While vastly different from each other, Chilean Communists and Iraqi insurgents call into question a view of history in which globalization and ELT represent the inexorable forces of progress. As Pennycook writes (1994), to view the spread of English as 'natural' and 'beneficial', it is necessary to:

> turn one's back on larger global forces and the goals and interests of institutions and governments that have promoted it...(and) ignore the relationships between English and the inequitable distributions and flows of wealth, resources, culture and knowledge. (Pennycook, 1994: 23)

Despite such critiques, the worldwide English teaching profession has collectively tended to view its work as indeed 'natural' and 'beneficial'. For example, one major professional organization (of which I have been for many years a member) in the last decade described its mission as promoting 'effective communication' amidst the 'constant flow of information from country to country...in our shrinking world' (TESOL, 2007). For many TESOL professionals and their students, this authoritative discourse about the value of English is *also* internally persuasive (Bakhtin, 1981), resonating with their own positive linguistic experiences. In fact, the hegemony discussed by Edge (2006) could perhaps be defined in Bakhtinian terms as the process by which authoritative discourse becomes internally persuasive.

Here, I would like to pause briefly and reflect on what I am doing in constructing the preceding two paragraphs. From a Bakhtinian perspective, I as the author am putting the voices of Edge and Pennycook in dialogue with the voice of the TESOL website. I am using the 2007 version of the mission statement, which I preserved in an earlier article, because it makes a clearer statement about the value of English than the 2012 mission statement, which I looked up online while writing this chapter (see Appendix 4), and which does not actually take a position on the now controversial question as to whether learning or teaching English is in fact a worthwhile endeavor.

Bakhtin, primarily a literary scholar, argued that the juxtaposition of multiple social languages allowed novelists to express entire social eras. Appearing in novels as the voices of characters from various social groups, such languages represent the ideologies among which all speakers position themselves: 'specific points of view on the world, for conceptualizing the world in words... drawn in by the novelist for the orchestration of his themes and for the refracted (indirect) expression of his intentions' (Bakhtin, 1981: 292). These voices analyzed by Bakhtin draw upon socially available discourses: characteristic ways of using linguistic resources (and related non-linguistic resources) to discuss particular topics, such as globalization. Moreover, for Bakhtin, 'voice is not just a reflection of societal codes and discourses, but always contains an emotional volitional tone (i.e. the emotions, desires, and ethics of the speaker)' (Vitanova, 2010: 52; citing Bakhtin, 1993). From this perspective, I am putting the 'mainstream applied-linguistics discourse' of the 2007 TESOL website in dialogue with the 'critical applied-linguistics discourse' of Edge and Pennycook, while keeping in mind that even academic authors and website developers have emotions, desires and ethics.

The discourse of the 2007 TESOL website, within my own profession, is (or at least has been throughout my professional lifetime) what Bakhtin called an *authoritative discourse*. In his words, such discourse 'demands that we acknowledge it, that we make it our own; it binds us, quite independent of any power it might have to persuade us internally; we encounter it with its authority already fused to it' (Bakhtin, 1981: 342). In fact, what Bakhtin calls *authoritative discourse* is very similar to what Foucault calls *discourse* (Foucault, 1984: 110), and clearly represents a 'power to be seized'. I had to internalize this TESOL discourse to some extent in graduate school in the 1980s, in order to become a TESOL professional – but was meanwhile beginning to encounter more critical approaches to applied linguistics around the margins of my studies (with the encouragement of my professors). These critical approaches (especially Wallerstein, 1983) in turn helped me make sense of my experiences teaching EFL (English as a Foreign Language) in revolutionary Nicaragua in 1988, or ESL to working-class immigrants and refugees in Washington State throughout the 1990s. For me, the discourse of critical applied linguistics was internally persuasive because it resonated with my own emotional–volitional tone (Bakhtin, 1993) as well as the student realities I was encountering in my classrooms.

Writing in small-town exile in the 1930s and unable to publish (Holquist, 1981), Bakhtin managed to fairly well describe my own teacher identity development:

> An individual's becoming, an ideological process, is characterized precisely by a sharp gap between these two categories: in one, the authoritative word (religious, political, moral; the word of a father, of adults and of teachers, etc.) that does not know internal persuasiveness, in

the other internally persuasive word that is denied all privilege, backed up by no authority at all, and is frequently not even acknowledged in society. (Bakhtin, 1981: 342)

Certainly, as Bakhtin points out, the struggle between authoritative and internally persuasive discourse helped shaped 'the history of (my own) ideological consciousness' (Bakhtin, 1981). However, the picture is more complicated than I am drawing here, since critical applied linguistics itself has become authoritative discourse within my academic circles, and yet I find myself continuing to draw upon mainstream TESOL discourse (by now disappearing even from the TESOL website) in order to affiliate with practicing ESL/EFL instructors (such as Diego, see Chapter 1), who tend to lack authority within their own institutions and in society at large.

In any case, Bakhtin in the 1930s managed to mount what I consider an effective challenge to the 21st-century mainstream professional view of ELT as a way to promote orderly communication. Rather, he described language as *heteroglossia*: an ongoing struggle between dialects, registers and genres, in which standardized national languages (such as 'American English') compete for space, and no one language variety can view its own place as secure:

The world becomes polyglot, once and for all and irreversibly. The period of national languages, coexisting but closed and deaf to each other, comes to an end. Languages throw light on each other: one language can, after all, see itself only in the light of another language. The naïve and stubborn co-existence of 'languages' within a given national language also comes to an end – that is, there is no more peaceful co-existence between territorial dialects, social and professional dialects and jargons…and so forth. (Bakhtin, 1981: 12)

Some might still argue that the inexorable march of history has caused this state of linguistic competition to be superseded by the ahistorical 'effective communication', which was once promoted in the mission statement of the TESOL organization, but which has now (with the inexorable march of history) disappeared from its website. However, while the ELT profession has historically remained 'closed and deaf' to other national languages, and to 'non-mainstream' varieties of English, perhaps it is wiser to look for ways that languages really do 'throw light' on each other, such that standardized English can only be clearly seen in relation to its competitors. Indeed, what the TESOL website currently refers to as its 'credo' now includes as a bulletpoint 'respect for diversity, multilingualism and multiculturalism' (TESOL, 2012).

Research on ELT within specific sociopolitical contexts indicates that the spread of 'effective communication' in English has been a conflictual process, which has more in common with Bakhtin's heteroglossia than either of TESOL's mission statements. As Kroskrity (citing Lippi-Green) remarks:

> The proclaimed superiority of Standard English rests not on its structural properties or its communicative efficiency but rather on its association with the political-economic influence of affluent social classes who benefit from a social stratification which consolidates and continues their privileged position. (Kroskrity, 2004: 502–503)

This is as true in places where English is a widely spoken first language (such as California), as it is in nations where English is truly foreign (such as Chile). In regard to the role of English in the latter type of context (often referred to as EFL), research has primarily been conducted in post-colonial Asian nations, but has begun to spread into other parts of the world as well. Reporting on a research study conducted at a Sri Lankan university caught up in civil war, Canagarajah described students' conflict as 'how to learn English...without being inducted into the values embodied by the language and (Western-influenced) curriculum' (Canagarajah, 1999: 96). These rural students found textbook images of Western culture baffling, and generally refused to participate in classroom 'communicative' activities based on discursive values that they did not share. Likewise, Sellami (2006) found that Moroccan university students connected the English language to offensive media images of illicit sex and alcohol.

As well as such cultural issues, researchers have explored the connections between ELT and social stratification in a variety of contexts, including Hong Kong (Lin, 1999), India (Ramanathan, 2005), and Peru (Niño-Murcia, 2003), with varying results. While Lin describes working-class students in Hong Kong as 'confronted with a language in which they had neither interest, competence nor confidence, but a language they recognized, though angrily, as a key to success in society' (Lin, 1999: 408), Niño-Murcia chronicles the eagerness of young Peruvian workers to learn English as a means of 'realizing the dream of emigration, increasing job opportunities...making money, (and) entering the global market' (Niño-Murcia, 2003: 130). However, there has been little research on how individual ELT professionals position themselves within these historical conflicts over globalization and the legacy of colonialism.

Moreover, just as Pennycook above questions whether the spread of English should be seen as 'natural' and 'beneficial', contemporary social critics (often referred to as 'Communists') similarly interrogate the neoliberal free-market capitalism on which Chile's contemporary economy is based (see Chapter 1). Such critics are apparently easy to find in Chilean public high schools, according to Alicia and other teachers I interviewed. In Alicia's version of the Che Guevara T-shirt story (audiorecorded 10 July 2006), which she said she had heard from a colleague at a teacher's meeting, she quotes the voice of the Communist student at length (Menard-Warwick, 2009d):

> **Alicia**: Well, you know Communists think, 'Okay, Americans are *Yanquís*[4] and they are stealing things from people,' so he didn't want to learn English. She had big issues with this student because of that. And it was like he was insulting her class all the time like, 'I don't wanna be in your *Yanquí* class. I don't wanna be here. I don't wanna learn English. English is for people who steal things.'

Introducing language ideologies, Kroskrity defines them as 'the perception of language and discourse that is constructed in the interest of a specific social or cultural group' (Kroskrity, 2000: 8); in a later article, he points out that in any society, language ideologies tend to multiply as different groups struggle for their interests (Kroskrity, 2004). Similarly, Bakhtin describes the centralizing forces of linguistic standardization (representing the interests of centralized authority) as always in conflict with the reality of heteroglossia:

> At any given moment of its evolution, language is stratified not only into linguistic dialects in the strict sense of the word...but also – and for us this is the essential point – into languages that are socio-ideological: languages of social groups, 'professional' and 'generic' languages, languages of generations and so forth. (Bakhtin, 1981: 271–272)

In Bakhtin's writings (1981, 1984), heteroglossia is portrayed in the novel through reported speech representing voices of different social groups. The Chilean groups whose ideologies clash in these narratives are English language teachers and their 'Communist' students, with Communism in contemporary Chile defined as advocacy against capitalism (Jaime Gómez, personal comment, 2007). Within the Chilean context, opposing groups connect ELT to Chile's participation in the global (capitalist) economy, but evaluate this participation positively or negatively in accordance with their own interests. Bakhtin does not discuss the rejection of any national language by members of a socio-ideological group, but this is an easy extension of his theories. As Irvine and Gal argue, 'Ideology often imagines languages as corresponding with essentialized representations of social groups' (Irvine & Gal,

2000: 77), while further assuming that 'identity and allegiance are indexed by language use' (Woolard, 1998: 16).

Thus, leftist Chilean students see English as pertaining to '*Yanquí*' capitalist aggressors, such that their own political identities and allegiances preclude learning the language. After recounting the Che Guevara T-shirt story, Alicia went on to describe similar problems with her own students: 'like they had their Communist ideas and, "Why do you like English? English is for *Yanquís*."'

Her pedagogical difficulties intensified when she assigned students to create a 'comic' about an English-language song of their choice. As one student told her:

> **Alicia**: 'I can't find a song, so I want to do with a song in Spanish with some Communist singer like Silvio Rodríguez,' [...] and I was 'No, you cannot do it in Spanish, you have to do it in English.' 'But I can't find anything in English to...' 'Okay, I'm going to try to find something for you and I'm sure...' 'No, because, no...' and he said something like, 'There's no American who sings communist lyrics.' And he said, 'There's no *Yanquís* who sing communist lyrics.' 'I'm going to find something.'

Whereas Communist students relate English to their essentialized image of Americans, and view language study as indexing allegiance to US capitalism, teachers like Alicia connect the language to fashionable and sophisticated images of English-speaking countries. These conflicting ideologies appear as competing voices in Alicia's narratives. To construct her own identity as a teacher, she orchestrates these voices in the way that Bakhtin describes novelists orchestrating the voices of their characters (1981). This phenomenon is termed *dialogic voicing* or *double-voiced discourse*, the linguistic construction of social worlds through reported speech (Bakhtin, 1981; Menard-Warwick, 2005). Moreover, Bakhtin reminds us that this orchestration is not solely the province of novelists:

> Our practical everyday speech is full of other people's words: with some of them we completely merge our own voice, forgetting whose they are; others, which we take as authoritative, we use to reinforce our own words; still others, finally, we populate with our own aspirations, alien and hostile to them. (Bakhtin, 1984: 195)

A variety of scholars have drawn on this insight that speakers and writers refract their own intentions through the voices of characters in narratives (e.g. De Fina, 2003; Koven, 2001; Menard-Warwick, 2005, 2007). Maybin, for example, used Bakhtin's theories to analyze stories told by schoolchildren, examining how 'reconstructed dialogue... enable(s) (tellers) to play on ambiguity and explore a variety of evaluative perspectives simultaneously' (Maybin, 1996: 37).

Similarly, Alicia's use of reported speech allows her to represent the variety of evaluative perspectives in her own context of English teaching. In this 'double-voiced discourse' (Bakhtin, 1981: 324), Alicia juxtaposes her own (reasonable) voice ('I'm going to find something') with her student's tirade ('There's no *Yanquís* who sing communist lyrics'). In so doing, she 'expresses (her) intentions' (Bakhtin, 1981) of demonstrating the value of English for articulating a wide variety of viewpoints, as well as confirming her agency as a teacher:

> **Alicia**: So I started to talk with my classmates from here at the university, my colleagues now, [...] and I said, 'What do I do with him? Don't you know any group or singer something?' I don't remember who told me *Rage Against the Machine*. 'Are they Communist?' 'I don't know but their lyrics are like the things that he want to hear.' 'All right, I'm gonna work with that.' And I look on the Internet, I started to read the lyrics, and yeah, it was very close to the things that the student wanted.

In this excerpt, Alicia continues to construct an agentive teacher identity for herself through multiple voices. As Varghese *et al.* write (see Chapter 1), identities are 'not context-free but (rather)... related to social, cultural, and political context(s)' (Varghese *et al.*, 2005: 23) where teachers have learned, used and taught languages. In this case, Alicia and her colleagues are constructing cultural identities for themselves as English language users through practices of popular culture consumption and the appropriation of discourses related to those practices: 'world views, trends, viewpoints, and opinions (which) always have verbal expression' (Bakhtin, 1986b: 94).

Moreover, the identities constructed by Alicia in this narrative for herself, her students and her colleagues must be situated in their historical context, in Chilean conflicts between capitalism and socialism, dictatorship and democracy (see Chapter 1) and within the decades-long process of cultural globalization. In Ariel Dorfman's description of Chilean youth culture of the 1950s: 'The first defiant beats of Elvis and Bill Haley... were invading Chile..., the preamble of a global culture which allowed any kid anywhere to sing and dance the same tunes being blared out halfway across the planet' (Dorfman, 1998: 119). Still today, the 'defiant beats' of global youth culture are often articulated in English, offering Alicia an opening with her recalcitrant pupil:

Alicia:So I took the CD, 'Listen to this.' 'But this is *Rage Against the Machine*, they're American.' 'Who cares? Just listen. And this is the lyrics in English, this is the lyrics in Spanish.' And he started to listen to the song and he's, 'This man and what...Yeah. Oh yeah! Yeah, yeah! This is going to work.' 'Okay, so now work please.' And he made this great comic with this idea, and I'm not a political person so I really don't understand. I really do not understand social, the social party, the Communist.

Here, I can extend my discussion of identity in Chapter 1 by drawing on Bucholtz and Hall's concepts of adequation and distinction (2004), noting that while identity involves belonging to a group of people and constructing a sense of similarity with them (adequation), it also involves not belonging to other groups (distinction). Here the student's Communist identity initially precludes the consumption of English-language music – while at the same time Alicia's teacher identity requires the non-comprehension of explicitly political ideologies ('I really do not understand social, the social party, the Communist'). Still, she finds the content of her student's 'cartoon' memorable enough to recount in detail:

Julia: What did he put in his cartoon?
Alicia: He put like slavery work. Like people who was, he took it to the level in which, you know when Mexicans go to the states without any...
Julia: Documents.
Alicia: Yeah, and they work in this factory where they are very bad paid, and abused and in very different ways. And he did something related to that. Related to a girl who goes...I remember there was something like, a girl that goes to the States and goes to work in a factory, I think they were making dresses or something.
Julia: Probably, yeah.
Alicia: And she was raped and she was very bad paid, and she ended dead because of an abortion and things like that. But he did something like very, very dramatic.

Through the song by Rage Against the Machine, a California-based band, the Communist high school student in Chile was able to explore a sense of identification with undocumented Mexican workers in the United States, experiencing how ideologies and discourses cut across national languages (Risager, 2007). This exploration finally allowed collaboration with his English teacher. Moreover, his trajectory helped Alicia to further develop her own bilingual identity as a Chilean English teacher who can work successfully with the full range of students in Chilean public schools.

From Bakhtin's perspective, identity construction is a process of 'ideological becoming' (Bakhtin, 1981: 341) through the selective appropriation of discourses. Some of these discourses may be considered authoritative, such as the discourse of globalization. However, as Bakhtin suggests, 'the history of an individual ideological consciousness' is shaped by 'the struggle and dialogic interrelationship' between authoritative discourses and other internally persuasive discourses, which are 'tightly interwoven with one's own word' (Bakhtin, 1981: 345) – as the leftist discourse drawn upon by Rage Against the Machine appears to be interwoven with the world view of Alicia's Communist student. Moreover, Alicia's recounting of his cartoon suggests that, to some extent, she finds this discourse internally persuasive. As a researcher, I note, for example, her use of simple present tense with the discourse marker 'you know', both of which suggest that the sufferings of Mexican immigrants are common knowledge in Latin America ('you know when Mexicans go to the States....'). Even a mostly apolitical Chilean teacher like Alicia has extensive background knowledge of the historical relations between North and South America that she can bring to bear on her interpretation of an alternative rock song.

While discussions of English teacher identity often fail to engage the full discursive and historical contexts in which development occurs, from a Bakhtinian perspective, identities get constructed through an intense (though not necessarily conscious) struggle between a variety of possible practices and perspectives. As Vitanova writes (2010), drawing on post-structuralist theory, 'discourses are actually the force that allows us to create subject positions. It is through taking up or not being able to take up a certain discourse that the subject is created' (Vitanova, 2010: 18). In Alicia's narrative, as she labors to counteract her student's view that English is inextricably linked to discourses of capitalism, she must at least temporarily engage with Communist discourses that are alien to her – but in doing so, she develops a stronger sense of agency. Teacher development advances as individuals learn to make sense of and position themselves within the complexity of their local discursive environment, in the way that Alicia portrays herself doing in these narratives. In fact, Bakhtinian theory emphasizes that individuals are not simply placed into social positions by available discourses but rather 'assume a more dynamic role by actively using speech genres (or discourses) to orient themselves in relationships and social interactions with others' (Vitanova, 2010: 132).

It is easy to observe these discursive struggles in the openly ideological Chilean educational context, where individuals take clearly contrasting positions on the place of English in their society, and on the historical relationship between Chile and the English-speaking capitalist countries. The Rage Against the Machine song enters the Chilean English classroom inhabited with the voice and permeated with the interpretations of California leftists (Bakhtin, 1981). The Communist student finds that word linguistically uncomfortable (i.e. in an alien language), but already inhabited with discourses that he recognizes and to which he has committed himself (Risager, 2007). In the case of Alicia, who expresses distaste for politics but fascination with popular culture, the *Rage* song forces her to interact with discourses that make her squirm – but offers new strategies for overcoming her students' resistance to English.

Dialogue in a California Classroom

In this next section, I bring this same Bakhtinian framework to bear on a very different context, where the ideologies are just as multiple, and just as powerful, but less explicit. Below, I draw on the theories elucidated through Alicia's narrative to make sense of a discussion I observed in a California community college advanced ESL reading classroom on 6 February 2006, in an 'emergent "border zone" within and between social groups' (Kroskrity, 2004: 512). It is in such border zones where meanings are least finalized (Bakhtin, 1981, 1984), where there is no one 'common sense' and where significance must be actively constructed in dialogue. As Vitanova writes, Bakhtin's insistence on the 'multiple and contradictory meanings' of texts, utterances and discourses remains 'especially significant for educators in adult second-language classrooms, where divergent discourses of culture, gender, race, and occupation frequently compete' (2010: 32).

The teacher of this class, Eric, appeared to be in his 30s; he had grown up in a rural California farming community, but had lived, worked and learned languages in French Canada, Europe, South America and Asia. A majority of his students were from Eastern Europe (such as Stefania and Anton, who speak below), but in the following dialogue, two men from South Asia (Simran and Kumar) and a Mexican woman and man (Rafaela and Saúl) also participate, along with several other students whose names I hadn't learned.[1] In a space where participants come from all over the globe, and have little sense of shared history, the development of English language identities remains a 'struggle... among various available verbal and ideological points of view, approaches, directions and values,' (Bakhtin, 1981: 346). However, through looking closely at an interpretive classroom exercise, where students and teacher use their own diverse and gendered life experiences to make sense of a textbook poem that seems to exist outside of time and space, we can see how structures of meaning within internally persuasive discourses are '*not finite*' but rather '*open*,' and 'able to reveal ever newer *ways to mean*' (Bakhtin, 1981: 346, italics in the original).

The data below is written in the form of field notes (Watson-Gegeo, 1988), originally typed on my laptop while I observed Eric's class on 6 February 2006, rewritten and refined while listening to the audiotape later that same day, and then checked again with the audiotape while writing this chapter in 2012. To set field notes off from the rest of the text, I put a box around them. The poem was written by 20th century Haitian writer Marie Thérèse Colimon-Hall, who was educated in Europe, but spent most of her life teaching in her native country, and who wrote in French (Martelly & Poujol Oriol, 2005). However, none of this historical information came into the classroom discussion, and the poem appears in Eric's class textbook in English (Baker-González & Blau, 1995: 26).

Not only does this poem illustrate the potential openness of meaning in Bakhtinian theory (1981), its publication history speaks to the issues of textual ownership raised earlier in this chapter. Originally published in a US literary magazine (Colimon, 1992), 'Encounter' was reprinted first in the ESL textbook used by Eric's class, which is now out of print (Baker-González & Blau, 1995), and later in the *Oxford Book of Caribbean Verse* (Brown & McWatt, 2005), where it still appears and can be purchased. Nevertheless, according to the Oxford University Press permissions department (email, 2013), it is not clear who currently holds copyright, especially since Colimon-Hall died in 1997. In other words, the history of this poem provides a good example of how the provenance of words cannot always be determined (Bakhtin, 1981) even in a society where establishing ownership is generally considered a necessary prerequisite for publication. For this reason, I quote only enough of the poem to clarify the classroom dialogue about it.

'Encounter' begins with a seemingly everyday conversation: 'I'd say: "How are you?" And you: "Fine, thanks"' (Colimon-Hall, 1995: 26). Perhaps for this reason, the discussion of the poem in Eric's class starts on a Bakhtinian note, with attention to voices:

Eric inquired, 'How many voices are there in the poem?'
A student replied that there was only one.
Eric agreed, 'So there is just one voice because the conversation is an imaginary conversation.'

> He wrote on the board:
> *Imaginary*
> Eric mentioned that 'imaginary' is the adjective form, then said, 'Very good. What's the perspective or point of view of the narrator? An omniscient narrator?'

Here Eric identifies himself as a teacher by drawing on a traditional literary discourse, using words like narrator, point of view, omniscient. The poem is rich with reported speech, but the class quickly accepts the conclusion that this is *imaginary* speech, and thus represents just one voice (although soon afterward the class comes back to the idea that there are two voices). So far, historicity appears only insofar as decontextualized literary analysis is itself a historically-based practice.

However, the next segment of the poem moves beyond basic greetings: 'I'd say: "We don't see you anymore."' (Colimon-Hall, 1995: 26). While the interlocutors in the poem continue in conversation, they increasingly seem to be talking at cross purposes. A couple lines later, the narrator states, 'I'd begin again very softly "Tell me..." And you, not hearing my mumbled words would go right on unsuspecting' (Colimon-Hall, 1995: 26). As Eric and his students continue their conversation, questions are raised about what type of relationship is represented in the poem, and with those questions, gender ideologies. This begins with discussion about the interlocutors' emotions, beginning with disembodied adjectives: 'uncomfortable... strange... distant...' Finally Eric directs them to 'make an inference' about the relationship. When I asked him about this in a later interview, he replied, laughing, that 'making inferences from a text is one of the key objectives of this course as stated in the curriculum and which I am trying to implement.'

In response to his prompt, Rafaela (young Mexican woman) takes a more definite stance than anyone so far by using a singular pronoun:

> Arguing that the interlocutors are 'romantic friends,' Rafaela said, 'If he don't care about this person, why does he think about this person?' After repeating her idea, Eric noted, 'You said a very interesting word. You said "he."' Students laughed. He asked, 'Who thinks this is a man?' Students laughed, and one said, 'no!' Eric went on, 'Who thinks this is a woman?' He had students raise their hands for the two possibilities.

Eric's initial question focused on the gender of the narrator, source of the two 'imaginary' voices (whom Rafaela had referred to as 'he'). In writing about voices in novels, Bakhtin argues that contrasting voices depict entire social worlds. Here, however, Eric and his students have the task of inferring which social world is being depicted by the voice or voices in the poem (which by now has lost its quotation marks). The author next portrays the voice(s) as remarking, 'Oh, (politely) you don't have your big straw hat anymore! But... No, not anymore. I'd answer And you, do you still like sugared almonds?'(Colimon-Hall, 1995: 26). Even in these lines where the imagery becomes more concrete, the poem remains radically unfinalized (Bakhtin, 1981), given that the specific items depicted, sugared almonds and straw hats, can be found in a wide variety of temporal and geographical locations.

In answer to Eric's question several students argue for one gender or the other without adducing evidence:

Perhaps to help students support their answers, Eric brought up the question of the hat in the poem, 'A big hat, that's interesting.' However, Saúl (Mexican man) did not take him up on this. Instead he commented, 'I think the gender is not really important. It's strongly about the situation inside everybody. Say 'hey, I think somebody is about um (...)?'" He began reading from the poem as if to support his assertion:

–Listen to that tune from the house opposite.

Then we would each go off across the city

Carrying in our hearts, full with silent sobs

Although Saúl had started the reading very tentatively, and he had not yet reached the end of the verse or even of the sentence, he concluded with strong falling intonation on the 'silent sobs' as if that was his point. Eric wrote on the board:

gender not important

Despite the unfinalizability of the poem, when Saúl says 'it's... inside everybody,' he suggests that this discourse is internally persuasive because he identifies with the emotions depicted, and expects everyone else to do the same. Throughout the discussion, in a process of adequation (Bucholtz & Hall, 2004), Saúl will argue for the universality of human emotion, and thus the ambiguity of gender in this poem.

Following up on Saúl's comment, and referring to a textbook question about the poem, Eric said, 'He's taken choice number five, gender doesn't matter....' Students laughed throughout Eric's comment, but

> he continued speaking 'which is perhaps a very interesting. . .good choice because the author doesn't identify it, so maybe that's the author's choice, but I and you usually have gender, so is there something in the text that supports your opinion about gender?'

Stefania, a middle-aged woman from Eastern Europe, then gave her own perspective, which was clearly based on a discourse of gender and emotion different from the one that Saúl had employed:

> Stefania said, 'I think the narrator is a man, and he is talking to a woman, and in the last sentence, they. . .like. . . "go across the city carrying in our hearts full with silent sobs." So I think that they have in the past some romantic friendship, and something is broken in this way, so they have something in their hearts. . .something warm ((laughing)) for each other but it cannot be thinking any more. So I think it's a romantic friendship between a man and woman (. . .) because two men can't be "full with silent sobs." ((laughing)) It cannot be between two men.'
>
> Eric said, 'That's interesting. Now, from my culture I would agree with that, but you from your culture, do you agree with that? If two men have a broken friendship, Simran, I am going to ask you very specifically, because your culture is very different. . . .' Simran (young Sikh man) did not reply.

Listening in 2012, I note how Eric offers his personal agreement, 'from (his) culture,' with Stefania's unmitigated assertion that 'two men can't be full of silent sobs.' This not only contradicts Saúl's argument that 'it's inside everybody,' but also raises the question as to whether Eric and I, both Anglo-Californians, are from 'the same culture,' given that I would be more inclined to Saúl's point of view. However, in 2006, when I first pondered these contrasting ideologies about gender, relationships, and emotion, my own gender ideologies and sense of historicity made a different (silent) contribution to the dialogue. Sitting in Eric's classroom with my laptop, I typed an 'observer's comment' to myself, putting it inside square brackets as I learned to do in graduate school:

> [I was thinking about the issue of homosexuality. It seemed a good time to bring it up, I probably would have. . .even if students are homophobic, and even if you don't have the goal of changing that, nevertheless, this is something that leaps to mind in the context of contemporary US culture, and they should recognize this. . . .But]

My own gender ideologies are apparent in the negatively evaluative word 'homophobic,' as well as the implication in 'even if' that a reasonable teacher might want to do something about this social problem; my sense of historicity appears as I write 'in the context of contemporary US culture,' a context in which I assumed that prejudices about sexuality should be rapidly diminishing.

In any case, no one else weighs in on the ideological question as to whether two men could have hearts 'full with silent sobs.' Instead, the class engages with the concrete detail of the straw hat, inadvertently triggering my gender ideologies and sense of historicity all over again.

> After an unrelated exchange about a coat that a student was wearing, Eric returned to Stefania's remarks. 'I made the same inference as her.' He then turned to another student, 'Is that the same for your culture? Do you think differently?'
> The student replied, 'I think the narrator is a man [. . .] because usually a woman has a big straw hat.'
> Eric said, 'I could agree with that.'
> Another student said this could be a man.
> Eric agreed that it could be a cowboy because of the big straw hat. 'From my perspective? Cowboys would never say that (. . .), because they don't talk about the past.' ((Many students laugh)). He went on, 'From my perspective, that is also a question. . .from a. . . .((speaking quickly)) it wouldn't be between two men, it would be a man noticing a woman's hat ((pause)). This idea of a big straw hat. My sister had a straw hat, none of my brothers did.' He made a note on the board, and asked for other ideas.

When I heard Eric's remark about cowboys, I wrote in my notes, again using square brackets:

[I was thinking about the fact that *Brokeback Mountain* just got nominated for a ton of Academy Awards, surely some of the students would be aware of this, whether or not they approved. . . . Gay cowboys thinking about their shared past? Isn't that what it's all about?!!]

Later, in an interview, I learned from Eric that his father had been an actual working cowboy on ranches in his youth, thus giving the word a greater emotional resonance and stronger historical trajectory for him than for me. For him, the discourse of cowboys is internally persuasive, whereas for me, it is something from the movies, almost entirely someone else's (Bakhtin,

1981). Of course, both Eric and his father presumably watched cowboy movies and picked up discourse from the actors to describe their lived experience ('cowboys never talk about the past'). Thus, like me, Eric brings historicity to his interpretation of the poem—but he draws on a different version of history than the one I have in mind.

Next, in order to return to the authoritative academic discourse that constituted his actual curricular objective, Eric employed a line from the poem that had been quoted by both Saúl and Stefania: '"We would each go off across the city." That's probably support that they are not farmers, not cowboys.' Knowing how to support arguments with evidence is part of the effective communication discourse that appears on the 2007 TESOL website (cf Kroskrity, 2004). When Eric asked for other support, and suggested the 'sugared almonds' as a possibility, a student finally addressed this detail, suggesting that 'he asked her' about them. After several turns in which no one was able to explain what sugared almonds had to do with gender, Eric tried asking whether men usually buy presents for women they like.

> Rather than respond to that question, Simran (Sikh man) broke in, using a strongly authoritative falling intonation, 'She's asking him.'
> Eric said, 'Ohhh, so you think the narrator is a woman? For the same reason?'
> 'No,' said Simran, in the same authoritative tone. 'Because he asked her about the hat, and she's asking him about the almonds.'

This exchange was followed by a closer reading of the poem to tease out the different voices, in which it was determined, as Simran had been contending, that the narrator was in fact the one who used to have a straw hat: it was clear that the first-person voice in the poem had just mumbled 'tell me...' at the point when his/her interlocutor went 'right on unsuspecting' and asked about the hat (Colimon-Hall, 1995: 26). At the end of this, at least two hands went up, and Eric called on Rafaela.

> Rafaela said, 'OK. I think...I am going to support him that he say it's a woman.' [Probably she is referring to Simran's comment].
> Eric clarified, 'Oh, that the narrator is a woman?'
> Rafaela replied, very definitely, 'Uh huh. It's a woman narrator. Because...it's a poem, maybe the poem talks...for love? And they were, there was a relationship? And maybe she fall in love with him. And it say that, "do you still like sugared almonds?" It's like she used

> to...give him almonds...for a present. And maybe, I don't know maybe he (left) her...'
>
> Eric said, 'OK. Maybe. Maybe.' Referring to Rafaela, he said, 'She is using the idea that poems about love...So you think that those usually come from women? Or?'
>
> Rafaela said, 'Men sometimes, I don't know...' ((She laughed))

In responding, Rafaela employs the concept of *support* that Eric has been promoting, although she does not use the word in the same way that Eric does; for her, 'support' seems to mean 'argue for.' She does not provide evidence, but simply her idea of what the poem is saying, based on Simran's insight about the gender of the interlocutors. The fact that she uses the word 'maybe' three times implies a belief that her ideas are plausible but far from certain (Eric uses the word 'maybe' in this way frequently, so she could have appropriated this discursive resource from him). Meanwhile, Eric is trying to get students to make explicit statements of their assumptions and stereotypes about gendered relationships ('poems about love usually come from women?'), but without much success. When I interviewed Eric about this discussion, he framed it as a critical thinking task: 'I wanted to help them try and vocalize and express those inferences, and understand that they were making an inference based on a possible gender or cultural stereotype, and so I was trying to bring that forward, get that out of them so we could analyze that.' Clearly students are drawing on assumptions and stereotypes to construct plausible scenarios, but they shy away from actually stating these (as Rafaela says, 'I don't know').

Having failed to obtain any concrete statements about sugared almonds (readers might ask themselves if they have any gendered cultural assumptions about sugared almonds), Eric went on to pose easier questions, such as whether the speakers are communicating well (Simran said no), and whether the conversation was taking place inside or outside. However, students quickly returned to gender issues.

> A male student said, 'Husband and wife. They are husband and wife.'
>
> Eric said, 'Maybe. If these people are in the same house, maybe they are husband and wife.'
>
> Several students, laughing, said, 'They are divorced.' [...]
>
> A female student quoted the poem, 'Because it says "I'd say: 'We don't see you anymore,'"' following which the male student reiterated, 'They're divorced.' A number of students spoke simultaneously, and Eric

said, 'Ahhh.' He commented, 'I think she gave us some good support. "We don't *see* you any more." ((He writes this on the board)). I mean, they're not together. I think that's pretty clear.'

A student said that they might be neighbors, and Eric agreed that this was possible.

Anton (middle-aged Eastern European) suggested that maybe they used to be husband and wife, 'they have children, but one of them left.'

Eric said, 'You know I like that? I never thought of that before, maybe the "we" is I and our children. This all goes back to Saúl's comment, maybe the gender is not really important. Why does the author make this so unspecific? We don't know for sure, if the narrator is a man or a woman, or the (other) is a man or a woman or how they are connected. We don't know for sure. Is there a reason for this? Why is this unspecific?'

Here Eric uses the word *support* again when a student quotes a line from early in the poem 'we don't see you any more' immediately after several students conclude that the poem is about a divorced couple. This in fact seems to be the most popular interpretation so far, both among the laughing students and to Eric ('you know, I like that.') However, none of the students use the word *support* the way Eric wants them to.

In any case, Eric has given an opening to Saúl to promote his view of the poem again. (My interpretation of what Saúl is saying appears in square brackets, of course):

After about ten seconds of silence, Saúl said, 'I think it is no...any conversation.' [In other words, the poem is not actually a conversation at all]

Eric agreed, 'Oh, you're right.'

Saúl continued, 'It is only everything...everyday happen. (Thinking) the way how it is, and then everybody go wherever. And taking your feelings (...).' [In other words, it is just a habitual internal dialogue].

Eric said, 'OK, keeping your feelings inside. All right.' He writes this on the board.

A female student said something softly.

Eric said, 'Did you hear that? Some poems don't have a gender so everybody can adopt the poem. It's a question of point of view, perspective. Maybe the author wants you to put yourself into the poem.'

Saúl's central point seems to be about hidden emotions, but he has earlier contended that emotions are not gendered. Building on Saúl's earlier point, Eric invites students to identify their own feelings with those depicted in the poem ('put yourself into the poem'). He then asks them to discuss the poem's message more generally with their neighbor, and report back to the class. When Rafaela 'reports back' it is clear that she identifies with the emotions depicted in the poem, and this affects her interpretation:

Rafaela said, 'They don't have gender and they don't have a specific passion. Because when I read the poem I remember my father.' She explained that they went for a long time without seeing each other, and when they finally saw each other again, they started a conversation like the one in the poem.
Eric said, 'Great! The author wants you to think about one relationship in your life that is broken.' [...] Kumar (middle-aged Sri Lankan man) said, 'The reader can apply this to themselves.'
Eric commented, 'That's a really good phrase. Remember that phrase. The author wants us to apply it to ourselves.'
He wrote on the board:
To apply it to ourselves
He asked, 'What's it?'
A student replied, 'the poem.'

Although many students in the class are not participating, a sense of intersubjectivity is being constructed through adequation (Bucholtz & Hall, 2004), and specifically through a discourse about the universality of emotions. This is strongly encouraged by Eric. When Rafaela says that the poem reminds her of talking to her father, Eric replies, 'Great!' Next, Kumar achieves a sentence in the same textbook discourse that Eric has been employing, 'the reader can apply this to themselves,' and Eric tells students to 'remember that phrase.' Stefania's statement that men can't be full of 'silent sobs' has fallen out of the conversation, despite Eric's earlier cultural identification with this sentiment. Rather, as this dialogue progresses, ESL students as readers of this poem are invited to remember their own broken relationships and hidden emotions—under the assumption that 'we all' have them. In fact, Saúl is the first student who has managed to present an abstract generalization as a possible message of this poem: the idea that keeping feelings inside is an everyday happening.

Eric, however, remains happy to have students constructing possible narratives (as opposed to abstract generalizations), as long as they are 'supported' by the text of the poem:

Eric said, 'When I thought of this at different times, I thought of different people, one woman, one man. (...) I never thought about until today, Anton's comment ((students laughing)). I never thought about this possibly being a husband with children, or the woman has the children, or a family situation, I never thought (...). Now I read it, and I think why not? I think it could work. ((pause)) Other questions? Other comments?'

Speaking softly, a female student pointed out the end of the poem: 'the empty pride of having kept our pain' (Colimon-Hall, 1995: 26). In her interpretation of the poet's intention, '(She) wants us to see the situation, inside of us, from this situation, we keep our pride inside ourselves, it's empty feelings.' Eric wrote *empty pride* on the board, and agreed, 'It helps us to think about pride, empty pride. They say 'pride is a cold bedfellow,' if you sleep with pride, it's very cold.'

As the discussion of the poem winds down, Eric returns to a point that he himself hadn't anticipated, the possibility that the protagonists were a divorced couple with children. A student, recognizing the importance in classroom literary discourses of finding the author's intention, concludes that we all know what it is to suffer from empty pride. It is indeed not too far of a stretch to argue that this might be Colimon Hall's intention as she orchestrates the imaginary voices in this unfinalized world (Bakhtin, 1981). Accepting this interpretation, Eric sums it up with a proverb I don't ever remembering hearing before, but which I recognize as an ancestral voice from an earlier stage of English when pride was sin, and shared beds were taken for granted.

In classrooms, histories and ideologies are not only invoked but also constructed. As Bucholtz and Hall point out, 'a common identity is a social achievement rather than a social artifact' (2004: 384): although not all students have participated, intersubjectivity has been brought into being in this classroom. To this intersubjectivity, participants have contributed their personal histories: Eric with cowboys, Rafaela with her father, Saúl with intense emotion, Stefania with men who won't admit to 'silent sobs.' This classroom dialogue illustrates Vitanova's contention that 'language and discursive practices give meaning to one's experience,' as well as her observation that these meanings are often 'multiple and contradictory . . . . in adult second-language classrooms, where divergent discourses . . . compete' (2010: 19). Although Eric keeps attempting to bring the class back to a literary exercise involving support for interpretations, a number of students engage with the text emotionally/volitionally (Bakhtin, 1993) and it is primarily on this level that intersubjectivity is constructed.

Conclusion: In Dialogue with Duane's Email, Alicia's Narrative and Eric's Students

In this chapter, in order to begin connecting Bakhtin's theoretical perspectives to language teaching, I have shared several events: an email interaction about the ownership of words; two Chilean teacher narratives about Communist students' resistance to English instruction; and a Haitian poem translated into English, depicting emotions that ESL students 'can apply to themselves'. I have used these artifacts to explore some theoretical ideas that appeared in English in the 1980s under the name of Mikhail Bakhtin, which are collectively known as dialogism (Holquist, 1990): words are shared; the context by which we understand words is historical; language varieties and societal discourses compete and conflict.

From a Bakhtinian perspective, events such as research interviews, classroom discussions and email exchanges are made up of utterances that arise from dialogue 'as a continuation of it and as a rejoinder to it' (Bakhtin, 1981: 222). He notes, moreover, that the dialogue in which a particular utterance participates may range widely across time and space, including all previous utterances which the current one 'refutes, affirms, supplements, and relies on' (Bakhtin, 1986b: 91). For example, Bakhtin (1984) sees the *Book of Job* in the Bible as an utterance with which Dostoevsky's *The Brothers Karamazov* is in dialogue. He also, however, refers to 'actual dialogue' (i.e. prototypical dialogue) as involving 'speaking subjects' whose utterances 'alternate' (Bakhtin, 1986b: 72), as seen in the class discussion of the Haitian poem. Indeed, the interaction between Eric and his students is filled with 'dialogic overtones' (Bakhtin, 1986b: 92). He and his students quote the poem directly, especially the words 'silent sobs', and they additionally draw on societal discourses and ideologies about gender, sexuality and emotion: Saúl's phrase 'inside everybody' is a common way to talk about human feelings.

In fact, Bakhtin states that all utterances have dialogic overtones (Bakhtin, 1984: 92). Nevertheless, he finds it necessary to contrast *monologic utterances*, which enforce a single point of view, with *dialogic utterances* that recognize a multiplicity of perspectives (Bakhtin, 1984: 279, 1986b: 92). White (2003) clarifies these ideas somewhat by referring to the former as dialogically contractive, while the latter are dialogically expansive. Alicia's story, in particular, portrays an experience of what might be called dialogical expansion (I expand here upon White, 2003), as she realizes that she must engage with her student's ideologies in order to provide appropriate pedagogical materials. In contrast, Stefania's assertion that 'two men can't be full of silent sobs' is dialogically contractive, since her words rule out any possibility that silent sobs might be 'inside everybody'.

The engagement of Eric's students with widespread ideologies and discourses points to the fact that a given utterance exists in dialogue not only with utterances directly known to the speaker, but rather comes as 'a *response* to preceding utterances of the given sphere' (Bakhtin, 1986b: 91, italics in original). While utterances often address previous comments and anticipate future remarks in face to face interaction, they also exist in dialogue with societal discourses, as when Eric draws on vocabulary and concepts from traditional literary analysis, or Alicia portrays her Communist student voicing the language of anti-imperialism. In broadly responding to previous utterances, each utterance in turn anticipates a response from interlocutors, who may be in the same room, or far distant across time and space: in fact, 'an essential... marker of the utterance is its quality of being directed to someone, its *addressivity*' (Bakhtin, 1986b: 95, italics in original). In our email exchange, Duane and I constructed dialogic utterances by drawing on specific texts, including most obviously the listserve email about Bronckart and Bota (2011), the cartoon in Ivanic's book (1998), and the plagiarism policies at his college. However, we were primarily engaged in dialogue with each other, regarding the value of Bakhtin's theories for our own work. Our priority was to comprehend each other, and only secondarily to engage the literature. It is only by including our emails in this chapter that I bring our words into a larger scholarly dialogue on the legacy of Bakhtin.

In this way, Bakhtin's concept of dialogue provides a way to analyze *discourse*, that is, language in use, as well as *discourses*, that is, characteristic ways of discussing and evaluating particular topics ('preceding utterances of the given sphere'). Moreover, the connections that remain mostly implicit in Bakhtin's work between discourse, dialogue and identity development have been elucidated further by later writers (e.g. Pavlenko & Lantolf, 2000). As Vitanova writes, we not only take on identities in interaction, but also engage in 'hidden' inner dialogues with discourses and 'as a result, a subject position is created' (Vitanova, 2010: 25). For example, in my own field note dialogue between Eric's class discussion and the film

Brokeback Mountain, I silently constructed a teacher identity for myself quite different from Eric's. However, it was never Bakhtin's intention to operationalize any of these ideas for language education, a task left to later authors.

Theorizing cultural pedagogy in the foreign language classroom, Kramsch sees dialogue occurring where 'speakers of different languages... struggle to keep the channels of communication open in spite or because of the ideological differences they recognize and maintain between them' (Kramsch, 1993: 23). This can be seen in Alicia's response to her student's challenges, which was clearly 'motivated by ambivalent feelings of both empathy and antipathy,... involve(d) a fundamental change in power' (in that Alicia gave up her privilege as a teacher to impose materials that reflect her own ideologies) 'and create(d) a special space and time at the boundaries between two views of the world' (Kramsch, 1993: 29–30).

Kramsch clarifies that dialogue involves not merely response and the anticipation of response, not merely the incorporation of others' words or societal discourses, but an effort at comprehension. As she points out, the goal in cultural pedagogy should be 'not only to exchange words with people who speak (the target) language but actually to understand what they mean' (Kramsch, 1993: 34). Eric clearly makes an effort to comprehend and engage his students. However, there is little other evidence in this class of 'speakers of different languages struggl(ing) to keep the channels of communication open between them' (Kramsch, 1993: 23), and still less 'actually... understand(ing) what (each other) mean' (Kramsch, 1993: 34). In the rest of this book, I will explore these ideas further, bringing them into dialogue with the contemporary literature on language ideologies, cultural pedagogies, and the development of teacher identities.

Notes

(1) This chapter draws upon data and analysis that first appeared in Menard-Warwick (2009d).
(2) In their 'translators' preface' to Voloshinov (1986), Matejka and Titunik state that Soviet semiotician V.I. Ivanov made the public claim in 1973 that Bakhtin was the real author of the works by Voloshinov and Medvedev. They add, 'Baxtin himself, then still alive, of course, had the opportunity to accept Ivanov's assertion or to deny it, but he remained silent and never made a public statement' (Matejka & Titunik, 1986: ix). They go on to say that when asked, he refused to sign a copyright affidavit as to his authorship of the books. Holquist states his belief that 'ninety percent of the text of the three books in question is indeed the work of Bakhtin himself' (Holquist, 1986: xxvi; cf Holquist, 1990).
(3) The introduction to the edited volume which contains 'Problem of Speech Genres' states that the essay was written in 1952–1953 (Holquist, 1986: xv). Stalin died in 1953.

(4) *Yanquí* is a derogatory term for US nationals used throughout Latin America. It has stronger political and economic connotations, as well as a more specific national reference, than *gringo*, the other common derogatory term used for Anglophone foreigners of European descent (primarily North Americans).

(5) I only give pseudonyms to students whose names I had access to while writing field notes—students whose names I learned were those who spoke a lot in class and whom the teacher addressed by name.

3 Language Ideologies in Chile and California[1]

The same day the Nazca plate slipped under the South American plate and Michael Jackson was acquitted (see Chapter 1), I interviewed Ruby, an adult-school ESL teacher in Farmington, California. I asked what she saw as the value of teaching ESL, and after a pause for thought, she replied as follows:

> **Ruby**: Well, I think, on an idealistic note, I think, ((pause)) English seems to be the de facto international language, so for people to understand one another, speaking English really helps, for them to be able to understand other cultures, speaking English helps. On a very practical note, and this one, I'm not as fond of this one, [...] I have taught a lot of people who just really are interested in hardcore capitalism, and they want to just climb the ladder, and English is a very important key, and that part is sort of sad to me.

Even more explicitly than the Communist student in Alicia's Chapter 2 narrative, Ruby draws discursive connections here between the English language and capitalism. She recognizes that many of her students want to learn the language out of economic motives (to 'climb the ladder'), and this seems 'sad' to her. She prefers the more idealistic side of her job, which for her involves helping people to 'understand other cultures' through learning English.

Similarly, Luke argues that teachers' work:

> requir(es) forms of intercultural capital, that is, the capacity to engage in acts of knowledge, power and exchange across time/space divides and social geographies, across diverse communities, populations and epistemic stances. (Luke, 2004: 1429)

This connection between English and intercultural capital represents a perception of language connected to the interests of Ruby's social group, adult ESL teachers in California, who benefit from their understanding of other cultures and have little chance to climb any kind of ladder. As Gal writes, 'language ideologies are never only about language. They posit close relations between linguistic practices and other social activities' (Gal, 2005: 24), such as international marketing and finance – or the kinds of cultural activities that lead to 'understanding' (e.g. hosting exchange students).

Language ideologies provide constant tension along ELT's discursive faultlines. In this chapter, I explore these perceptions of language that align with the interests of particular social groups (Kroskrity, 2000) in Las Peñas, Chile and Farmington, California. For each geographical context, I begin with ideologies that elucidate the purpose of English learning, as in Ruby's interview excerpt above (for more about Ruby, see Chapter 5). I then examine ideologies about the processes of language teaching, including questions as to which varieties of English should be prioritized, and why. Throughout this chapter, I will connect language ideologies to authoritative discourses (i.e. discourses that are widespread and dominant in society) as well as to internally persuasive discourses (discourses with which teachers seem to personally identify) (Bakhtin, 1981, see Chapter 2).

In discussing my research findings, I use *discourses* to refer to concrete ways of 'conceptualizing the world in words' (Bakhtin, 1981: 292), which construct evaluations of particular topics by using characteristic vocabulary, collocations and expressions. While discourses (often) instantiate ideological beliefs, ideologies themselves may be unspoken, and reproduced in practices (Olivo, 2003). To varying degrees, both ideologies and discourses can have material causes and consequences (Blommaert, 2005; Holborow, 2012a). For example, 'English is the universal language' discursively manifests an ideology, aligned with the interests of international business, which leads English to be a required subject in Chilean public schools. It is important to note that people (teachers) can enact ideologies (in their classrooms) that they are not aware of, and that they do not necessarily agree with. As Godley *et al.* (2007) write:

> Language ideologies influence...instruction in significant ways by framing particular uses of language as acceptable or unacceptable and by positioning particular students as more- or less-skilled language users... (They are) expressed through the patterns of classroom participation and through teacher and student talk. (Godley *et al.*, 2007: 103–104)

Thus, in this chapter, I draw on a range of data: in some cases, ideologies are explicitly stated; in others, they are enacted in practices. The data I use here come from classroom observation field notes and audiotaped interviews[2] conducted in both California and Chile, as well as from the videotaped 2006 intensive course on language and culture, which I co-taught for the Masters in English Teaching program at the ULP, including teachers' final essays for the class. In this chapter (as well as in Chapter 4 and parts of Chapter 6), I draw on data from many teachers without introducing individual teachers in depth; however, I do mention each teacher's context of teaching. For basic demographic information on teachers as well as dates of interviews and observations, see Appendix 2.

In my thematic coding of these data, I defined language ideologies as evaluations of language or linguistic practices in the interests of a specific social group, and in this chapter, I present, categorize, juxtapose, and problematize teachers' specific ideological statements. I do this first with my Chilean data, secondly with Californian data and then discuss common and contrasting trends. The section on Chile is partly based on Menard-Warwick (2013).

Language Ideologies in Las Peñas, Chile

While Chilean teachers at times equated English learning and teaching with economic success, they also called this equation into question based on their own life experiences and student critiques. Some teachers connected English learning to social stratification in Chile but also to its possible transformation, while others valued English for its perceived connection to a broader global culture rather than as a means to financial gain. In this regard, some teachers emphasized the cultural dimension, access to cultural products provided by English competence, while others emphasized the intercultural dimension, opportunities for cross-cultural communication. Many teachers spoke at length about how issues of social class and international politics complicated their work. In their own ideological positioning as English teachers, they were forced to take these factors into account.

The power of a global language

Azucena, a university instructor, first learned English in the 1970s as a high school exchange student in rural Minnesota. Upon returning home and starting university, her initial career choice was law, an undergraduate major in Chile. She told the following story about why she changed her major to English:

Azucena: I was in law school one years, and I didn't like it, because I don't like to memorize, I didn't like to study, and it was a time in which there was a lot of political problems, and my school was um very uh....they were in favor of the government, Pinochet in that case, and all my classmates, girls, we were all 18, 19 years old, and I wore jeans and they all wore skirts, high heels, and pearls, so I was like, I didn't fit in that environment. And I still wanted to be a teacher. But I wanted to be an elementary teacher because I liked to work with children. And my parents were very upset with this idea, and said, 'Well, but you know a little bit of English so why don't you at least be an English teacher?'

In this narrative, Azucena's rejection of her classmates' polished image (pearls and high heels) went along with her rejection of their politics. Choosing to work with children and wear jeans meant opting out of the pursuit of power in Pinochet's Chile. While the narrative does not imply that her 'upset' parents supported the dictatorship, it seems clear that they wanted her to choose a profession with more social clout than elementary education. Nevertheless, the discursive association between the English teaching profession and the prestige of the English language provided Azucena's parents some consolation for her rejection of a legal career. From their comment in the narrative, it appears that 'at least' an English teacher has more social power than an ordinary elementary school teacher in Chile.

Although Azucena does not explain why her parents preferred her to teach English, one common justification for the importance of English in Chile is the ubiquity of the language in global society (Seargeant, 2008). When I asked an older teacher at a public high school what she tells her students about English, she replied:

Sofía: Well, as I said before, 'Although you don't like it, you have to learn as a (cultural language), you see? It's part of your life, it's part of your environment, it's part of society, if you want to study in university, all the books are written in English. Okay? If you go to Internet, it's in English, if you listen to music, it's in English, and all the jobs are required a person that's trained in English.'

It is important to note that what Sofía is saying is not literally true; she overstates her case. Not all the books in the university are in English, the internet has a great deal of Spanish content, it is very possible to listen to music in Spanish and many Chilean professionals get by with minimal English competency. Nevertheless, this is a clear statement of a common ideology about the importance of English learning in Chile.

Norma, at that time the director of the foreign language department at the ULP, draws on authoritative discourses (Bakhtin, 1981) to argue for the economic value of English:

Norma: Ever since they started with this free trade treaty,[3] there was an awareness of a need of improving the levels of English, and that's one thing. The second idea is that since Chile is viewed as a safe place to visit, then there is tourism on the other side, and so that's another area where English is absolutely necessary. Those would be the two areas, right? Uh, even to trade with Chinese, and that's why I think we should encourage kids to learn English.

The belief that English is essential for international business has become a self-fulfilling prophecy around the world. Writing about Korean families in Singapore, Park and Bae (2009) note that they share the language ideology that 'good English skills are an indispensable requirement for success in the global economy' (Park & Bae, 2009: 368). However, not all teachers who saw English as 'universal' emphasized its value as a business language. There are similar authoritative discourses about the universal cultural value of English, as in Alán's interview statement below:

Alán: English takes you anywhere, you can read about almost anything you want if you know English, or if you speak English, you can speak to almost everybody on the planet and also because it comes from these countries that show a wide variety of cultural aspects, you know, different people, different races, different religions, yeah, so I think it's all connected.

Alán, one of the younger ULP English instructors, had spoken at length in his interview about his interests in art, film and literature. I had asked if he saw a connection between these cultural interests and his work as a language teacher. Although my question was potentially a personal one about his cultural identity, there was nothing personal about this particular answer, which highlights both cultural and intercultural dimensions of English as an international language.

Other teachers talked more directly about their own experiences in this regard, so we can see what these authoritative discourses look like as they become internally persuasive. As one adult-school teacher stated in my intensive MA class:

Rita: I realized last night that when I decided to study English, was because I thought, 'Okay, English is going to be the future, right, so let's do it . . . .' And I decided to study because of that and now that I can speak English, right, I have noticed, that because of English, I have had the opportunity to experience so many wonderful things, right? Not because of money, not because of jobs, not because of travel, but because I have had the opportunity to meet so many people. And for me that's so important, right? because I have the chance to know about other peoples' culture just because of English.

Here we can see an opposition constructed between the illusory economic value of English and the more concrete intercultural value: 'the chance to know about other peoples' cultures'.

Moreover, despite claims that English is important for success in Chilean society, few teachers gave me concrete examples of times when English had been actually necessary for them. The narrative below, recounted to me by Maritza, a 5th-year undergraduate prospective teacher, is particularly interesting because stories of actual English use are rare in my Chilean data:

Maritza: I have a friend that is a making a post grad. . .in physical education, and she asked me, 'Please help me, because all the handouts that the teacher gave me, are in English,' 'Okay, I'm going to help you,' and I translate all the handouts, [. . .] and all [her] classmates that day, tell me, 'Oh, you're great, you are fantastic,' oh, I was like a queen, ((laughing)) [. . .] because they said, 'We never have the opportunity to learn English, and now we know that it's very important.' [. . .] Because even the teacher was going to make the class in English, [. . .] but they said, 'No, it's awful,' they have to ask for the teacher that (they) have to speak in Spanish, and it was difficult for him because he was Chinese, and he speaks Portuguese, ((laughing)) and English, [. . .] and he has to make the class in Spanish, [. . .] It was difficult, very difficult, and English, now, it's like the language that everybody in the world speak.

This ethnically Chinese Portuguese-speaking physical education instructor is a good example of the kind of global citizen who depends on English competency to communicate across national borders; however, the Chilean graduate students described by Maritza see English as 'awful' and 'difficult', and are able to insist on having their needs met as monolingual Spanish speakers. Although in this context a proficient English speaker is like 'a queen', Maritza's narrative does not substantiate Sofía's argument that high school students will not be able to access higher education without English (or even Maritza's own argument that 'everybody' speaks English).

When I asked Maritza's classmate, Edith, about the value of English, she mentioned the economic reasons such as trade agreements and trade with China cited by Norma, then noted like Rita that English is the language of 'the future' (cf Blommaert, 1999), finally ending like Maritza with the argument that 'everyone has to be speaking English'. Thus, although few Chileans are currently fluent in English, there is widespread belief, at least among English teachers, that this needs to change.

Complications of social class and politics

If English competence in Chile is not yet necessary or sufficient for general academic or professional success, it is nevertheless associated with the higher social classes, who have traditionally received high-quality language instruction in private educational venues. While teachers themselves did not necessarily identify with the upper classes or with standardized Spanish, they valued standardized English as part of their own professional competence and as a potential asset for their students. For those few teachers I interviewed who were working with elite students, this was an easy argument to make. As Diego (see Chapter 1) described his private high school students:

> **Diego**: They know they are going to study in university. I told them if you are going to study in the university, medicine or architecture, you need to speak English. You need to know the language. 'Oh sure, I know that, I know I want to be a doctor...' 'But how about if you are going to study in the United States, you need to know the language.' They know that. They know that. Their parents know that.

Students like this were not very common in the experiences of the teachers I talked to, and many of the teachers themselves had been unable even to travel to an English-speaking country.[4] Nevertheless, this connection between English and the elite then raises a question: if English is associated with the upper classes, can we work toward social equity by teaching English? As one elementary school teacher, Amanda, wrote in an MA class essay:

> English would be the language able to change the relationship between these specific individuals (those from the lowest strata) and the given social group (Chilean society). But, the most important point is that English could permeate in these individuals' very thinking and way of viewing the world. To open their eyes and know other realities and

understand that inequality must not be seen as something 'normal'. English would be the weapon against this unequal system.

This is an idealistic view of the value of English for social change. However, a far more common way for teachers to talk about working-class students is to note their belief that English is irrelevant (MA classroom videotape):

> **Hector** (elementary school teacher): I have this huge problem with my school. I work with very low social class students, and they see English as an un-useful subject. And it's my everyday struggle, that I am trying to teach them... that English could be a plus for them, a cultural plus, because in the society that we are living now, [...] in which a large amount of information [...] is everything. They need to get involved with these changes, and they need English because it's the global language, so to speak. So that's what I have to do almost every day because I come to a classroom for example, and... I have 45 students, and 13 students are not motivated to learn language, because [...] they think they are not going to use it, because they think that when they finish high school, they are going to work I don't know, cleaning houses, being mechanics.

It can be noted that it is a minority of working-class students who complain, but this minority tends to stand out when teachers talk about their work (and even the majority is usually not very successful in learning English). Similarly, Alicia, who taught public high school (see Chapter 2), described to me 'two or three very mature students, thirteen fourteen years old' who told her, 'You shouldn't teach us so many things or try to make such a big effort for us because our parents are in jail or are lost or whatever, so we are never going to be able to pay university studies or anything.'

In discussing which variety of English to teach in order to help students advance socially, most teachers agreed that standardized English would be the most valuable (Godley et al., 2007; Milroy, 2001a, 2001b; Wortham, 2001). As Alán (see above) argued in the MA language and culture class:

> **Alán**: Students need to know standard English because it will be better for their future communication, I mean, it will allow them to communicate everywhere, to not be discriminated by certain social groups, if you speak good English without a slang accent, original accent from your original language.

Here Alán distinguishes standardized English, necessary to avoid discrimination, from both a slang accent and a foreign accent, thus indexing ideologies that privilege 'native speakers' (who do not have a 'foreign' accent) while depreciating speakers of non-standard dialects who have a 'slang' accent, as African-American English is at times described (Godley et al., 2007). Aware of the prevalence of non-standard English in pop culture, teachers had different perspectives on how to deal with this in the classroom.

For example, in Genaro's professional development class for English teachers at ULP, there seemed to be a general consensus that error should be avoided, that 'language use is prescriptive, governed by rules that are determined and enforced by authorities' (Godley et al., 2007: 117), even when practicing the differences between formal and informal English, as seen in my field notes:

Genaro told them, 'Now I would like you to write down two letters, one formal and one informal of the same length. In the informal letter use the same vocabulary [from the text]. For example, "last night I got in so exhausted that I had a bite to eat and then went to sleep."' He said they should also write a formal letter, 'maybe to your principal.' There was some laughter at this. He said, 'Write a letter and then we will project it on a transparency.'

The students asked if they should do this in groups, and he said yes.

Genaro clarified that it should not be the same letter as in the text, 'Use your own insight, but use the same vocabulary.'

A student asked if the letter should involve apologizing. Genaro said not necessarily, it could be a secret or an anecdote.

The groups all started working noisily together. Genaro attempted to get their attention unsuccessfully. Finally he said loudly, 'Colleagues! Yoo hoo! After you have written the letters, write them on the transparency with this pen, and be sure not to make mistakes because this one is permanent.'

One of the men said, 'Oh my god.'

Although 'oh my god' indexes the ideology that 'the goal of language learning is correctness rather than effectiveness' (Godley et al., 2007: 113), the exclamation seemed at least partly tongue-in-cheek, since there were no negative consequences to making a mistake on a transparency.

At the same time, teachers reported that many Chilean students negatively associated English with the United States or the United Kingdom.

While teachers themselves held positive views of the English language (regardless of their own opinions of US politics), they had to deal with their students' ideologies. The following question commonly arose: if English is associated with the United States and the United Kingdom, does learning English index favorable attitudes toward those countries – and to their economic structure and foreign policy? While Diego taught private high school students during the day (see above), he taught at a public adult school in the evening, and found his students' political questions challenging:

> **Diego**: I am always trying to be positive about the cultural burden of the language. Because there are many students who feel that English language could be negative. They don't agree, for example...when I say English, they say Bush. Or Iraq. Or the war there. 'No, it's an empire...' OK. So I take the positive things. What can be good for you about the English language? This is what I am trying to do with my students [...] [at the] night school. Adult people. So they have lots of prejudice about United States.

This was not a problem for all teachers, but a huge problem for some. In the following narrative, Alán, currently a university instructor (see above), describes in an interview why he stopped teaching public high school after a year spent improving his English in the United Kingdom. Here, he connects anti-imperialist, anti-capitalist politics with a rejection of English learning – but notes that the same students wanted to learn the non-standard English of rap lyrics:

> **Alán**: [The students] didn't care about English, they didn't like me, when I came back from England, [...] they thought that I was, like I belonged to a higher class or something like that, you know, they felt rejection, they showed rejection towards me [...], they said that 'the English people were imperialists, like the Americans, that they were capitalists, they only wanted to conquer us, with their ways and their methods, that if I liked it so much, why didn't I stay there.' And I'm talking to you about very young people, you know, fourteen, thirteen years old. Or, well they wanted to learn about, if they wanted to learn, they wanted to learn about uh bad words, they wanted to learn about rap lyrics, hip-hop lyrics, things that I didn't know, anyway, because I couldn't translate them, you know, because they use lots of slang [...] In the end, I didn't want to do anything, I just wanted to leave, I didn't spend much time struggling for finding a solution, I felt very upset, and

like disenchanted, especially after coming back, I talked to the principal, and I talked to our counselor, the counselor in the school, and I was very honest with them, so they said that if I was feeling like that, I should stay till the end of term, and walk away ((laughing)). That's what I did.

A number of teachers told similar stories about leftist youth in high school. Sofía convinced one such student, a talented athlete, that he might need English if he were invited to compete in Australia. However, the teachers who were most successful with these students were often those who could incorporate the popular music (and to some extent the non-standard English) that they enjoyed and appreciated. This can be seen in Alicia's story from Chapter 2, in which she uses a Rage Against the Machine song to change a Communist student's attitude toward English learning. Diego, too, mentioned using songs as a way to motivate learners. However, he found that student attitudes toward English additionally affected how much English he could use in the classroom, so his practices in this area varied considerably between the elite high school and the adult school. He said that at the private high school he spoke English about 90% of the time in class, but that sometimes with his senior students he used it even more:

Diego: Some of my classes? 100%. Some of them, 100%, no Spanish. ((laughs)). 'Don't say anything in Spanish, I don't understand Spanish. I don't speak Spanish. Say it in English.' 'Ohhh, pero, teacher...' 'Sorry, what did you say?' 'Oh, but teacher...' 'OK. I understand.'

However, things were very different with his working-class adult students:

Diego: Well, I start my classes in English, you know, 'How are you? Sit down. Today we are going to talk about...This is the activities...,' you know? But then, no, you know, 'Teacher, what are you talking about? I don't understand! Why do you say so? I am not from the United States!' ((harsh voice tone)) They want it in Spanish, right? So, OK, no, in Spanish. Then I explain in Spanish, and have a little moment of English. [...] Just one drop ((laughs)) of English.

In fact, he said his administrator at the adult school had pressured him to use Spanish in the English class to make it easier for students to pass. Diego quotes him saying, 'Remember, those are workers.' In other words, working-class students need to pass tests and earn a high school diploma but are never expected to actually use English. In contrast, the university classes I observed were primarily in English with very brief codeswitches into Spanish, as noted in one set of field notes from Alán's classroom:

Alán said laughing that essays were due Tuesday July 12 'because I need to correct them before the end of July. If you don't like it, it's just the way it is, I'm sorry. Essay number 2, sería bueno en esta fecha, so I can correct it and give it back to you the next week before the oral tests, the final tests.'
On the board he had written:
July 12th-13th essay 2
Final test semana del 26 al 29 julio.

Spanish with these intermediate students was not strictly necessary but was used to emphasize certain points, or perhaps simply because codeswitching felt natural ('sería bueno en esta fecha' translates as 'it would be good on this date' and 'semana del 26 al 29 julio' translates as 'week of 26–29 July').

Thus, teachers could easily state reasons why it is valuable to learn English, very frequently repeating the discourse of English as important for economic success. Certainly, many Chileans, especially middle-class Chileans, do want to learn English for a variety of reasons. However, many Chileans who are required to study the language do not anticipate ever using it; many of these reluctant students have learned to argue back against the rather vague reasons ('globalization') that are enough to convince English majors. Thus, teachers have had to confront social class and international politics, often finding that few people could see the value of English in the current context. And teachers almost never offered examples of their students actually using English, for example, to get a job.

Rather, teachers tended to employ discourses around English that they found 'internally persuasive', based on their personal experiences. In my interview with Tomás, a prospective teacher, I asked him whether he had known foreigners or other multilingual people as a child, and he replied:

Tomás: No, I haven't, no, not really, but it always caught my attention the English language, because Las Peñas...is a very small town, and maybe well, when I watched movies, I don't know, ((pause)) I wanted to know something about it because it...was so strange for me and compared with a small town like Las Peñas.

Later in the interview, when I asked why he wanted to teach, he came back to this same expansive sense of being part of a larger world:

> **Tomás**: I want to say to my students that 'the world...doesn't end in the corner of their street' [...] because I realized very young, very child, that the world was very huge [...] but there are lot of students, lot of young people, that doesn't know that, they think that just, the only city in the world is Las Peñas and there is no more, I don't know, it's just like they just em blind their eyes and think, 'Well, I live here, and I got some drugs, so I am happy,' and that is no good, that is no world, and this is something, but uh I like to do something for it....

In fact, when teachers talked about their own experiences with English, as opposed to reasons why people in general should learn English, they, like Tomás, often mentioned encounters with popular culture that had given them a broader outlook (Tomás specifically mentioned *Schindler's List*, a Hollywood film about the Holocaust). A few cited experiences with foreigners. English had not made them wealthy and successful, but it had connected them with the world beyond northern Chile. As Rita (see above) wrote in an MA essay:

> The concept of international language means that English is no longer the property of a few countries where it is spoken as the native language, but it belongs to everybody [...] If you want to be part of the world you must speak English, otherwise you are out. So integrativeness should be the most important reason to learn English. People who have not understood this yet are the ones who see English only as a way to get a better job or more opportunities to get success.

In this view, English is an important asset, not so much for the global marketplace, but rather for global citizenship, for participation in an expanding global culture where 'English belongs to everyone'.

In this way, teachers responded ideologically to the general status of English and Spanish in Chile, which corresponds to the relation between these languages under globalization. As Mar-Molinero writes:

> While both languages are often the official languages of international organizations, it is well known that English will in the vast majority

of places be the one chosen for communication .... Equally significantly, much popular cultural activity which expects to cross national boundaries is in English, such as pop music, sports events and cinema. Despite the large numbers globally of speakers of Spanish, in all these scenarios Spanish takes a back seat to English. (Mar-Molinero, 2000: 204)

However, none of the teachers seemed to find it problematic that English was so 'universal', especially because Spanish dominance was such a powerful trend in Chile (and neighboring countries). In Chile, they could see English promoted by the government and international business, resisted by leftist movements and consumed (e.g. as music on the radio) but not learned or used by most of the populace. This is similar to the way Hawkins describes English in Tunisia: 'All students must study English, and it is widely regarded as a very useful language. In practice however, its usefulness is somewhat limited' (Hawkins, 2008: 371). Indeed, since economic success as a result of English learning seemed illusory in northern Chile, teachers tended to redefine globalization to focus on cultural rather than economic aspects.

Language Ideologies in Farmington, California

When I asked California teachers about the value of ESL teaching, I got two kinds of answers. One, less ideological, stressed the joy of teaching motivated students. As Eric, a community college instructor (see Chapter 2), explained his work, 'I am feeding hungry people. . ...and it's very satisfying to work with people who want to learn.' The other type of answer emphasized the value of English for helping immigrants socially and economically to 'fit' into communities (see below).

Throughout their interviews, teachers also extolled the value of diversity and cross-cultural communication, which they saw facilitated by their work in the ESL classroom; in other words, they stressed the intercultural value of teaching English, as some of the Chileans did. Their view of English as *the* intercultural language may have contributed to the unease most felt with students' use of their first language in the ESL classroom. Teachers' resulting efforts to restrict classroom L1 use took place in a larger context where many Californians view immigrants and their languages as problematic. Thus, ESL teaching straddles a powerful faultline as multilingual teachers who value 'diversity' attempt to maintain (primarily) monolingual classrooms in a society that devalues multilingualism.

'Fitting in'

The five younger Californian teachers were current MATESOL students or recent graduates. They were far more likely than the practicing teachers I interviewed to stress the value of ESL instruction for 'fitting in', a term that Charles used explicitly: 'older people want to find jobs, they have more personal reasons, perhaps fitting in, interacting more.' In Linnea's words, 'if you know English better you'll be more successful, at life and at school, getting a job and communicating better with people.' While these remarks describe both economic and social values for English, other younger teachers' answers reflect the tension ('not only...but also') between economic and cultural reasons for learning English so prevalent in my Chilean data. As Molly commented:

Molly: I think in order to not only gain just a good fiscal income but also being engaged in the larger community that's English speaking. It's important [...] Just because it's an English speaking environment I think you limit your opportunities for yourself and your family if you don't learn the language.

Similarly, Jokwon in a follow-up email stated, 'It would open more doors not only for practical reasons (job, basic communication, etc.), but for personal enrichment reasons as well.'

These are clear statements of a widespread authoritative discourse about the value of English instruction in California, or anywhere where English is the dominant language. As in Chile, this authoritative discourse probably overstates the case, since English learning does not necessarily lead to a good income or engagement in the larger community (Warriner, 2007). At the same time, two prospective teachers implied that English was less dominant than it used to be. Linnea, bilingual in Mandarin Chinese, described English as 'the dominant language alongside Spanish', while Martin, in explaining why his mother had not learned Spanish from her immigrant parents, put the reasons in the past tense: 'I don't know, you came here, and you spoke English. We're talking about the 40's and 50's.' Moreover, Jokwon hedged his answers by adding the disclaimer, 'While I agree people do get by without adopting the language to a functional level...'

Of the more experienced teachers, Susanna, a community college instructor, was the only one who emphasized concrete economic and social values for learning English:

Julia: What do you see as the value of teaching ESL? What makes your job worthwhile and meaningful?

Susanna: ((pause)) I guess I mean just the basics of I know(ing) that I'm helping make someone's life better, that I'm making a direct impact into someone's life, you know, giving them these skills whether or not they go on and get a college degree or not, they're learning English that will help them participate more in the community, that will help them get a better job, that will help them, you know, sometimes just even communicate with their family members, you know, and so I feel like I'm making a direct impact on individuals.

Thus, Susanna's answer was similar to the younger teachers, but for her the authoritative discourses had become internally persuasive: she could see herself making a 'direct impact on individuals'.

Valuing diversity

While not all teachers stressed the importance of English for 'fitting in', I found more uniform agreement with Ruby's statement that 'for people to understand one another, speaking English really helps, for them to be able to understand other cultures, speaking English helps'. The desire to 'understand other cultures' is prevalent among English language teachers (see Chapter 4); in Seargeant's words, 'the ideology of universal communion is still a key factor in many people's relationship with foreign language education' (Seargeant, 2008: 227). As Ruby went on to say:

Ruby: And I have had many students over the years express many times how they learned so much besides English, in that classroom. It was just learning and the friendships that they made with people [...], and they say, 'you know, I've never in my whole life met a Japanese person.' 'I've never in my whole life met a...such and such or a such and such' and there they are sitting with those people.

The value of diversity is a widespread authoritative discourse in California, if not yet universally shared. In a history of recent decades in California, Starr explains the state's 'theory' about diversity:

According to this theory, the more diverse an organization or an enterprise might be along the lines of race, ethnicity, gender, and sexual orientation, the more vital it became...A diverse society (is) by definition a better society. (Starr, 2004: 209)

Similarly, Leeman and Martinez argue that diversity has become 'commodified' in education and 'constructed as beneficial for the majority as well as the minority' (Leeman & Martinez, 2010: 51). This celebration of diversity can extend to linguistic diversity as Bucholtz *et al.* found:

> [Some Californians] espouse a multicultural language ideology wherein linguistic diversity is viewed as inherently valuable...Some respondents point to the sociolinguistic harmony and tolerance that they associate with this situation, stating that speakers in such areas learn to communicate with and adapt to speakers of other languages and dialects. (Bucholtz *et al.*, 2008: 73)

Teachers' support of this ideology is illustrated by Susanna's comment about student nationalities:

> **Susanna**: One of the things I really like about Farmington Community College is that it has a very diverse population, there's a lot of students from Asia, Latin America, Russian, and the various Russian...Ukraine, Uzbekistan, a wide variety of Eastern Europeans, also from, you know I have students from Africa, the Middle East, and so it's really a very diverse population and I really enjoy that about teaching here.

A few minutes later, she again included the diversity of the students in a list of things she liked about her job, along with 'support from the dean'. Veronica (see Chapter 1) described her high school classroom with similar enthusiasm:

> **Veronica**: I love that world, I love that world, I love being in that classroom with that [students speaking Spanish], and I have kids, I have kids from Belarus, and some kids from Pakistan, kids from India, so there (are) different languages in (there).

I found that younger teachers were less likely to mention 'diversity' explicitly but more likely to embody it. All six of the experienced California teachers I interviewed were of Anglo-American descent (including Ruby who was born in Brazil to expatriate parents, see Chapter 5); out of the new teachers, two were Asian-American (Filipino and Chinese), one was part-Latino and two were white. Their generation perhaps takes 'diversity' more for granted, although Molly, a second-year MA student, who had grown up in an all-white rural community, displayed the same excitement as the older teachers:

Molly: Getting to meet people from all over the world, and just amazing, like, it's been an amazing experience, just sitting in a classroom teaching [ESL], and having students from a variety of countries, some of these countries, they don't talk to each other, there are political issues and they're sitting in the same class together, learning, and so I just think it's exciting.

Similarly, Jokwon, in his follow-up email to me, wrote, 'learning English in California will make one more aware of interculturality and learn to appreciate the wonderful diversity the state has.' Jokwon here states the authoritative discourse common in California about valuing diversity, which becomes internally persuasive through concrete examples such as Molly's. This is also something that he has lived as a Filipino-American from San Francisco involved in both Japanese anime and hip-hop dance (see Chapter 4). These excerpts highlight how English instruction discursively connects to diversity, in that English facilitates positive experiences with 'students from a variety of countries', or in other words, intercultural experiences. In Ruby's example, without English class, 'they' would never meet a Japanese person.

The value of diversity had in fact become an institutional ideology at Farmington Community College, which held a diversity fair on Melinda's campus during the weeks I came to observe her class. As she explained after a classroom discussion about the fair:

Melinda: I wanted them to see that diversity isn't just ethnic and cultural [...] but we like to talk about diversity on our campus to be very inclusive, in that the things that make us different from the groups that others would link us to, can bring us together with people who are from different groups. For example, if you have a physical disability, that kind of diversity helps you belong to another micro-society of some kind, or if you're a gay person, ethnic and linguistic diversity is diminished by the commonality that you share. And so diversity is very, very important to understand in ways that go beyond the things that people can see or hear.

Whereas ethnicity is what Californians think of first when they say 'diversity', Melinda and her college were trying to take this value further into other categories of identity, to recognize that students had multiple identities. She saw opening her students' eyes to diversity, broadly conceived, as an important part of her job. When I asked her how she taught culture in the ESL classroom, she replied:

Melinda: My job is not so much to acculturate or to teach directly about culture, but to bring students to an understanding that [...] different isn't bad, that different is different. [...] You can't say 'well, my way is the only way.'

This statement by Melinda could have been made by almost any of my interviewees: cultural relativity is one of the first lessons that contemporary language teachers learn about culture, and most are happy to inculcate the value of cultural diversity in their classrooms. However, as Melinda also indicates, there are many kinds of diversity, a lot of dimensions on which human beings can differ from each other – and some of these dimensions are easier to accommodate than others. Ironically, linguistic diversity (in the form of L1 use) constitutes a significant discursive faultline in many California classrooms.

L1 in the L2 classroom

Of all the teachers I interviewed, Susanna (see above) had the firmest policies against the use of student languages in her community college classroom. She had been a Spanish major in college, had studied abroad in Spain, was married to a Latino immigrant and spoke the language with his parents who lived in the Farmington area. Knowing all this, I asked if she ever spoke Spanish with her students:

Susanna: Never in class, for a variety of reasons, one is they're there to learn English, and I don't necessarily want to let them feel like they have an out that they can start talking in Spanish, and then the other reason, of course, is because my classes are usually very culturally mixed, and so it would be unfair to speak to one group in their language when others can't, and then I have an English-Only policy in my class where the students can only speak English [...] Sometimes out of class, not often, because again I want to encourage them to use their English as much as possible, but every once in a while, especially if there's a student who is particularly struggling with something, and I think an explanation in Spanish would just be really helpful for that student, then I will [...], and I do tell them 'not in class'.

This explanation, that using the students' first language would be unfair to students who did not share that language, was a common way for teachers to explain English-Only policies. Linnea, a recent MA graduate, specified that she would not use her Mandarin Chinese skills in a linguistically mixed class: 'I feel like it would be an unfair advantage, if someone speaks Chinese and someone speaks Spanish, I can only help the Chinese.'

Similarly, MATESOL student Molly argued:

Molly: Well, that's hard because if you're dealing with like a class, say, a high school class and there's two Vietnamese speakers and five kids from Mexico, and two from Honduras, [...] and you only know Spanish and like you're helping five, six, seven kids out of the whatever by being able to explain to them a little better the issue, and not this other population that's sitting there going 'ok, well they just got extra help there and everything's clarified for them, but what about us? I still don't understand what you're talking about.'

Thus, in order to make an argument for (primarily) English-Only pedagogy, Molly dialogically voices hypothetical Vietnamese students surrounded by Spanish speakers and feeling lost (Bakhtin, 1981). However, she went on to say that even in a linguistically homogeneous class, she still would expect teachers to use English: 'I think that most teachers, their goal is to get the students to learn the second language, [...] they're not going to be using a significant amount of that first language.' Continuing to mull the issue, Molly said that she was not sure: that it could be good for students to see that their teacher is bilingual, but that she herself was disappointed when her German instructor taught mostly in English. Veronica displayed similar ambivalence (see Chapter 1), stating her personal preference for L2-only pedagogy, then additionally noting that when she did use Spanish in her high school classroom to build rapport with Latino students, she had to be cautious 'because the non-Spanish speakers, one in particular gets, they get really angry'.

Susanna, however, displayed no ambivalence, seeming quite sure that English-Only was best, regardless of the preferences of the students. I asked specifically about her beginning ESL computer skills class, and she said she maintained her English-Only policy in that context:

Susanna: I do encourage them to help each other, but to try to help each other in English, and I try, you know I work really hard to give them the vocabulary, to do it, and, you know, hopefully they're able to do it, sometimes, you know, there are some students who just, you know, between the frustration of English and computers, sometimes just can't do it, so I encourage them to maybe get help from (their) friends out of class. But not in class, because again, I don't want to break down the policy, and usually it's more of a problem with Russian students, but once I give them a little foothold of 'Okay, we can use Russian,' then they just completely take (over). [...] [At our satellite campus] it's a really big problem, because there the classes are 90 to sometimes 100 percent Russian, and so if I am not very strict about the English-Only policies, then it becomes a Russian-speaking zone.

Thus, from Susanna's perspective, it is important not only to maintain English-Only policies for reasons of fairness in a linguistically diverse class, but also to prevent overuse of the first language in a linguistically homogeneous class. Moreover, prohibiting classroom L1 use remains a priority even in situations where students are experiencing 'frustration' and 'just can't do it'.

Other teachers had more nuanced policies. Charles, an MA student who had taught in Korea, said he would like to see 'more L2 usage just in general' but that he considered L1 use necessary for certain purposes, 'especially for difficult grammar points or lower level instruction'. From Ruby's perspective as an adult-school instructor:

Ruby: I think basically your first language is a huge resource, and I would not, I don't like it when students just sit there and are constantly talking in their first language and generally I take care of that problem pretty easily by saying, you know, 'Here's your big chance to speak English,' you know, 'You can speak your language any other time.' But on the other hand, I sometimes tell my students, if I try to explain something, if they don't understand, I try to explain in other words. If they still can't, I just ask [another person from] their country, and I say, 'Can you translate for them and just tell them what it is?' And I'm usually surprised because they. . .never have a quick translation. It seems to always ((laughing)) be complex and involve a lot of words.

In explaining a similar policy around vocabulary translation for his community college students, Eric stated that, on the one hand, 'I don't want to alienate my two Farsi speakers and my two Vietnamese speakers just because twenty-five people in the class speak Russian,' but that, on the other hand, 'a quick translation can sometimes be the best, fastest way to learn'.

Out of all the teachers I interviewed, whether in California or Chile, Melinda (see above) was the most outspokenly positive about L1 use in her community college ESL classroom:

Julia: Under what circumstances would you consider it appropriate to use a student's first language in a second language classroom, if any?
Melinda: ((pause)) If I could speak them all, I would try to do it intentionally as much as possible, just to demonstrate that I value their first languages.

Melinda also said that she encourages students to maintain their first languages at home, telling them that 'your first culture is precious' and that bilingualism has cognitive benefits for children. Her academic background in theoretical linguistics had led her to value native-speaker competence in all languages. However, it is important to note the 'if' in Melinda's response above. She did not in fact speak any of her students' languages fluently (although she was fluent in American Sign Language). Thus, Melinda was able to demonstrate the value of first languages, but only minimally. She said that she would at times ask students to write sentences in their first language, and then the class would analyze the different structures in different languages, for example to 'talk about how adverbial information is put into the sentence'. I did not observe this kind of activity, but I did see her using Spanish in a linguistically diverse class during a discussion about an upcoming campus talk by Guatemalan indigenous rights activist Rigoberta Menchú:

Melinda said, 'The people who lived here first, we call Native Americans or Indians. In the Spanish- speaking countries, the people who lived there first were? What's the word in Spanish?'
A student replied, 'Indian.'
Melinda corrected, 'No, in Spanish.'
The student said, 'Oh, en español (in Spanish).'
Melinda agreed, 'Uh-huh, en español, ¿cómo se dice? (in Spanish, how do you say it?)'
Several students said, 'Indios (Indians).'
Melinda queried, 'Indios, ¿o? (Indians, or?)'
Students: 'Indígenas. (Indigenous people, feminine form).'[5]
Melinda accepted this answer: 'Indígenas, so it is the same word as in English, indigenous, indígenas, same word.'

This interaction points up a potential issue with using students' L1 if the teacher does not know the language well enough to avoid problematic vocabulary: *indio* is a derogatory term in Spanish. When I asked Melinda about this in my interview with her, she said that she was looking for the word *'indígeno'* but had not realized that there was anything wrong with *'indio'*. Moreover, despite this example of teacher-initiated L1 use, it is very common for multilingual teachers who value diversity to impose classroom policies that discourage the use of students' first languages, or for institutions to impose the policies, which are then enforced by teachers. Susanna's approach to student L1 use is not unique to her classroom: the English-Only policy at her community college campus extends to banning bilingual dictionaries:

[A student had just given a difficult-to-hear explanation of the word 'revolt,' which had come up in a reading.] Susanna responded, 'Good guess, and I see Lyudmila is looking it up so I am going to wait and have her give us the definition ((pause)). A Russian dictionary! ((mock scolding intonation)) Come on! ((lengthy pause, student laughter)). When you looked it up in your Russian dictionary, was it a meaning you could explain in English?'

Of course, just because an institution has an English-Only policy does not mean that an individual teacher will follow it. Cherie, an adult-school teacher who also worked with children, told me that she ignored her school's policy:

Cherie: I know that we have been told we're not supposed to be using ((pause)) the first language. [. . .] Well, with these low-level Spanish-speaking students in the elementary school, I've gotten that feeling very, very strongly, that they ((pause)) aren't really interested in listening to me unless they know that I have some sensitivity to the issues they face, and their language, and so on.

Given that all the ESL teachers I interviewed are to some extent bilingual or multilingual, and given their claim to value diversity, there is some contradiction in discouraging linguistic diversity in the ESL classroom. Teacher monolingualism provides 'an audible reminder to the students of the position of English as the language of power in the school and in the larger society' (Olivo, 2003: 53), and I do not think it is coincidental that English-Only pedagogy has taken root in areas where monolingual ideology is strong in society. However, English-Only classroom policies do not necessarily represent monolingual ideology (especially when other languages are used outside the classroom), but should perhaps be seen more accurately as 'purification practices' (Bauman & Briggs, 2003: 302) which enact an ideology against language mixing (Dalmau, 2009; Choi, 2003). As Guardado points out, 'there can be a gap between explicit discourses about language use and actual socialization practices' (Guardado, 2009: 105), given that Susanna did not actually prevent Lyudmila from using her Russian dictionary. These gaps reflect ambivalence about just how far linguistic diversity should go.

As in Chile, standardized English was the variety taught in California, but sometimes non-standard English was discussed, especially when it appeared in a text that the class had read, as in this field note excerpt from Cherie's adult-school class:

[In discussing the language of a Shel Silverstein poem] Minoru asked about 'ain't.' Cherie said, 'Here it means "isn't."' Minoru noticed that "ain't" isn't usual English.' She told them this is called 'non-standard,' not the kind of English we speak in school. Not the kind educated people speak, for example, a professor lecturing. 'When we hear "ain't,"' we think the person isn't educated.' She talked about the pronunciation of writing as 'wridin',' saying that sometimes educated people speak that way but never write that way.

Thus, on the rare occasions when non-standard English was discussed, teachers discouraged students from using it. As Achugar explains, 'Standard varieties usually have more social prestige because they are associated with speakers who are in power. The standard needs to be constantly maintained through processes of legitimation' (Achugar, 2008: 2). In fact, associating standardized English with speakers who are in power *is* a process of legitimation, as when Cherie tells her students that 'educated people' avoid 'ain't'. In a state characterized by 'vast linguistic and cultural diversity' (Bucholtz et al., 2008: 65), California ESL classes tend to promote a single linguistic norm:

US English correctness norms carry a strong moral charge: there is a widely accepted belief that because 'good' English is assumed to be naturally available, people living in the US have no excuse for not acquiring it. They should acquire it, especially since acquiring it facilitates the 'American Dream' of class mobility, which is also considered a moral imperative for citizens or potential citizens, i.e., immigrants. (Urciuoli, 2008: 258)

Comparing Language Ideologies

In this section, I first contrast language ideologies related to English teaching in California and Chile, and then go on to mention similarities between the two contexts, as well as ways that individual teachers followed trends that were more common in the other national setting.

First of all, language ideologies around English are necessarily different in the two countries because the place of English in society is different. In Chile, English is a prestigious international language but is rarely used in daily life, whereas in California it is the main language of the majority of homes (almost 60% of Californians speak only English at home, according to census figures, Statistical Abstract of the United States, 2012) and also in workplaces. Therefore, speaking English in Chile is considered an accomplishment, whereas speaking English in California is considered a 'basic skill'. No one in California would refer to English as 'the future'; the language is seen as powerful, essential even – but slowly losing ground. No one would refer to Chile as an 'English-speaking environment', or mention English as necessary for 'fitting in', still less for 'basic communication'. Discussing the difference between Korean sojourner families in Singapore and Korean immigrant families in the United States, Park and Bae write:

> While [sojourner] families evaluate success in English language learning with respect to the community to which they will return (ie Korea), immigrant families understand competence in English within the context of the US society, in which the children must live as ethnic minorities under scrutiny of mainstream racial ideologies. (Park & Bae, 2009: 369)

Perhaps because English in Chile is connected to a particular vision of 'the future' rather than to 'basic communication', the need to learn English is far more contested. In California, the main political choices are between monolingualism in English and bilingualism in English and another (immigrant) language (Achugar, 2008). English monolingualism is often seen as 'the normal and ideal human condition' (Valdés et al., 2003: 7; cf Wiley & Lukes, 1996). In this view (which is not shared by any ESL teacher I have interviewed), immigrant bilingualism is believed to result in cognitive confusion and a life of failure (Jeon, 2008; Zentella, 2008). It additionally represents a betrayal of American ideals (Achugar, 2008; Blommaert, 1999). As Pomerantz explains:

> (US) society…conflates language expertise with assumptions about race, class, and national loyalty. For Latinos and other linguistically defined

groups, expertise in a language other than English can be a detriment, threatening their identities as Americans and limiting their potential for social and economic mobility. (Pomerantz, 2002: 277)

In Chile, the main political choices are between monolingualism in Spanish, and bilingualism in English and Spanish. Bilingualism is seen by many (including English teachers) as a way to success in a globalizing society, but by some leftist individuals as a lack of allegiance to socialist ideals and Chilean patriotism. In both California and Chile, elite bilingualism – speaking two languages equally well, never mixing them and using them skillfully for professional purposes (Valdés *et al.*, 2003) – is seen as difficult to attain and not realistic for most of the population.

Perhaps because English is seen as 'basic', there are stronger prohibitions against the use of other languages in California English classrooms than there is against the use of Spanish in Chilean English classrooms, at least according to my observations and interviews. In both contexts, I observed intermediate to advanced classes, where students were capable of communicating in English. In these classes, the overwhelming majority of classroom communication was in fact in English, and this did not seem to be problematic to anyone: students were generally on task-completing activities in English. What many California teachers perceived as problematic was the possibility (or reality) of some classroom talk occurring in other languages.

Whereas Chilean English students share Spanish, it must be emphasized that California English students may have no common language other than English; in California, the use of a language other than English can be seen as 'unfair' if not all the students speak it. However, according to my interviews, Susanna insisted on students using English with each other even if they all spoke Russian, and even if some of them were unable to complete classroom activities due to non-comprehension – whereas Melinda provided some space in whole-class activities for student languages that not everyone shared. Other teachers got around the 'fairness' issue by allowing students to translate vocabulary for each other as needed. Moreover, allowing bilingual dictionaries does not seem to raise issues of fairness, as long as all students have access to dictionaries, but they are still often prohibited in California ESL classrooms (Menard-Warwick, 2009a).

Of the three Chilean teachers I observed (all at ULP), Genaro was the only one who explicitly stated a prohibition against Spanish use in the classroom. At one point during the activity on formal and informal letters mentioned above, he told one group (who had presumably slipped into Spanish) that 'Spanish is forbidden'. However, my field notes also show that soon afterwards he helped a group translate the expression 'meter la pata' (put one's foot in it) into English, and he encouraged another group to use a bilingual dictionary to translate some phrasal verbs needed for the activity. Thus, the strictest English-Only policies I observed in Chile were similar to the less-strict policies common in California. Moreover, Genaro (and the other teachers I observed) occasionally used Spanish words for concepts difficult to translate into English, such as the school administrator position 'sostenedor', or even 'asado', which translates easily as 'barbecue', but has stronger affective connotations for a Chilean speaker than the English term. Alán, as illustrated above, at times codeswitched into Spanish to emphasize important announcements, and would also help students translate vocabulary:

> Alán said, 'You mentioned that the students didn't have money, so what did they do?'
> José said that they sold hot dogs and rifas.
> Alán corrected this to 'raffles.'

A teacher following a strict English-Only policy would have pretended to misunderstand 'rifas', as Diego quoted himself pretending to misunderstand 'pero (but)' in a conversation with one of his most-advanced English students.

Nevertheless, the overwhelming use of English as a language of classroom communication was similar in the two contexts, at least in the classes I observed. Another similarity was teachers' sense that there are both economic and cultural reasons for learning English. In both contexts, there seemed to be some tension between these reasons, and in both contexts, teachers expressed personal preference for emphasizing interculturality over monetary gain. It should be emphasized that in both California and Chile, teaching English is not well reimbursed: teachers go into the field for cultural or linguistic reasons, and do not expect to become wealthy. Therefore, it is not surprising that they wish to share their cultural and linguistic enthusiasms with students.

The ideology of diversity was particularly strong in California, but Chileans were also aware of the emphasis placed on this concept in contemporary English-speaking societies. Alán mentions this above in defining the cultural value of learning English: 'it comes from these countries that show a wide variety of cultural aspects, you know, different people, different races, different religions.' To some extent, teachers promoted this among their students. In Paloma's class for fifth-year undergraduate prospective teachers at ULP (Maritza and Edith were students in this class), I observed an activity in which students acted out qualities of good teachers, based on a list given to them by Paloma. One quality on the list was 'appreciates the culture and ethnic diversity of students in the classroom'. This part of the activity went as follows:

Marina stood up, and asked, 'I want to know if anyone knows Aymara[6] language here?'
Claudia said some words in Aymara.
Marina said, 'We are mixed cultures, so we have to respect cultures. Ming, can you share some words?'
Ming [a Chinese immigrant to Chile][7] said, 'Nihau (hello).'
Francesca [who had studied abroad in Denmark] said something that I assume was Danish, and then added, 'Bonjour (good day).'
Paloma said, 'Arigato (thank you). That is hello in Japanese. [...] So what is she demonstrating?'
Several students said, 'Respecting diversity.'
Paloma said, 'Appreciating other cultures. [...] We have to learn many languages.'
Marina wrote on the board, and Paloma read aloud:
'Appreciates the culture and ethnic diversity of students in the classroom.'

Paloma had lived in the United States for many years, and had studied multicultural education in graduate school there (see Chapter 5), so she was familiar with the ideologies of North American teachers, and maintained a commitment to sharing them with her Chilean students.

However, other teachers besides Paloma had also lived abroad, and encountered divergent ways of viewing the English language and related teaching practices. While English in California is commonly thought of as the basic language of daily life, it is also an international language, as Ruby mentions in the quote at the beginning of this chapter. This is similar to the way it is seen by Chileans, who repeatedly told me that English is the language of international business. However, of the Chileans I met, only one had actually taught English to international business people: Gonzalo, who was a student in the language and culture class, but whom I did not interview. My only interviewee with personal experience of teaching English for international business was Martin, an MA student in California:

Martin: In Prague it was interesting. I taught three guys who were customer service representatives. So they were speaking to people literally from all over the world. One guy told me he had correspondence with some guy in Afghanistan, tucked in the mountains in the middle of nowhere. They spoke in English, if you're going to talk to someone in the middle of nowhere and you're in the Czech Republic you're going to speak English.

After teaching in Prague, Martin had moved on to Santiago, Chile, where he continued teaching Business English:

Martin: I gave classes at [Name of Business], a quality control place where they would make sure that kitchen, bathroom appliances worked correctly. So I worked with people who were in various departments at that company and they did need to know English, because the boss of the company was from France and his English skills were pretty good, I think he was fluent, I don't remember exactly. But they needed to communicate with him because a lot of his people were communicating through English, not in Spanish. [...] A lot of people from France were coming over [to] Chile so they needed to know English.

Thus, ironically, the teacher I interviewed whose work had most exemplified the authoritative discourses about English in Chile was not Chilean but rather Californian.

Notes

(1) ·This chapter draws on data and analysis that first appeared in Menard-Warwick (2013).
(2) For more on my classroom observation methodology, see Chapter 6. For more on my interview methodology, see Chapter 1.
(3) Chile and the United States signed a free trade treaty in 2003 (United States Trade Representatives, 2003).
(4) For Diego's travel experience, see Chapter 1.
(5) Probably the student was using the feminine form because Menchú herself is a woman.
(6) Aymara is a local indigenous language in northern Chile and in neighboring areas of Peru and Bolivia.
(7) See Chapter 6.

4   Representing Cultural Identities[1]

Culture is a difficult word to define, and is a deeply contested notion in its home discipline, anthropology. Nevertheless, culture is widely used within foreign language teaching to mean the practices, perspectives and products shared among groups of people (Phillips, 2003); indeed, culture has become a concept that is 'loose on the streets' (Eriksen, 1997: 104), employed for self-definitions by individuals and communities around the world. For this reason, Hastrup and Olwig argue that the term culture should not be discarded but rather 'reinvented...through an exploration of the "place" of culture in both the experiential and discursive spaces that people inhabit or invent' (Hastrup & Olwig 1997: 3). To that end, here is a brief narrative about 'cultural difference':

Norma: The first day [we were in Iowa, the neighbors] came and said, 'We have this open house, for the neighbors, and we would like you to come in,' and the incredible thing was that Dirk who, you could tell that he was typically American, and from the Midwest [...]. And he told us that he had found out, because there were some people from Venezuela (and us), that he had been 'born in the wrong place,' he said, because he would come and visit us and stay there for hours, just chit-chatting. [...] Or and there were these times, when I would be walking very fast to class or to teach, and then I said, 'Oh, Dirk is coming, what am I gonna do?' because I knew [...] he would stop and would like to chat, and it was funny because it was like me, a Latin-American, thinking of not meeting with him, an American, because he would stop and start talking to me, the way we used to do here.

If I combine a language-teaching definition of culture as practices and perspectives shared within groups of people (Phillips, 2003) with a definition of identity as based on negotiated group membership (Blackledge & Pavlenko, 2001; Wenger, 1998), I can roughly define the compound term, cultural identity, as 'a sense of belonging to a group of people who share practices and perspectives'. Although Norma had lived most of her life in northern Chile and taught English for many years at Universidad de las Peñas (ULP), she had earned an MA degree in Iowa, the setting for her narrative above. Telling narratives is a significant way for human beings to come to self-understanding, and also to share their understandings with others (Ochs & Capps, 1996), both within and across cultural boundaries. Even simple narratives construct representations of particular realities: Norma's narrative represents, and thus makes sense of, her own cultural identity as well as the cultural differences that she perceived as a Latin American graduate student newly arrived in the US Midwest. Thus, this brief narrative illustrates the 'mutual construction of identities through cultural encounters' (Hastrup & Olwig, 1997: 5) during Norma's time in Iowa.

From a Bakhtinian perspective, Norma's narrative is not entirely 'her own', but draws on socially available discourses. In theorizing heteroglossia (see Chapter 2), Bakhtin wrote that all language varieties and discourses represent 'specific points of view on the world, forms for conceptualizing the world in words,...(which) encounter one another and co-exist in the consciousness of real people' (Bakhtin, 1981: 291–292). From this perspective, identity development occurs as 'one's own discourse is gradually and slowly wrought out of others' words' (Bakhtin, 1981: 345), that is, as individuals appropriate discursive resources and practices in order to accomplish social goals (Assaf, 2005; Clarke, 2008; Pavlenko & Lantolf, 2000; Vitanova, 2005).

However, as Bakhtin also points out, when discourses are 'juxtaposed to one another (and)...interrelated dialogically' they may 'mutually supplement (or)...contradict one another' (Bakhtin, 1981: 292), and in fact Norma's narrative illustrates the frequent inadequacy of available discourses for voicing lived experience. The cultural discourses to which she has access assume a sharp divide between North Americans and Latin Americans in regard to time management; however, her narrative emphasizes an 'incredible thing' – that is, an ironic exception to these patterns: a 'typical Midwesterner' who wants to stop and talk juxtaposed with a Latin American (Norma herself) who watches her own practices changing across time and space. These processes are illustrated through Norma's use of dialogic voicing (Bakhtin, 1981), first quoting Dirk's comment that he had been 'born in the wrong place', then her own private speech, 'Oh, Dirk is coming, what am I going to do?' (for more discussion of dialogic voicing, see Chapter 2).

Analyzing Cultural Identities in Interview Data

In this chapter, I give an overview of the range of cultural identities that English language teachers referenced in interviews with me in 2005–2006. In order to do so, I explore teachers' interview comments about culture and the cultural groups with which they identify. Generally, when I asked teachers to define their cultural identities, I referred to this as a 'difficult question'. If interviewees hesitated, I would follow up by saying, 'How do you see yourself culturally? What kind of person are you?' Culture is a word that most English teachers use imprecisely, it is part of their language teaching curriculum, usually not the most important part. It is often conflated with nationality (see discussion in Risager, 2007, and also in Chapter 5 of this book), and for this reason many teachers answered my question about cultural identity by talking about national identity. However, this still proved challenging because identity was not a word they were accustomed to use.

Below I share some trends in teachers' answers to my 'difficult' question, as well as trends in talking about their own practices, their own perspectives, the groups they belonged to or did not belong to. In many cases, the data excerpts I am presenting are narratives, or fragments of narratives, about discursive faultlines that teachers have experienced: events and situations when they saw themselves in tension between different cultural groups. At times, as in Norma's narrative above, societal discourses prove inadequate to make sense of events and relationships in their lives. In other cases, teachers are able to present straightforward explanations of their identity constructions using varied discourses as a convenient resource.

Given the contradictions inherent in identity development, it is important to keep in mind that the appropriation of discourses for self-definition is a risky undertaking. Narratives often explore instances in which one interlocutor refuses to accept the identity claims of the other, depending on the ideologies at play within that social context. In Norma's narrative above, Dirk's statement that he was 'born in the wrong place' is an implicit claim to a Latin American identity based on his discursive practices, a bid rejected by Norma when she refers to him as 'typically American and from the Midwest'. Thus, there is often tension in narratives between the identities that individuals claim for themselves and those they are assigned by interlocutors (Blackledge & Pavlenko, 2001; Ochs, 1993). In this chapter, based on what teachers said about themselves in interviews, but keeping all of these contradictions in mind, I illustrate how identity is authored by individuals using available discursive resources (Pavlenko & Lantolf, 2000; Vitanova, 2005).

When I began writing this chapter, my first step was thematic coding of interview data for all references to identities, which I operationalized for coding purposes as self-descriptions, or discussions of specific categories of people. In my interview transcripts, I color-coded all data that referenced identities, then cut and pasted those data excerpts into a new document, where I coded for types of identities: linguistic, national, local, ethnic, political, religious, social class, gender, generational, popular culture, professional. Most data excerpts that referenced identity at all were coded for more than one type of identity. For example, the following narrative fragment was coded for national, intercultural, popular culture and professional identities because it describes Paloma's effort as a university English instructor (professional identity) to broaden students' cultural horizon (intercultural identity) by bringing into her Chilean classroom a Scotsman (national identity) playing the fiddle (popular culture identity). In calling this a 'narrative fragment', I refer to it as *narrative* because it recounts and evaluates an event, and as *fragment* because I do not present Paloma's complete account of the incident.

> **Paloma**: And that's why I appreciated also having Ian, bringing music from Scotland, bringing something absolutely different, they listened, they were not very happy with the ( )
> **Julia**: ((overlapping)) With the fiddle?

Through a further process of cutting and pasting, I created separate files for each type of identity, allowing me to see which identities were most prevalent in my data. I then picked out excerpts that seemed prototypical for each category, or that exemplified clear trends. The excerpt above illustrates how teachers portray themselves introducing students to unfamiliar cultural practices. Selected data became the basis for this chapter, in which I compare the cultural identities of Chilean and Californian English teachers. Due to my emphasis on presenting trends across groups of teachers, there is tension in this chapter between thematic analysis and narrative analysis (Riessman, 2008), with thematic analysis tending to predominate. Nevertheless, it should be kept in mind (as discussed above) that interview excerpts are best seen as discursive representations of cultural experiences – rather than as objective information about teacher identities or about Chilean and Californian culture.

The Cultural Identities of Chilean Teachers

In this section, I write first about Chilean teachers' portrayals of their own national identities, then about the ways they represent their local and ethnic identities and finally about the identities they have developed through professional and personal choices.

Norma's narrative above employs addressivity (Bakhtin, 1986b) in that she draws on background knowledge that she assumes I share about (stereo) typical differences between Latin Americans and North Americans: in Iowa, Norma (the Chilean) would be 'walking fast' (like North Americans are typically assumed to do) and Dirk (the American) would 'want to stop and talk' (behavior seen as more typical of Latin Americans). The data excerpt below shows how another ULP instructor and I draw on similar assumptions in negotiating when to end an interview:

> **Paloma**: Perfect, yeah, no, I have another fifteen minutes because I was (late).
> **Julia**: Oh, you have another fifteen minutes? Oh, well, well, you have to get downtown, too.
> **Paloma**: It's okay, remember what Chilean time is about.
> **Julia**: Chilean time, okay, well, that's fine, if you want to go on Chilean time, that's just fine, I'll put another tape in here. [...] Edith's coming any minute now, but you know she can be on Chilean time too.

In order to extend our interview conversation, Paloma and I draw upon a discourse about 'Chilean time' which is part of the Chilean English teachers' larger discourse about cultural differences. Within this discourse, Chilean attendees are expected to arrive somewhat later than the announced time for meetings, while North Americans are typified as obsessively punctual. Moreover, in this discourse (also employed in Norma's narrative), attitudes toward time are felt to indicate attitudes toward unscheduled socializing. Ability to use this discourse is part of the professional competence, and thus the professional identity, of Chilean English teachers. My appropriation of 'Chilean time' could be seen as evidence for my acculturation into the local context, while Paloma's reminder to me of this discourse perhaps shows her efforts to socialize me as a foreigner in Latin America. However, my final comment implying inconvenience to Paloma's student Edith allows me to subtly justify my original suggestion of ending the interview on time, even as I accept Paloma's offer to continue longer.

At an earlier point in my interview with Paloma, I asked how she talks to students about 'culture', and she responded by recounting a ULP classroom conversation. In this narrative, she attempts to elicit from her students a common discourse about Chilean national identity:

> **Paloma**: And I said, 'Well, how about our culture, can you tell me some characteristics?' Long silence. Long silence, because we tend to wear

jeans that are in fashion but are French or American, so what is it that makes us Chilean [...]? And someone said, 'That we are friendly,' 'Ayyy, very good point, because there are other cultures that do not have that trait, very, very friendly [...]' I said, and they all smiled, but um well, 'that we have good wine, and that we like this, so if you go to Chile you will find people that are like that, that they like to eat, that they like to share.'

Paloma's narrative presents a contradiction: 'jeans' is a reference to globalization, widely seen to be changing Chile irreparably; in contrast friendliness[2] is a key part of the discourse of Chilean national identity. This is not to argue that all Chileans are in fact friendly or even want to be friendly, but simply that they see this as part of their national heritage. The students' smiles in Paloma's narrative perhaps show their relief at being positioned as patriotic Chileans, who still make time to relax with friends despite their global consumption practices.

Further elaborating this discourse of identity, Alán, a ULP English instructor, connects these values of food and relaxation (which he sees as more broadly 'Latin American') to the natural environment:

Alán: Um, the love for nature, that's good. Eh the fact that a lot of the continent is still, you know, just vegetation and wildlife, I think that's the best, the food ((laughing)). And uh the relax, the way in which we live is definitely I think more relaxed than in other countries, and that's good, that you take your time for everything, and that you sometime, sometime in the day you stop, you disconnect and you go to the beach to look at the sea.

Alán and Paloma are voicing the same discourse of Chilean (or Latin American) identity: there is a lot of commonality between Alán's words, and the turns of phrase that Paloma quotes herself employing with her students. However, when Alán begins describing how 'sometime in the day you stop', his comments undergo a subtle shift from authoritative to internally persuasive discourse (Bakhtin, 1981). He uses the general pronoun 'you', but appears to be talking about his own unscheduled trips to the beach: going to look at the ocean perhaps seems to him an essentially Latin American part of his own identity. As for me, I cannot read these words without picturing the beautiful beaches of northern Chile – so even as an occasional sojourner, I easily find Alán's discourse about identity to be persuasive.

Moreover, just as Paloma mentioned that Chileans 'like to share', several interviewees invoked *solidarity* as a national value. When I asked Tomás, a fourth-year undergraduate, what he appreciated about 'Chilean culture' (and here I am the one conflating cultural and national identities!), he responded, 'Ah, Chile, it's a, I don't know what is the right word, solidary? [...] The community is very strong, and they want to, they like to give. When the people are in need, people respond.' To the same question about Chilean culture, fifth-year English major Maritza responded as follows:

> **Maritza**: If you have a problem, something like that, even if you are not part of the family, we as a family try to, 'Okay, we are going to help you,' and I think that in every family having that, here in Chile, we try to help other people from other countries, from other places, from other regions here, 'Ah, you are poor, okay, I can give you a place with food.'

However, Francesca (Maritza's classmate) had developed negative views toward this authoritative discourse after spending a year in Denmark as an exchange student. From her perspective, she is 'not a typical Chilean girl' because she is outspoken about her opinions. In explaining this, she pointed out contradictions between the common Chilean discourse of sharing and her own transnational identity:

> **Francesca**: Because here it's like you are forced to share, you know, 'You have to share, or you are a bad person,' you know [...] [but] I'm really direct to the person, like 'Don't do that in my home,' you know, I'm like really strange for being a Chilean and my sister is the same, it's because we have lived with other exchange students, and you cannot just open and eat something, like if they have a bar of chocolate, why should you? 'It's not yours, why did you take it?' and here it's like that, you know.

Furthermore, while Chilean national identities were prominent in any discussion of cultural identity in Las Peñas, teachers distinguished northern Chile from the rest of the country. As Alán described the location, 'We live here in this part of Chile, which is in the middle of the desert, and it's like we're so abandoned from the rest of uh, you know, other cities are so far away.' Moreover, many teachers drew on common discourses about the indigenous Aymara culture to explain the local area, even though few self-identified as Aymara. When I asked Tomás about his own cultural identity, he immediately invoked this regional culture to which he had no ethnic connection, saying that he felt 'like a mixture. . . .I feel close for, from Aymara culture, I don't have any traits of Aymara culture, in my blood, but I feel close about it, I feel close about the highland culture.' Francesca, who worked as a part-time tour guide, explained to me that the indigenous culture 'is the best part of us': she enjoyed taking visitors to the geoglyphs, traditional designs built out of rocks on desert hillsides.

Lydia, a fourth-year undergraduate who actually had an Aymara background, explained that no one in her family spoke the language nor celebrated the traditional New Year,[3] but that her father 'likes those things about that culture, the flag, I don't know if you know the flag? Yeah, it has several colors, and each colors means something.' As a university student, she said she felt responsible to be a good role model:

Lydia: I'm the example for my cousins, and for my brothers, because I'm the only one who is studying in here in university. [...] It makes me feel um well [good] because (yeah) I could achieve my goal to enter here (in) university, but at the same time, I have to be focused in my career and not to fail, because that (will) be 'Ohh, she failed, so maybe (it's) difficult, uh maybe (that's no good).'

Thus, while all local Chileans can potentially take pride in the Aymara past, as represented by the geoglyphs on their hillsides, people from Aymara communities have to position themselves within the more complex discourses of the Aymara present, involving language loss, cultural celebration (New Year and the flag), as well as ongoing efforts to overcome poverty and discrimination. Lydia uses dialogic voicing to explain the responsibility she feels toward other young people in her community: if they see her fail, they will perhaps say that education is 'difficult' and 'no good'.

While Aymara heritage connected teachers to the local environment, to the desert and the Andes, some teachers also claimed an immigrant heritage that linked them to the larger world. Francesca's family had an Italian background, and she reminisced, laughing, about Sunday afternoon spaghetti dinners:

Francesca: They used to talk really loud, really loud, it's like they are fighting, but some people were like, 'Oh, are they fighting?' 'No, they are just talking you know.'

Like Lydia, she employed dialogic voicing, but in this case to contrast Italian from non-Italian identities. Renate, an older high school teacher, explained her German heritage through the traditions that her father had maintained throughout her childhood:

Renate: My father played the violin, he played the guitar, violin, acordeón, accordion? Yeah, and piano, and uh, well it was quite different from people here, yeah, we used to have our Christmas dinner early, early, yeah, at about 8, but before opening our gifts and something, everything, my father used to play the violin, and we had to sing, we had to sing German songs [she sings a verse of O *Tannenbaum*[4]]. [...] I have many, many characteristics that German people have, for instance, I think that I'm really practical, practical person, I'm very sharp, punctual, Chilean people don't ((laughing)).

We then talked about the fact that she had arrived for her interview 20 minutes early, as her father had always advised. Thus, Renate invokes the discourse of 'Chilean time' to make a claim to a German identity.

These identities were open to interpretation, and could be practiced on a daily basis (as in Renate's punctuality) or allowed to slip away (as with the German, Italian and Aymara languages) – but they arose from biographical detail: Renate chose to be punctual but she did not choose to have a German-identified father who stressed punctuality. Furthermore, she describes singing German songs at Christmas as something she 'had to' do when she was a child, an obligatory rather than an optional practice which reinforced the inescapability of her ancestral heritage, even though she did not understand the words of the songs she was singing.

In contrast to ethnic background, English proficiency was attained by these teachers because of decisions made in adolescence, but also as the result of hard work and passionate interest over many years. Lydia, who grew up in a rural Aymara community, said she was inspired to learn English by a good teacher:

Lydia: Then, in the high school, I like it because of the professor that I had in that time, [...] and I felt that she like her career because she did a good job with us, with her course, she teach us about songs, lyrics of some songs, videos, and handouts and she motivates us to make posters in English and to stick it on the wall, so that [...] caught my attention, and I asked her how many years take to learn English and she explain me, and she also gave me some names of some scholarships.

Thus, the inspiration to learn English came not only from her teacher, but also from English-language music.

In this way, Lydia connects an authoritative pedagogical discourse from her course of studies (e.g. words like 'motivate'), with English as a vehicle for popular culture. This discursive connection between pedagogy and popular culture was common in my Chilean data, and appeared to encourage the use of English to search for positive messages in song lyrics, as a way to overcome the contradiction between English music as a leisure pastime and English study as an academic endeavor. Setting herself apart from Chileans who listen to English lyrics they cannot comprehend, Lydia says that Phil Collins is one of her favorite musicians because of his anti-discrimination message:

> **Lydia**: Yeah, the songs are very interesting, I like 'Another Day in Paradise,' and that says that we don't have to discriminate others, and we have to be conscious that there are homeless people and for those, for everybody, there is a paradise, yeah, for all of us.

In this way, Lydia's appreciation for the music of Phil Collins *intra*textually connects with other parts of her interview (Moonwomon-Baird, 2000) where she mentions reading Martin Luther King's 'I Have a Dream Speech' in her English class, and decries discrimination against Aymara communities in Chile. Lydia thus connects her Aymara heritage and popular culture preferences with her developing professional identity as an English teacher. Although the connections that Lydia draws are based on personal experience, making this discourse internally persuasive (Bakhtin, 1981), such popular culture encounters had been influential for the second language identity development of many of the English teachers I interviewed.

Indeed, young Chileans have been sharing English-language popular culture with their friends for decades, as noted by Diego in Chapter 1. Genaro, a ULP professor of English, explains how he and his friends pursued their 1960s fascination with rock and roll, especially the Beatles:

> **Genaro**: Because when I was very young, I was a teenager, in our country, the most popular music was in English, the unique music, you know, rock-and-roll, [...] So we wanted to know, when I say 'we' I mean, my friends, all those guys of that time, we wanted to know what the meanings of the songs meant and you know that was a sort of triggering element or motivating element [...] We worked with dictionaries, we helped each other, you know, in a group, there is always a guy who knows more than the other ones.

Using 'we', Genaro explicitly situates himself generationally (among 'all those guys of that time'). Like Lydia, he draws on the pedagogical discourse of motivation to explain connections between music and English learning, such as the use of dictionaries to understand song lyrics. For Lydia's classmate Tomás as well, comprehending the English lyrics of his favorite band is essential to his appreciation of their music:

> **Tomás**: A band, it's called Tool from California, from Angeles. It's difficult to label their music because it's a mixture from a lot of things, but basically it's rock [...] But, yeah, they are very spiritual, because the spiritual is different than religion, they talk about the spirit and the souls, and how the ... body changes, but the soul remains [...] There is a phrase or a sentence that I like from Tool because, I always sign my e-mails, because it's a 'We are eternal, all this thing is an illusion.'

The fact that Tomás signed his emails with an English-language message implies a personal identification with Tool's discourse of non-traditional spirituality. Moreover, this establishes the seriousness of his interest in English language music as part of a larger process of personal growth.

Reuel, a classmate of Tomás and Lydia (all three were in Alán's class), also identified with English-language popular culture, especially the fantasy film trilogy *Lord of the Rings*. In a Spanish-language conversation, translated here, we discuss how Reuel recognizes himself in this imaginary world:

> **Reuel**: Let's see, I don't know, maybe ((pause)) in my past life, I lived in that time, I don't know, it's because I like all that so much, I like everything in epic literature, where there are princesses, dragons, magic, and all those things. [...]
> **Julia**: In 'Lord of the Rings,' which character do you like the most?
> **Reuel**: Gandalf.
> **Julia**: Gandalf, me too ((laughing)) [...] And why?
> **Reuel**: I don't know, I think that he's the mediator, the mediator of everything, like everything depends on him, well, he's like an angel, I don't know.
> **Julia**: Uh-huh, ((overlapping)) he *is* like an angel.

Later, while explaining how he shares video and music files with a group of friends, Reuel stated his identification with the wizard Gandalf more directly: 'I am the mediator, I am Gandalf ((laughing)) [...] I organize the group.' Our previous agreement that the Gandalf is 'like an angel' makes Reuel's remark humorous (thus the laughter) but also lends gravity to the practice of file sharing, which could otherwise be seen as purely frivolous.

Alán seemed to have less interest in music than most other participants, but more in film, to the point where this appeared to be a significant part of his identity: 'I've always been very em...a fan of film and a serious one.' He spoke at length of his student days:

> **Alán**: I had some other classmates who were also very good in English, and we always got together in those times to, you know, watch movies [...] ((laughing)). All the Steven Spielberg things. I'm speaking about the 80s. So yeah, you know, 'Indiana Jones,' and what else?, and 'E.T.,' and 'Poltergeist' and things like that ((laughing)). [...] It was like the golden age of Spielberg.

Alán's narrative implies a clear relationship between watching Spielberg movies and excelling in English as an academic discipline. Diego (see Chapter 1) said similar things about watching films with friends during his university days, and described himself keeping a vocabulary notebook and a bilingual dictionary at hand while watching shows like *Married With Children* on cable television.

However, it is also important to stress that popular culture is only one motivating factor for English learning in Chile. When I asked Norma, then director of the foreign language department at the ULP, why she had become an English teacher, she referenced music, but rejected it as the reason for her career choice:

> **Norma**: I really cannot point to anything, but probably, for instance, some people talk about music, I mean, I'm not that kind of person, I can tell you what I'm not, probably, it wasn't the lyrics [...] but it was communicating with people actually, and that would be it, I mean, it would be the chance to talk to foreigners.

Norma's prioritization of 'communicating with people' connects to the pedagogical discourse of communicative language teaching (Savignon, 1983) which forms part of her professional expertise. Here, however, she is speaking personally, so it appears that this discourse is internally persuasive to her. It also connects intratextually (Moonwomon-Baird, 2000) with her narrative above about making friends in Iowa. Foreigners are in short supply in the far north of Chile, however, and travel to English-speaking countries is prohibitively expensive, so enjoying music and movies provided a more realistic way for many of my interviewees to encounter English.

Having constructed English-speaking identities from a wide array of experiences, teachers then need to make decisions about the kind of settings where they hope to teach. Discourses of social class are widely employed in this latter exploration (see Chapter 3). Sofía, who had taught for decades in working-class high schools, describes her deliberate choice for this (less prestigious) environment as a young teacher after one year of employment in a Catholic high school:

> **Sofía**: I just work one year, although I was offered to continue working, 'No,' I say, 'No, that's enough,' because the students were terrible, just women, you see¿ But as their parents pay the education, they think that we have to do everything they like, they misbehave, and we have to accept it, you see¿ They couldn't get a bad mark, because their parents pay for the education and if I don't give them a good mark, I will be fired, that's the kind of student, so 'No, I'm so sorry, I'm not going to work anymore,' [...]
> **Julia**: Uh-huh. And was the new job better¿
> **Sofía**: Yes, because eh it, a public school, you see¿ [...] The problem, big problem, physical problem, emotional problem, economic problem, so I (had to help) people, so I prefer those kinds of students than those who have beautiful houses, beautiful cars [...]. But in the other school, they don't have (a radio), students don't have a pencil, don't have a pen, sometimes they don't bring books, [...]. But I like it. I like it, it's a challenge for me, I like that kind of job.

Here is another narrative that deals with contradictions between social expectations and lived experience, in that private schools are widely viewed as a 'better' teaching environment. Sofía uses dialogic voicing to represent her younger self at the point of resigning from the Catholic school, 'No, that's enough, I'm sorry...' Through listing possessions, she sets up a contrast between spoiled rich students at the private school and poor students with problems at the public school. The word 'but' (in 'But I like it') further contrasts the societal prestige of higher-class schools with her own preference for helping poor students.

Maritza, likewise, fondly recalled her recent teaching practicum at an impoverished school:

> **Maritza**: They were ((laughing)) like devils ((laughing)) because you have to say 'Okay, please listen to me,' and nobody listens to you, they were running in the classroom, ((laughing)) they also has a hole in the wall, and they go through the hole and go outside of the classroom, ((Julia laughing)) you have to sit there, trying to cover the hole... .
> **Julia**: Wow.

Maritza: ((laughing)) It was awful, but (I) liked (it) ((laughing)) [...] When I go there, I arrive there, and I have a lot of girls and boys [...] ((laughing)) and they try to kiss me, they 'May I carry your bag? May I carry your eh?' 'Okay, okay, okay,' and everybody was hugging me [...] And chocolate, when they kiss me... ((gestures to face))
Julia: It's all over your face.
Maritza: ((overlapping)) I have all in my face, and I don't going to clean my face in front of them ((laughing)) [...] They were very sweet, I think that they loved me a lot.

In the interviews, it was common for teachers to employ a discourse of poverty, drug abuse and parental neglect to enumerate the difficulties of teaching students from the lower classes. Nevertheless, following Alán's narrative about quitting his job at the public high school (see Chapter 3), he negatively evaluated himself in comparison to teachers like Sofía and Maritza:

Alán: I kind of blame myself, because I wasn't the right person for them, I was not doing a good job with them, and I always thought or believed that someone else could come, someone [...] with a different attitude towards them. Somebody who could like children like them, with so much trouble in their lives.

However, Alán found ways to draw on his own gifts when he took a job teaching literature at a university in Peru. A self-described 'fan of film', he engaged students with screen adaptations of classic English novels, like *The Razor's Edge* or *The Red Badge of Courage*:

Alán: They had to read the novels, and then we would watch the film [...] For instance, one part of the book, we would go and search for this part in the movie, and do comparisons, and, you know, compare the characters, if they thought that they were like they had imagined in the book, (we) compared the situations and the plots, and then in the end, we would watch the entire movie to you know, have like a global vision. And also films adapted from literature are very useful to give your students a real sense of the atmosphere, the setting of the books, because you can see actually how people dressed, and you know, the streets, how their lives were.

While teachers like Sofía and Maritza found an appealing challenge in working with impoverished students, Alán had discovered that the high school environment did not allow him to 'develop a sense of professional identity that successfully incorporates (his) personal subjectivities' (Alsup, 2006: 27), nor to fully use the professional knowledge that he had developed through education, travel and artistic participation. As Genaro said, recounting his own decision to leave high school teaching, 'I realized [...] that was not ((pause)) the (space) I was looking for, and I considered that probably that could be found at the university.'

Indeed, opportunities to impart professional knowledge to the next generation of teachers gave meaning to the work of English professors such as Genaro and Paloma. One significant aspect of their professional knowledge was the discourse of 'cultural differences'. To inculcate an open-minded attitude, Paloma invited a Scottish teaching assistant to play traditional music for her class:

> **Paloma**: And that's why I appreciated also having Ian, bringing music from Scotland, bringing something absolutely different, they listened, they were not very happy with the ( )
> **Julia**: ((overlapping)) With the fiddle? [...]
> **Paloma**: Eh, they ... kind of, they looked at each other ( ) 'This is different.'
> **Julia**: Yeah, it is different.
> **Paloma**: Very different, but also I am promoting the idea that different should not be bad.

This value, which perhaps could be seen as an ideology, that 'the different should not be bad' is widespread among language teachers around the world (see Melinda's comments in Chapter 3). Teachers viewed their own experiences of language learning and cultural sharing as personally enriching, and they wanted to encourage their students to develop cross-cultural respect. While this desire is certainly strong among Chilean English teachers, it is perhaps even stronger among ESL teachers in California.

The Cultural Identities of California Teachers

In this section, I again analyze teachers' discursive identities, as they portrayed themselves in interviews. I write first about how teachers described their own national, local and ethnic identities. I then explore how teachers constructed identities based on (sub)cultural practices, cross-cultural encounters and educational and professional endeavors.

When I asked Molly, soon to graduate with an MA in TESOL, about her cultural identity, she replied with some puzzlement:

Molly: I try to stay away from the stereotype of like Americans have no culture or white people, white Americans don't have culture, so I guess I do have a culture, but it just, for me it seems like I don't know how to explain it and I don't know how to set it apart from other cultures.

Like the Chilean students described by Paloma above, Molly had difficulty defining her national identity. Like Norma, she employed addressivity (Bakhtin, 1986b) by assuming (rightly) that I was familiar with the same stereotypes that she was, but whereas Norma and I had assumed that we belonged to 'different cultures', Molly and I saw ourselves as having 'the same culture', given that we were both Anglo-American Californians. However, for Molly and me, it was likewise paradoxically clear that Anglo ethnicity conflates with US nationality and that 'white Americans' stereo-typically 'have no culture'.

Interestingly, Veronica's newly arrived immigrant high school students (see Chapter 1) made similar comments about their Anglo classmates:

Veronica: One of the things I've heard is that kids, newcomer kids, ( ), they're, 'Anglos don't have a culture,' [...] and then María said, '(Well), the food isn't very good [...], you don't eat breakfast,' and you know, so it's (more) curiosity about what seems to be a really relaxed family structure, and kids are on their own, and they're kind of curious about that.

In this way, a discourse has grown up around the notion that whiteness implies a lack of culture (and family). While Molly could assume my agreement with her sentiment that stereotyping was wrong, this seemed to leave her without any means of constructing her own sense of cultural identity.

However, some California teachers had an easier time discussing the complexity of their national identities. Cherie, a 'white American' adult-school instructor, had grown up in Africa; when I asked about her cultural identity, she began by stating that she was 'typically American' until she went overseas at age 12, but then went on to describe her sense of alienation:

Cherie: I've always kind of said 'Well, I'm a citizen of the world.' Because that's easier than saying I don't have a cultural identity, which is more of what I actually feel.

Julia: Mmhmm, mmhmm. How does that interact with being a language teacher?

Cherie: ((pause)) Well, I can feel really neutral, or, or equally enthusiastic about everything. And, I mean, I'm constantly having to explain American culture to myself, so explaining it to them is really easy. ((laughs)) And, I truly do see how odd American culture can seem from the outside, having come back to United States as a seventeen-year-old, and been plunged into high school.

Thus, Cherie constructs a national identity that is American, but not entirely American, that sees America from the outside. In specifying that 'world citizen' is how she has 'always kind of' described herself, she dialogically voices herself in conversation with multiple interlocutors, who demand that she specify her identity. In stating that this is what she 'has said' rather than how she 'actually feel(s)', she suggests that her discourse of world citizenship is authoritative (likely to be accepted by interlocutors), rather than internally persuasive (Bakhtin, 1981). Thus, like many people, Cherie makes sense of her own identity by drawing on a discourse that conflates cultural and national identities. However, this discourse highlights the contradictions in her own lived experience: her sense of being no longer 'typically American' is what leads her to 'actually feel' that she does not have a cultural identity.

Susanna, a community college instructor, had a different perspective on what it meant to be 'American' when I asked about her cultural identity:

Susanna: I probably identify myself with my job, and you know, that certainly comes with, people who are interested in language, people who are interested in culture, and then, I guess, you know, of course I identify myself as an American, but at the same time, maybe not, I hope not a narrow minded... ((laughing)), but someone who is also interested in the world at large.

For her, being culturally 'American' to some extent contrasted with being interested in language and 'the world at large'. She uses the word 'but' to express a sense of incompatibility between her professional and national identities: for Susanna, being 'American' apparently involves risk of being narrow minded, a risk to which she 'hopes' she will not succumb.

Interestingly, Molly, almost tongue-tied when she thought I was inquiring about her national identity, became quite voluble when I asked her about being a Californian:

Molly: Everyone in my family is very outdoorsy and energetic [...] I mean, I grew up where the Gold Rush started and there's tons of gold mines and the big American River, the South Fork, the North Fork, the Middle Fork, it's all right there and that was our playground and I remember walking up the river as a kid, like some sort of Mark Twain story, you know, I was picking crawdads[5] up and I think that's a very California cultural thing for me, or even northern California. My family like has a really negative view of southern California...

Like Chilean English instructor Alán (see above), Molly draws discursive connections between local identities and the natural environment such that picking up small river creatures (crawdads) is a 'very California cultural thing'. She immediately specifies that this does not apply to southern California, which her family views as a dangerous urban landscape: when her brother went there, someone stole his truck. The images she uses to portray her own identity also appear in the discourses of the California tourist industry: the Gold Rush, gold mines, rivers, Mark Twain. This authoritative discourse about her home region appears to have become internally persuasive for her as a resident. When she had a chance to design a mini-course for international students, she drew on her background and focused on California travel destinations, such as the Napa wine country and Lake Tahoe.

Eric (see Chapter 2), a community college instructor like Susanna, offered a different perspective about growing up Anglo-American in rural California:

Eric: When I think about the kids on my street, it was the Gonzalez family, Jorge senior, Glorieta was the mother, and Glorieta was my mom's best friend, and so she (would) come over and teach my mom to make tamales[6] [...]. And her son Rufino and I (and) their other son Jorge, we were best friends [...]. And then there's the Ortega family down the street, and Christmas was not complete unless the Ortega family brought us some tamales, so Mexican culture, I was very, very comfortable, very comfortable with that, and, you know, there's a lot of Spanish words I didn't learn in class.

Rather than invoking the natural world, Eric describes his local identity ('my street') in terms of his family's friendship with Latino neighbors, and thus in terms of cultural diversity, a widespread authoritative discourse in California. As Starr writes (see Chapter 3), Californians tend to believe that 'a diverse society (is) by definition a better society' (Starr, 2004: 209). Instead of spelling out this ideology, Eric evokes it through a long list of Spanish names and the mention of tamales, trusting that I as a fellow Californian will share similar memories of homemade spicy food. It is our shared memory of tamales that make this discourse internally persuasive. Eric additionally connects cultural diversity to linguistic diversity and even to informal language learning, using the image of tamales as well as the adjective 'very comfortable' to evaluate this diversity positively. Given that we share background knowledge about racism against Latinos in California, the repetition of 'very comfortable' serves to distance Eric from such negative attitudes, and to demonstrate his allegiance to ideologies of diversity. Thus, there is a lot of addressivity in this part of the interview (Bakhtin, 1986b), as Eric shapes his remarks to what he can assume will be my interpretation.

Whereas Eric details fond childhood memories of Mexican-American traditions, Molly first encountered and learned to appreciate California diversity when she left her small town in the mountains to attend an urban university: 'it was very visible that most of my friends were not white for the first time and coming back home for the first time felt weird, being around all white people.' For Susanna, born in Utah, a family visit to Los Angeles at age 12 served as an introduction to the cross-cultural experiences that she later sought out as an adult. In her account of this trip, she dialogically voices her own excitement and amazement at the unfamiliar practices she encountered:

Susanna: We were invited to dinner to a family from, I think they were from Mexico, and they had all of their extended family there, which I thought was really interesting, so it was this huge party, and I think they had music and dancing and I thought, 'Wow, my family doesn't do this,' ((laughing)) and so I, you know, I thought it was really fun and interesting, and I can remember having watermelon juice and thinking, 'This is watermelon!' ((laughing))

Linnea, who had recently graduated from our MA program, likewise connected a California background with cultural and linguistic diversity:

Linnea: I was born and raised in California, my parents are originally from Taiwan [...]. Growing up in California, I didn't grow up speaking English, I also grew up speaking Mandarin Chinese, which I would say is my second language, so I grew up bilingual which is how I would describe myself. I grew up watching American TV shows and learning English through shows. When I was younger, I would mostly speak Chinese, watching old videos of me.

As a second-generation Chinese American, Linnea had learned Mandarin from her parents, along with other aspects of her heritage that her parents considered important to pass on, such as Chinese history and holidays. Similarly, Eric, whose mother's ancestors emigrated from Germany, identified with being German American, and had made an effort to gain fluency in the language. Like Renate's family in Chile, his family had always sung 'O Tannenbaum' on Christmas Eve.

When I interviewed Jokwon, however, I found that his ethnic identity had been complicated by his Filipino immigrant parents' refusal to use Tagalog at home:

> **Jokwon**: It wasn't till high school that I started learning a second language with Japanese, and I continued that ever since high school. I consider that my second language, it's a little weird for most of my family, my extended family, to see me not learning any of the Filipino languages, it's just Japanese out of nowhere. But it wasn't totally random; a lot of it was influenced by my dad. [...] He was also a martial artist growing up [...]. And he was very much into that part of Japanese culture and that was a big deal for me and my sister growing up. That was his form of discipline for us. He taught us martial arts. [...] So ya, that's kind of, I guess, the mix of culture there, I don't know...I guess being raised here, so being an American boy but taking some aspect of Japanese culture and also Filipino culture into my life, and integrating all of it.

A native of San Francisco and a first-year MA student, Jokwon had traveled and worked briefly in Japan; he was fairly fluent in Japanese, and a long-time fan of Japanese anime movies. Along with practicing Japanese martial arts, he had become an expert breakdancer (an African-American dance style). He even mentioned breakdancing 'for fun' to 'Japanese pop music from Korea'. Thus, in discussing Jokwon's cultural identities, it is hard to say that either his ethnic heritage (Filipino) or his national identity (American) should be given priority. His discourse of multiculturalism, which he connects with California ('I guess being raised *here*') conflicts with the related discourse of cultural heritage, which led Eric to study German rather than Spanish.

However, for most of the California teachers, it was clear which identities they had inherited based on family origin and geographical location and which they had actively chosen. Like the Chilean teachers, the Californians without exception had put effort into language learning. In some cases, teachers' career paths followed a complicated linguistic trajectory. For example, Melinda had gone from being a ballet teacher who knew some French, to learning American Sign Language (ASL). She then became a sign language teacher and interpreter through the 1970s and 1980s, before deciding to teach ESL at Farmington Community College:

Julia: But why, why not just be a sign language teacher, why, why ESL? **Melinda**: Well I suppose it's cultural, not being the child of deaf adults, and coming into sign language as an adult, I could never hope to achieve a central position in deaf culture, [...]. And my sign language accent, if you will, was always going to be there. So I realized that if I wanted to have a career that provided a lot of growth opportunities, I needed to not be in a career where I would always be subject to being marginal. And also jobs were fewer and further between for sign language teachers [...] So it had economic elements to it as well, but also because I think a language teacher needs to come from the core of the language speaking community.

Although Melinda had been a successful teacher and interpreter of ASL, she saw her non-native-signer status as a barrier she could not overcome. In answering my question about her career choice, she draws on a discourse of 'deaf culture' that excludes Melinda from the 'core' of the ASL 'community', a discourse connected to native-speaker ideology (in which a non-native accent is a fatal flaw), as well as with a widely used discourse about professional opportunities. It is through orchestrating all these discourses (Bakhtin, 1981) that Melinda portrays the contradictions represented by her relinquishment of ASL after decades of investment in the language. Likewise, Susanna said that it was her non-native background that made her decide against becoming a Spanish teacher.

Both Melinda and Susanna invested a lot of effort in learning languages (Norton, 2000). By definition, this effort as young adults was what separated them from native speakers. Unlike the Chilean English teachers, they believed that their conscious efforts as learners disqualified them from serving as teachers. Ultimately, native-speaker ideology limited their second language participation and their ability to fully identify as teachers of these languages – while reinforcing their identities as English teachers. Melinda stated that her local California accent gave her confidence in teaching ESL pronunciation, since she knew she sounded like the news anchors on television.

Some younger teachers were still developing multilingual and multicultural identities, and like the Chileans, they used popular culture for this purpose: Martin tuned into Spanish-language radio, Charles listened to Russian pop music, Jokwon watched Japanese anime, and Linnea was fond of Taiwanese movies. Molly, actively learning both Spanish and German at the time of the interviews, had found Facebook helpful for communicating with speakers of both languages. A recent stint of volunteer work in Nicaragua had inspired her Spanish-learning efforts, while German was a heritage language in her family. Generally, she found popular culture consumption to be the least stressful means of second language participation, especially after she began exchanging music online with a Colombian graduate student at her university:

> **Molly**: Well, on his part, there's this band from Uruguay, like one of my favorite bands now and it's called El Cuarteta de Nos. And it's like Spanish rock [...] Well, yeah, just tons and tons of music. And on my part just kind of inspirational, everything from hip hop to rock and roll, he's incredibly political, [...] so a lot of my music is from people who've struggled here and are uplifting [...] I listen to the song as I read the lyrics, and then any time there's a word I don't understand I use google translate, and it's so quick that I can just look at the word right away and then pretty much, I mean, they're on my ipod everyday I'm going to school riding my bike, or riding my skateboard, I'm listening to these songs [...] so it's just helped in expanding my vocabulary because it's fun and it's music I like, it's rock and roll, it's hip hop, it's youthful and energetic.

Here, Molly draws on pedagogical discourse ('expanding my vocabulary'), along with a discourse of new technology ('google translate', 'ipod'). This discourse identifies her with the current generation, as a person who is 'youthful and energetic' (who rides to school on a bicycle or even skateboard), and who thus likes music that is also youthful; at the same time, contemporary discourses of technology in language learning connect to her teacher identity. Furthermore, listening to this music supports her developing leftist political identity, shared with her Colombian former student who is socializing her through a discourse that links (certain types of) popular music to 'people who've struggled'. In explaining these interrelationships, she repeatedly uses words like 'uplifting' and 'inspirational' to show the strong influence of all this internally persuasive discourse on her identity development.

Conversely, very few of the California teachers over thirty had done much to explore media products in other languages. The exception was Veronica (see Chapter 1). When I asked her about cross-cultural experiences, her answer included active interests in West African and South African music, Argentine tango, Jewish and Sephardic music and finally Balinese music. Going far beyond the international consumption practices of any other teacher I interviewed, Veronica attributed her interest in world music to a Los Angeles radio show that she had listened to in childhood. However, unlike Molly or the Chilean teachers, Veronica did not use music as a means for language acquisition.

Moreover, while other teachers of Veronica's generation had not had the same chance to develop globalized tastes in music, both Cherie (adult-school teacher) and Susanna (community college instructor) had married men from other countries, and this had necessarily resulted in intercultural experiences. As a Peace Corps volunteer in small-town Tunisia, Cherie had appreciated the strong emphasis on family among her hosts. In explaining her marriage to me, she drew on a widespread discourse of American family breakdown to justify her decision to marry her Tunisian boyfriend, as well as to establish a family-oriented identity for herself and her husband:

Cherie: All the men I knew there [at US graduate school], were either ((pause)) married ((pause)) or getting divorced because they'd been cheating on their wives. Or gay? or bisexual. [...] And to me, the idea, of marrying ((pause)) an American ((pause)) was so bizarre because I didn't understand the way they thought, I didn't understand their value systems? [...] With all that, I decided that marrying an American would be more cross-cultural for me than marrying in Tunisia.

Susanna had married into a transnational Guatemalan extended family, whom she described as 'overprotective... but at the same time, much more open with love and affection than my family is'. Falling into the popular California discourse about cultural diversity, I then asked her about food and music, and she said she was looking forward to her in-laws 50th wedding anniversary:

Susanna: They're having a huge party, they're gonna do a celebration of their vows....and have a big party afterward, and yeah, there's gonna be Latin music there, and probably a Mariachi band, [...] and people will be there dancing (to) salsa and (the) merengue ((laughing)) and you know, a lot of that kind of music, and definitely Latin food.

In this way, her marriage had brought her back to her first cross-cultural experience (dancing and Latin food) during the family vacation in Los Angeles (see above), but from a different social position.

In explaining career decisions, a desire to work cross-culturally was often connected to the desire to 'help people learn' as MATESOL student Charles remarked, or as Cherie explained at more length:

Cherie: So I thought about it and I said 'Well, what is it I like to do? What is it I want to do?' and I said 'Well, I love learning languages. I love meeting people from different cultures? I love going to other countries and learning about their country from underneath, not as a tourist. And, um ((pause)), I love being able to contribute something that I'm good at! ((pause)) And that people want,' and I said 'Okay, what am I good at? Well, I'm pretty good at English.'

Here, Cherie represents her mental processes as an inner dialogue (Vitanova, 2010), with her questions and answers illustrating reasons that many California teachers shared for becoming an ESL teacher: a desire to make a positive difference in society; a background in language learning; and an interest in cross-cultural encounters (similar to Norma's predilection for 'talking to foreigners'). Indeed, crossing cultural and linguistic boundaries remained an important aspect of their professional life. Eric described himself gradually adapting to his community college students' cultural practices:

> **Eric**: I find sometimes myself reflecting what's been given to me from my students' culture. [...] Because I have a Korean student, and when she gives me her tests when they're finished, she hands them to me with two hands? ((gestures this)). Slight bow. And I find myself accepting it with two hands [...] ((laughing)) I don't do that with any of my Russian students!

In this way, Eric's teacher identity included the adoption of culturally significant body language from his students. His words 'find myself' imply that this adoption is not wholly voluntary or conscious. Ducking his head and holding out an imaginary piece of paper respectfully with two hands, he employed what might be called 'dialogic gesturing' to share this insight with me. He expanded on this theme by describing interaction strategies he had learned from his Russian students, whom he initially saw as 'in (his) face... kind of rough and harsh'. He found most useful a certain shrug that his students had often used on him. In his words:

> **Eric**: I do find myself sometimes being like them when it comes to issues now...as far as just...there's kind of this ...I want to say a blasé...matter-of-factness? Which I often inter...which as an American I interpret it as blasé or...they don't care about not turning in an assignment or something, where they'll say 'oh...' ((he shrugs)) and they'll walk away [...] So sometimes I've found myself reflecting that back, when...you know [they say], 'Oh, you know this was a hard test, too hard.' [I say] 'Yeah?' ((he shrugs)).

Julia: Kind of 'so what.' ((laughing)).

In explaining his own growth as a teacher, Eric dialogically voices (and dialogically gestures) his Russian students' 'blasé, matter-of-fact' attitude – or what he is careful to describe as what he 'as an American interprets' to be a 'blasé, matter-of-fact' attitude. Since it appears to him that students shrug their shoulders to demonstrate lack of concern for his opinion, he 'finds himself' giving the same shrug right back to them – to show that he is impervious to their complaints. Continuing the dialogism, I voice my interpretation of this shrug as 'kind of "so what"'.

As well as acknowledging students' influence on them, teachers also sought to influence students culturally, for example to familiarize them with contemporary US gender ideologies. In the following interview excerpt, we were discussing the fact that Melinda had written 'divorce' on the board in her classroom as part of a list of reasons for sending a greeting card:

Melinda: So you know, they're always really curious about my marital status and so on, I say 'I'm a happily divorced woman' [. . .]
Julia: So they, so at the point (when) you wrote that on the board, they were already familiar with the fact that you were happily. . .
Melinda: Happily divorced.
Julia: ((overlapping)) divorced, uh-huh.
Melinda: It could be.
Julia: You're not sure if they were or not. . . .
Melinda: I'm not sure, you know, if anybody asks me, that's my standard answer, yeah.

As the adverb 'happily' usually collocates with 'married' in discourses of gender, its use with the word 'divorced' potentially sparks reflection on the advantages of autonomy and individualism, an ideology that resonates in popular California discourses about sexuality and family life. Melinda's own positive experience with divorce lends internal persuasiveness to these discourses (Bakhtin, 1981), which pose a challenge to the ones about American family dysfunction drawn upon by Cherie above (and alluded to by Veronica's immigrant high school students when they say that 'Anglos don't have a culture'). These antithetical discourses of family present a significant faultline in California classrooms; to manage the resulting tension, Melinda said her philosophy was 'to get students to value what they already have, and use it as a starting point and be observers and non-judgmental of others'. Thus, like Paloma, she tried to inculcate her students with a discourse of cultural relativism.

Eric, in contrast, saw acceptance of difference as a lesson that his community college students had already learned. In appreciating his students' willingness to interact peacefully across ethnic boundaries, he employs below a venerable discourse about immigration and American exceptionalism to claim that 'the miracle of America' happened all the time in his classes. However, he prefaced this sentiment with a narrative about a historical faultline that called this discourse into question, a faultline activated when he told a colleague about his German-American heritage:

> **Eric**: She said, 'Oh, you're not German, you were born here, right?' [...] and she really made a point of saying, 'No, you're just American,' and it turned out. ...I said, 'I'm proud of it,' you know, she said, 'Well, uh,' then she just got very, kind of angry, and said well, uh, 'I'm Russian-Jew, and the Germans killed my family,' and walked off.
> **Julia**: Wow.

Almost the entire narrative here is dialogic voicing: two contrasting ethnic identities each tied to a particular view of history and heritage. By 'walking off', Eric's colleague makes clear that dialogue is impossible for her across this particular faultline. However, Eric's internal dialogue continued (Vitanova, 2010). In making him think about his own relationship to German history, he said this encounter had made him 'more German', and also caused him to ask himself whether 'a German American and a daughter of Russian Jews (can)...get along and make a go of it here in America?' It was in this context that he sought resolution to the contradiction by mentioning what he called the 'miracle of America' in his ESL classroom:

> **Eric**: You know, I've got Vietnamese, Japanese, and Russians all together, and you know the war history of those [...] It just astounds me when I stop to think about it, that we can be here together peacefully and you know, it just is really kind of amazing that that can happen.

Comparing the Cultural Identities of Teachers in Chile and California

In this section, I compare trends across contexts, noting first the differences for teacher identity that are tied to the status of English in each context. In California, immigrants and sojourners who lack knowledge of the dominant societal language are viewed as disempowered and in need of 'help' –

whereas speakers of English in Chile are seen as specially empowered to participate in the contemporary globalized world. Moreover, there is an inevitable difference between being an English teacher in a large English-speaking country that is politically and economically powerful – versus being an English teacher in a small Spanish-speaking nation with a recent history of being dominated by the economic and political power of English-speaking countries.

However, it must be noted that teachers spoke little about these political and economic issues when talking about what it means to be 'Chilean' or 'American'. In their most prevalent discourse of national identity, Chileans portrayed themselves as friendly, affectionate, relaxed people who love good food and help the poor. California teachers did not have similarly complimentary things to say about their nation. Molly was at a loss to say anything at all about 'American culture'. Susanna equated being American with being narrow-minded and insular. The most positive thing that any teacher said about America was Eric's final comment about the peaceful coexistence of Vietnamese, Japanese and Russian immigrants – but this came at the end of a narrative in which an angry colleague discounted his German-American heritage.

In both Chile and America, discourses of ethnicity are most useful for teachers who stand out from the mainstream in some way. Ethnic identities at times connected to local identities, such that an Aymara indigenous heritage was seen by many Chileans as intrinsic to their home region. Since there has been more recent immigration in California, more of the California teachers could potentially draw discursive connections between their family histories and their immigrant students' experiences. However, I saw little evidence of this. Rather, teachers saw an appreciation for diversity, regardless of one's own family heritage, as key to a California identity. Jokwon's family had even downplayed their own background (Filipino) in favor of another (Japanese). My most vehemently Californian interviewee was Molly, who identified herself as '5th generation'. Like many of the Chileans I interviewed, she employed discourses that connected her local heritage to the natural environment.

All the teachers I interviewed, regardless of context, shared a similar commitment to language learning, and thus to the development of multilingual identities. They drew on common professional discourses to describe these experiences, using terms such as *motivation* and *communication*. The older Chilean teachers had enjoyed studying French as well as English in high school, and suffered through Latin in university. The younger teachers had been raised on discourses of English as the universal language. California teachers, regardless of generation, had found a wider array of languages to learn, especially at the university level or through living abroad, from Spanish to Tunisian Arabic. However, in many cases, they had learned these languages only to a certain extent before abandoning them. They had constructed identities as 'people who are interested in language, people who are interested in culture' (as Susanna said), but not necessarily as active multilinguals. In contrast, the Chilean interviewees appeared dedicated to English fluency and lifelong learning, both as a professional commitment and as a personal avocation. Of all my interviewees, Linnea (bilingual in Mandarin) was the only one who had learned a language besides English (in the United States) or Spanish (in Chile) at home.

One of the greatest contrasts I found between groups of teachers involved the use of L2 popular culture materials. A striking finding in Chile, across generations, was the long-term, widespread, committed consumption of English language popular culture products, both as a means of learning and as a context for active use. Chilean teachers repeatedly used discourses of motivation and of technological change to describe connections between English and cultural consumption. Older teachers described unrelenting efforts to locate and translate song lyrics; in recent years, the internet and cable television had become the preferred sources of a wide variety of English-language media products. Younger California teachers took part in similar internet and media practices to reinforce their language learning, and connected these practices to discourses of motivation and new technology, just as the Chileans did. However, this was not true of most California teachers over 30. Thus, I can tentatively say that advances in global media distribution are in fact changing the way California teachers learn and use their second languages, to more closely resemble the popular culture practices of Chilean teachers – but only in the youngest generation of English teachers, born in the 1980s.

On the other hand, while California teachers were less likely to have cross-cultural experiences on the internet, they were more likely to have them face to face. Just as they had more opportunity than Chilean teachers to study a variety of languages, they also had far more options than the Chileans to travel, live and work abroad, from Molly's recent internship in Nicaragua to Melinda's 1976 attendance at a choreographic conference in Cologne. More strikingly, while Chilean English students are almost entirely Chilean, California ESL classes include learners from many parts of the world. Thus, California teachers see the cultivation of cross-cultural skills as important to their professional identity, and they find learning from their own students to be a resource in this endeavor. While Chilean teachers find discourses of cultural difference to be a valuable part of their professional competence, California teachers end up using these discourses far more to make sense of their daily teaching practice.

This is because teachers in both California and Chile define their professional identities in terms of the kinds of students they teach. When I asked teachers to describe their students, Chilean teachers spoke of social class, while Californian teachers compared nationalities. In Chile, teachers are aware that economic realities prevent most students from traveling abroad, even as Chilean society is increasingly shaped by economic, political and cultural contact with English-speaking countries. The professional choices they make represent varying responses to this contradiction, with teachers often expressing strong preferences for particular socioeconomic environments – as in Sofía's narrative about quitting her job at the Catholic school. California teachers, on the other hand, live and work among highly visible immigrant communities, which are widely seen to be irrevocably changing the state. Discourses of diversity provide a way for many Californians to see these changes as positive. Eric's narrative about adopting different body language from Korean and Russian students thus represents a larger California experience in which local communities are increasingly multiethnic and shaped by cross-cultural contact. In the next chapter, I examine intercultural identity more closely, with case studies of transnational teachers.

Notes

(1) This chapter draws on data and analysis that first appeared in Menard-Warwick (2011a).
(2) In Spanish, *friendly* translates as *amable*, which has less connotation of extroversion and more connotation of kindness.
(3) In many indigenous communities of the Andes, New Year is celebrated on June 21, the winter solstice.
(4) *O Tannenbaum* is a well-known German Christmas song; it translates as *Oh Christmas Tree*.
(5) The Gold Rush refers to the discovery of gold in California in 1849, followed by the rapid arrival of miners from all over the world. The South, Middle and North Forks are branches of the American River. Mark Twain, the famous 19th-century US writer, lived and wrote in California for a brief part of his career. *Crawdads* are small edible freshwater crustaceans, more formally known as crayfish.
(6) *Tamales* are a traditional Mexican dish made of *masa* (ground maize dough) wrapped in leaves and usually stuffed with spicy pork or chicken.

5 Intercultural Case Studies[1]

> *In the realm of culture, outsideness is a most powerful factor in understanding. It is only in the eyes of another culture that foreign culture reveals itself fully and profoundly ....We raise new questions for a foreign culture, ones that it did not raise itself; we seek answers to our own questions in it; and the foreign culture responds to us by revealing to us its new aspects and new semantic depths.*
>
> Bakhtin, 1986a: 7

In the previous chapter, I explored English teachers' sense of their own cultural identities, including their accounts of identity development through encounters with people whom they perceived as culturally distinct. In this chapter, I explore processes of intercultural identity development, and begin to more closely examine the reciprocal relations between intercultural identities and intercultural pedagogies.

At the end of Chapter 1, I briefly addressed the unfortunate dichotomy that has persisted in the field of TESOL between 'native-speaking' and 'non-native-speaking' English teachers, whereas in Chapters 3 and 4, I noted the 'native-speaker' ideologies and identities that were referenced by some teachers. This chapter, in turn, contends that more attention needs to be paid, and more value needs to be placed, on multilingual, intercultural teachers and learners who have experienced what it is like to cross boundaries – especially those like Ruby, who do not fit neatly into the 'native-speaker/non-native-speaker' dichotomy. Born in Brazil to English-speaking parents, she grew up Portuguese-dominant, and does not feel that she was really proficient in English till after she moved to the United States in her early twenties:

Ruby: When I first came to the United States ... people definitely knew I wasn't American. And then, after living here for two years, they just thought I was from a different part of the United States, and most people still think that, and some people who really key into what they're hearing in language will say something like, 'Are you from ((pause)), uh, Canada? Or New York?' Somewhere far away, you know. (Menard-Warwick, 2011b)

Although many English learners end up using the language for purely local needs (Kumaravadivelu, 2006) or not at all, vast numbers of other learners deploy the language in cross-cultural contexts, whether over the Internet; with people from other nationalities in their own communities; or while living and working abroad. Rather than 'native speakers' or 'non-native speakers', what the language teaching profession needs is teachers, like Ruby, who understand what it is like to come from 'far away', who have experienced what Bakhtin refers to above as outsideness: reflective practitioners whose life experiences have led them to intercultural competence and who 'just as importantly have a meta-cognitive awareness of their competence' (Byram, 1997: 20).

If this is the case, it is important to closely examine the kinds of life experiences that can lead teachers to intercultural competence and to meta-cognitive awareness. In this chapter, after reviewing the literature on interculturality, I conduct this examination in two ways. First, I discuss the transnational life history narratives of Ruby and of Paloma, a Chilean English teacher who spent two decades in the United States, to illustrate what intercultural development can look like over the lifespan, and how interculturality might affect pedagogy (Menard-Warwick, 2008). Second, for a different kind of case study, I look closely at interaction data that illustrate the short-term development and display of intercultural competence. This data comes from one eventful week during a telecollaboration project that was carried out in April and May of 2006 between my linguistics graduate students in California and a class of undergraduate students studying to be English teachers at University of Las Peñas (ULP) in Chile.

Although interculturality (Byram, 1997; Kramsch, 2005), that is, seeing cultural issues from multiple perspectives, should not be viewed as synonymous with transnationality (Risager, 2007), that is, having significant interests or experiences that cross nation-state boundaries, the case studies in this chapter illustrate intercultural identity development through transnational experiences (Menard-Warwick *et al.*, in press).

Interculturality and the Cultural Identities of Language Teachers

Cultural awareness comes from dialogic encounters between distinct cultural groups – most typically face to face, but increasingly online, and at times through critical engagement with texts (Bakhtin himself was a literary scholar), including music and the media. When we are immersed in a set of cultural assumptions that pertain to a culture that we regard as 'our own', it is difficult to avoid taking our own beliefs and behaviors for granted. Profound encounters with cultural difference are usually necessary for us to see ourselves as cultural beings. In an early essay, Bakhtin reminded his readers that we cannot see our own faces, but when two people 'gaze at each other, two different worlds are reflected in the pupils of (their) eyes' (Bakhtin, 1990: 23). Similarly, as he suggests in the opening quote to this chapter, when we are faced with a 'foreign culture', we raise 'new questions' for it, and 'seek answers to our own questions in it' (Bakhtin, 1986a: 7). In this way, we begin to develop interculturality, which Kramsch defines as 'an awareness and a respect of difference, as well as the socioaffective capacity to see oneself through the eyes of others' (Kramsch, 2005: 553).

As Risager points out, within the long-standing national paradigm of culture learning, it is taken for granted that cultural identities are equivalent to national identities. However, to enable students' development as 'multiculturally aware world citizens' (Risager, 2007: 1), she argues for a new transnational paradigm that places language teaching in a global context, incorporates a recognition of contemporary linguistic and cultural flows, and recognizes identity development as a historically situated process that takes place both within and across national borders. If, as in Chapter 4, we see cultural identities as individuals' sense of belonging to multiple cultural groups, ranging from nations to extended families to musical fandoms, the transnational paradigm emphasizes that many of these cultural groups cross the boundaries of nation states. Risager argues that this dynamic awareness of cultural flows in the contemporary world is crucial for the development of interculturality, which occurs within language learning as students find ways 'to mediate between a number of cultural perspectives' (Risager, 2007: 114) (Menard-Warwick et al., 2013).

Since interculturality has become a goal of language teaching in Europe, Byram and his colleagues have worked to define this term in ways that language teachers can apply in the classroom. As these scholars explain, intercultural development involves beginning 'to understand and accept people from other cultures as individuals with other distinctive perspectives, values, and behaviors' (Byram et al., 2002: 10). To further clarify this concept for language teaching, they have identified specific components of interculturality. The first component is an *attitude of curiosity and openness*, 'readiness to suspend disbelief about other cultures and belief about one's own' (Byram et al., 2002: 7). Another component is *knowledge*, although specific knowledge about particular cultural groups is considered less important than more general knowledge about 'the processes of societal and individual interaction' (Byram *et al.*, 2002: 8). Interculturality additionally involves *interpretation* skills: the 'ability to interpret a document or event from another culture, to explain it, and relate it to documents or events from one's own' (Byram *et al.*, 2002: 8). Such interpretation requires distancing oneself from one's own culture, in order to see cultural phenomena from the perspective of another culture. Interpretation skills collaborate with a fourth component of interculturality: skills in *discovery*, which allow learners to gain cultural knowledge quickly from interlocutors and texts, and to draw upon this newly acquired knowledge in their interpretations and explanations. Finally, interculturality involves *critical cultural awareness*: the ability not just to understand and explain but to evaluate cultural practices using explicit ethical criteria.

Clearly, teachers' ease at modeling an intercultural stance will arise partly from their own cultural backgrounds and experiences with cultural difference. However, research on teachers has often portrayed them as prototypically monocultural (e.g. Kubota, 2003). While identity in L2 education has been seen in recent years as complex, multiple and dynamic (Norton, 2000), these ideas have been primarily applied to language learners. A number of articles during the last decade have instead emphasized language teachers' lack of cultural knowledge and confidence (Lazaraton, 2003; Sercu, 2006). For example, in one survey of European language teachers, respondents 'referred to their lack of preparation for teaching culture. They exposed a lack of confidence in themselves and stated they had only limited contacts with the foreign culture' (Castro *et al.*, 2004: 101). While some authors have noted biculturality or interculturality as an asset of 'non-native-speaker' English teachers (Nemtchinova, 2005), not much has been written on how these proficiencies influence their teaching practice.

In contrast to the rather bleak picture of teacher identity drawn by researchers in foreign language education and TESOL (an exception is Morgan, 2004), scholars of bilingual education detail teachers' pedagogical resources. Through biographical case studies, authors such as Galindo and Olguín (1996), Weisman (2001) and Monzó and Rueda (2003) note the gifts that bilingual teachers bring to the socialization of language minority children. As Weisman explains, such teachers are 'vital role models who can offer their students the opportunity to imagine possibilities for their future that do not negate their cultural worldview' (Weisman, 2001: 222). Moreover, bicultural 'teachers bring ... worldviews ... shaped by the sociocultural and historical contexts of their lives' (Monzó & Rueda, 2003: 72), which enable them to address the linguistic and social concerns of students from diverse communities. However, little research has been conducted on the bicultural or intercultural identities of second and foreign language teachers (Menard-Warwick *et al.*, 2013).

Transnational English Teachers: Paloma and Ruby

As an Anglo-American English teacher, who has taught and conducted research in Latin America as well as in US Latino communities, I have always found interculturality (to the extent I have it) to be a significant resource for my work. Therefore, I am interested in learning from the perspectives of truly transnational English teachers who have become immersed in other cultural contexts to the point where they consider themselves bicultural. The next section of this chapter provides case studies of the intercultural identities of two transnational teachers, Ruby and Paloma (Menard-Warwick, 2008). In this exploration, I define interculturality as an openness to seeing the world through the eyes of others, while being aware of one's own cultural assumptions (Kramsch, 1993; McKay, 2002); I define identity as a negotiation between how one sees oneself and how one is seen by others (Blackledge & Pavlenko, 2001). Drawing on Norton's insight that learning involves investment in cultural capital (2000), I view an intercultural identity as a negotiated investment in seeing the world through multiple cultural perspectives.

At the time I observed them, both Paloma and Ruby were teaching advanced general English classes, Paloma to Chilean students at ULP, and Ruby to a mixed-nationality class at an adult school in a middle-class area of Farmington, California. Having decided to write a comparative case study of these two teachers, I conducted a thematic analysis of their interview and classroom data using NVivo7 qualitative data analysis software. I constructed the Transnational Life Histories section below by going through their interviews and selecting data related to major life events: education, marriage, emigration, long-term employment and current activities, arranging the same chronologically. The '(Inter)cultural Identities' section is a synthesis of data coded for cultural identity, defined in my coding system as 'a sense of belonging to a group of people who share practices and perspectives' (see Chapter 4).

It was while coding that I found the need to operationalize a definition of culture that could be applied to different types of data across research contexts, and especially in the classroom. Drawing on the American Council of Teachers of Foreign Language (ACTFL) National Standards (Phillips, 2003), I coded data as having cultural content when it concerned practices, perspectives and products that are shared among groups of people (see

Chapter 4). As a definition of culture, this is simplistic, because it does not recognize the way these 'shared' understandings and practices are inevitably subjective, heterogeneous and dynamic (Kramsch, 1998; Ros i Solé, 2003); however, due to its simplicity, this definition served as the basis of a workable coding system. For example, in data from Ruby's class below, tattooing is a practice shared by fashionable youth worldwide, which results in a product (body art) and arguably exemplifies values of individual self-expression. Although it could be asserted that linguistic forms are cultural, I excluded most form-focused activities, for example, vocabulary exercises, from my cultural coding.[2]

I also coded data for approaches toward culture taken by participants (see Chapter 6 for an extended discussion of approaches in the classes I observed). Ruby's most common approach was cultural comparison (Byram, 1997; McKay 2002): discussion of how the practices or perspectives of one group (she focused primarily on national groups) differ from those of another group. Paloma also used this approach, but more often focused on cultural change in Chile: discussion of how contemporary practices and perspectives compare to those in the past. I selected classroom data that exemplified observed trends in teaching culture. Then, in my analysis of classroom data below, I point to evidence of interculturality within typical activities in the two classes, drawing on the components of intercultural awareness identified by Byram *et al.* (2002), such as 'interpretation skills'.

In presenting this analysis, I know that the eight hours I spent in Ruby's and Paloma's classes may not be representative of their teaching practice, and that my presence may have affected the approaches they took during my observations.[3] As discussed in Chapter 1, their accounts of their lives, identities and pedagogies should not be seen as a transparent representation of factual information, but rather as their perspectives on past events in the light of the present, and in relation to the context of telling (Ochs & Capps, 1996). In interviews, they represented their transnational identities to me through narrative, and in this section, I re-construct a more condensed representation of their stories, in order to further our dialogue by sharing the understandings I gained from them with a larger audience.

Transnational life histories

In this section, I present accounts of my focal participants' life histories, spanning many decades and two continents, to contextualize my later discussion of their (inter)cultural identities and (inter)cultural teaching practices. These narratives recount both women's viewpoints on how they came to distance themselves from their original cultural context (Byram *et al.*, 2002), as they encountered societal conflicts and new cultural perspectives.

Ruby

Born in Brazil in the 1950s, Ruby was a middle child in a family whose fortunes fluctuated over the years of her childhood. Her father had moved to Brazil from the United States after a stint in the Navy as a young man, while her mother had come from England as a child. Both were bilingual in English and Portuguese, and spoke both languages at home in Ruby's early childhood. Her father, 'very much of a nerd [...] a computer person', was initially successful in business, but later the business failed. Her parents divorced when she was five years old, and Ruby describes her family life during childhood as 'spinning in such chaos'. For the most part, she lived with her mother, who used only Portuguese at home after the divorce. After her mother remarried, Ruby at 13 temporarily joined her father and stepmother in Holland. There she relearned English, also picking up Dutch and some German. This European sojourn interrupted her Portuguese-language schooling, and she ended up behind her age group when she returned to live with her mother in Brazil.

As a 17-year-old student, she was faced with the need to work full time: 'I was living with my mom and she didn't have money, so I really needed to have some money and since I spoke English, [...] I was working as a freelance tour guide in Brasilia.' This work didn't leave time for school, so she dropped out. Her mother by this time had started teaching English, and Ruby was soon offered a job at a private English school because although she 'didn't speak that well at all', she 'did speak without an accent'. Ruby quickly learned to teach 'cookbook style. Everything you had to do was written there [...] and I sort of jumped in the classroom and being an extrovert, just went ahead from there.' Outside class, Ruby spent time with expatriate English teachers, who urged her to continue her education; with her 'staunch capitalist' but now impoverished family; and with a 'very left-leaning' boyfriend, critical of the military regime in Brazil. By the time she left Brazil in 1977, 'I knew that people disappeared, I knew there was torture, I knew there was harassment, I knew that you couldn't talk about politics [...] but at the same time I was just a rebellious teenager [...] I wasn't very conscious.' When she got the opportunity to move to New York and live with her uncle, she remembers telling her Brazilian English students, 'I'm gonna be zipping around in this convertible Mercedes and isn't life great.'

In New York, she finished high school, took junior college classes and regained a native-like proficiency in English. She enjoyed her science classes, but wanted a warmer climate, so in her mid-twenties, she moved to California, got a degree in Agronomy and met her husband Matt, a university lecturer. They married and had two daughters. Ruby initially planned to be a full-time mother, but then she was offered a job teaching ESL at the local adult school. They initially hired her to teach a night class, saying that she had 'the right energy' and would be able to 'keep the students' attention', but when her daughters started school, she requested to change to a morning class. 'So I got that class but it was a little higher level and [..] this particular woman from Spain wanted to know a lot of grammar and I didn't know the grammar at all [...] and so I decided that if I was going to teach English, I needed to go back to school.' Ruby earned a Master's degree in TESOL, and continued teaching mornings at the adult school.

Both her daughters are now adults, and at the time of the interview had recently spent six months in Brazil to improve their Portuguese. Along with teaching English, Ruby is active in the local community helping to organize yearly Latin American music festivals, as well as more frequent Brazilian community gatherings: 'We have a Yahoo group and any information we have of any event that has to do with Brazil we just send it to everybody on the Yahoo group [...] So it's pretty fun, I'm really happy about it.'

Paloma

Born in the 1940s, Paloma was the youngest child in a middle-class family in Las Peñas, the Chilean city where she now lives. Spanish was her home language, but her older siblings had been successful foreign language learners in school. Her high school French teacher inspired her lifelong love of languages and cultures. English class was less rewarding: 'But for some reason I always told my mom that I wanted to be a teacher of English.'

Paloma's father 'did not believe that women had to study' past high school. Her mother had health problems, and as the youngest child, 'I was the one that had to take care of my mom.' However, her mother and teachers convinced her father to let her study English teaching at ULP. 'And (then) I met Javier, and Javier was going to study law in Santiago, and so we fell in love and he said, "So, I'm going to come study TESOL with you."' They got married two weeks after they graduated in December 1970, and six weeks later, Paloma was accepted for a Fulbright grant to study for a Masters degree in TESOL in Cedarville, Iowa. Although Javier was not offered support from Fulbright, 'it was wonderful because he was a good husband [...], he sold everything he could, he took money, and he cleaned dorms.' On this basis, Javier got his MA in literature at the same Iowa university.

When they returned to Chile in 1973, the country was enduring severe shortages of consumer goods in the final days of Allende's socialist presidency. 'We left admiring what was happening, and then we came back, and we saw so much pain [...] and everybody blaming it on the President.' The coup and military dictatorship soon followed: 'We saw many of our colleagues leaving and not coming back again, going to Canada, France, etcetera [...] and I remember that the ... day of the coup, [...] I was worried, and somebody said, "But it will be only for a year, Paloma."'[4] Because the couple had lived abroad during most of Allende's presidency, they kept their teaching jobs while colleagues viewed as 'leftist' went into exile. 'But things turned out very, very bad and then we just devoted ourselves to working.'

They taught English at the university in their hometown under military rule until 1985, when Javier was accepted into a PhD program in Iowa, and Paloma found a job as a coordinator of teaching assistants in the Spanish department at the same university. At this time, their son was nine years old. Over the next decade, Javier finished his doctorate and taught Spanish literature at two small colleges on temporary work visas, while Paloma got a second MA in Spanish and continued to coordinate teaching assistants. Their son acculturated to life in the United States and for the most part abandoned Spanish. In the late 1990s, Javier lost his teaching job and received an offer to teach English literature back at ULP. Chile had returned to democracy in 1990, and he and their son wanted to go back. Paloma was just starting a PhD program in Education, so she tried staying in the United States on her own, but found it too hard on their marriage. Returning to Las Peñas in 2003 without finishing her doctorate, she began teaching English part-time again at the university.

Although transitioning back to Chile was not easy for Paloma, it eventually brought new opportunities to promote cultural awareness. She felt out of place in her homeland until a friend talked her into attending a leadership diploma program. This was the same *emprendimiento* program mentioned by Diego in Chapter 1. The first time she attended, Paloma said that she felt 'reenergized'. As a project for the leadership program, she started an exchange program for Chilean English teachers to spend a month in the United States, living with US Spanish teachers and assisting in their classes – this was, in fact, the program that brought Diego to Iowa in 2004. As she explained to her *emprendimiento* group: 'I want to take teachers of English that have never been abroad, and I would like to have a program for them to go and just see the culture, be immersed with the language.' Two years later when I interviewed her, she was excited about the results of this program, as a life-changing experience for Chilean teachers. As one participant told her, 'Now I believe I can do things. Now I trust myself that I can bring change.'

(Inter)cultural identities

As discussed in Chapter 4, probably the most challenging interview question I asked was, 'How would you define your own cultural identity?' Paloma and Ruby answered more readily than most (although with laughter). In this section, I look at how they represent themselves as identifying with different cultural groups over the course of their transnational lives.

Ruby

When I asked Ruby how she defined her cultural identity, she immediately laughed, and replied, 'Split. Definitely split. [...] I feel like a hybrid of some sort, you know. It's um, it's mixed. ((pause)) I think at this point ((pause)) I'm probably more American than Brazilian.' At times, she said, she had felt alienated from other Brazilians in the United States, because of being married to an American, and of having lived, in some ways, a 'gringo' life even in Brazil. Although not particularly close to her father, she had picked up some of his values: 'In Brazil [...] if you grew up in the middle class or higher, you have maids and you have all the working class people who will do all the various different things. [...] You don't have to cook, you don't shop for things, you don't do your clothes, you don't fix anything, you don't garden.' However, from her father Ruby had learned pride in knowing and using practical skills: 'I'm very American that way.'

At the same, she saw herself as still possessing a Brazilian communication style. She explained this through an extended narrative about the abrupt end of a recent discussion with her husband: when she told him that she wanted to depart for a musical event, he picked up a newspaper and started reading – while she remained sitting, frustrated that he had stopped talking and was ignoring her body language:

Ruby: I suddenly said, 'Wait! I know what's happening. I am acting like a Brazilian...' who is thinking the context is what means a lot. My words didn't mean that much. My words were, 'I want to go there,' but my body was, 'I sat down here. I'm here. I'm available to you. I'm available to talk.' In his mind, [...] he heard, 'She wants to go there. She's not here anymore.'

Here, a narrative about a faultline in Ruby's own family is used to illustrate discourses about cultural difference and in this way to make sense of her transnational life experiences.

As well as maintaining the communication style she had grown up with, Ruby saw herself passing on to her daughters Brazilian values: having fun, socializing, eating and spending time with friends and family.[5] This was possible because she had actively reclaimed her Brazilian identity during the years of her daughters' childhood: 'When my kids were very little, I was so immersed in the world of little kids and...other moms and playgroups [...] so I had very little chance to speak Portuguese.' The Portuguese she remembered best was 'rebellious teen Portuguese' with 'a lot of cuss words', and she realized, 'Oh my gosh, I can't talk to my baby in Portuguese because I can't coo and do any, you know, things like that.' All she remembered was 'songs, a few songs'. Indeed, it was through music that she re-connected with her Brazilian heritage: at last she met 'somebody [who] really loves Brazilian music [..] and didn't have somebody to sing, and I love to sing', and although she had 'never imagined' performing, 'next thing I know, it's been ten years and we've been singing together ever since.' It was her involvement in music that led to her work with Latin American cultural organizations.

Paloma

Like Ruby, Paloma laughed when I asked her to define her cultural identity. Still laughing, she replied, 'My cultural identity. Um, I was born white, Catholic, I went to the States, they told me that I'm not white, I'm Hispanic, and a Catholic, I am not a majority, but a minority.' The North American tendency to draw a racial line at the US–Mexican border presents a significant discursive faultline for Latin Americans with different histories. Nevertheless, Paloma felt that her level of education brought her some acceptance in her new home: 'I liked when they said, "Well, you're a near-native Iowan," And I said, "Thank you for saying 'near' because if you say native, I am not, and I will never be."' At the same time, she appreciated being called 'near-native' in recognition of all that she had both gained and suffered while living in the United States. As with Ruby, she noted that the hardest thing to adjust to was the style of conversation. She illustrated this faultline with a narrative about an older couple who helped her and Javier get settled when they first arrived in Iowa:

Paloma: Um, so we learned that we could not stop by and say hello at any moment, we had to call, so I ... love them dearly, but it was something that was always, there was something empty, because I'd say, 'I have a problem and I wish I could talk with you,' he'd say, 'Okay, today is Tuesday, how about Sunday?' ((laughing)) 'Whew, ah, okay, I will go Sunday,' [. . .] in the meantime, I had talked to friends and I had the problem, everything solved by Sunday ((laughing)).

Despite these differing ideas about time management, Paloma described her relationship with her Iowa friends as 'beautiful'. Eventually, she says she realized that 'I belong to both cultures. I am a multicultural person.' Nevertheless, it had been a struggle to raise 'a bicultural kid [. . .] sometimes I'm talking to him, I sound like a person from Las Peñas and he responds as an American, and vice versa, and my husband cannot accept that [. . .], he gets very, very upset if [our son] says a four letter word in English, it is so typical with kids there.' She felt that after several years back in Chile, her son was still 'search(ing) for his center'.

As for herself, Paloma spoke of metaphorical 'umbilical cords' connecting her to Chile but also to Iowa. She described watching movies in English as a way to maintain her umbilical cord to the United States, but later in the same conversation, she said that becoming American and staying in the United States would have meant cutting her umbilical cord to Chile: 'It wouldn't be fair in my life to the place I was born.' Nevertheless, rejecting a US identity 'would feel unfair to a country that has given me so much, that has opened my horizons'. At the same time, she was deeply aware of both positive and negative changes in Chile during the years she was away. As a teacher, she identified herself as an 'agent of change' – but one transformation she hoped to enact was deeper appreciation for the traditional Chilean celebrations now being displaced by globalized consumer holidays like Valentine's Day.

Teaching interculturality

According to Sercu (2006), European teachers are now expected to incorporate the intercultural dimension of language learning in their classes. However, her survey findings indicate that this is still difficult for many teachers (cf Castro et al., 2004; Duff & Uchida, 1997; Harklau, 1999; Lazaraton, 2003). Teachers who have experienced and reflected upon cultural differences are perhaps best equipped to help language learners understand them. However, effective pedagogical responses to students' confrontation with cultural otherness will vary across contexts. As seen in the transcribed classroom observation excerpts below, the contrasts between Paloma's and Ruby's approaches show possible ways that cultural pedagogies might arise not only from biographical identities, but also from institutional settings

(Duff & Uchida, 1997). In both classrooms, teachers and students are constructing and evaluating representations of globalized cultural practices, specifically tattoos and 'fake smiling'. However, in the California classroom, the emphasis is on comparing different countries, while in the Chilean classroom, the central comparison is between the past and present.

Ruby

Ruby said that for many years she taught culture 'incidentally, only if a question (came) up'. In so doing, she drew on her own background, sometimes thinking through issues in Portuguese so she could identify students' sources of confusion with English concepts. In recent years, however, she said she was influenced by an article she had read on the Cultural Orientation Framework (Buckley, 2000), which presents a model for understanding cultural assumptions and values, for example, 'individualism vs collectivism'. Although she found this article useful for understanding differences between herself and her 'very American' husband, she discovered in classroom discussions that her students did not fall into the neat patterns that Buckley predicted. To illustrate this, she told a short narrative about a conversation with a Turkish student, employing dialogic voicing to represent the contrast between her own expectations based on Buckley and her student's account of Turkish norms:

Ruby: Like the Turks, um, they are actually very punctual according to my student, and I was so surprised, and, 'The Turks are punctual? They're Middle Eastern!' I was thinking they have this more flexible ( ) thing, and 'No, no, we have to be on time, we can't like, you know, 'Ten minutes." 'Like, (whoa), okay, whatever.'

Although she voices herself at the end of this narrative using the popular expression 'whatever' to accept the complexity, Ruby said she continued to use the article's concepts to illustrate values and assumptions that underlie cultural behaviors.

In her classroom, I observed discussions of tattoos, eating contests, political dissent and punishment for children. In each case, Ruby would relate specific issues, for example, eating contests, to more general themes such as affluence and waste. After introducing the topic with a form-focused exercise, in the case of tattoos, a poem used to teach pronunciation, she would direct students to talk in groups about how this issue is regarded in 'your countries', and then report back to the class. She asked students to share personal experiences, and also recounted experiences of her own. In connecting eating contests to affluence and waste, she mentioned being shocked as a child when her 'American cousins' staged a 'food fight' during a visit to Brazil: 'It was a perfectly good egg and there it went.' When students from the same country disagreed, she encouraged both to share opinions, a dialogically expansive approach (White, 2003) that emphasizes the heterogeneous nature of cultural practices (Kramsch, 1998). Thus, cultural comparison, contrasting national cultures from subjective perspectives, was Ruby's principal orientation to teaching culture in my analysis.

In the following excerpt, an older and a younger woman from Argentina have just disagreed on the prevalence of tattoos in 'their country' and Ruby, demonstrating her own skills in cultural interaction and discovery (Byram *et al.*, 2002), has asked the younger woman to elaborate on her answer. The following excerpts are from an audiotaped observation on 11 May 2005:

Cecilia: It's like a fashion in Argentina (we have to go) to have tattoos
Ruby: ((overlapping)) To get tattoos,
Cecilia: Yes.
Ruby: So, it's a recent fashion, so the health concern has emerged recently.
Cecilia: For example, I used to work at McDonald's and [...] if you have tattoos, you can't work there.

Ruby asked the class if they thought this would be the same at McDonald's in the United States, and when several said they did not know, she gave her own opinion, then asked students to interpret her answer (Byram *et al.*, 2002):

Ruby: I would guess not, I would guess you can work at McDonald's with a tattoo, in fact I would guess probably many people do have tattoos who work there. So why do you think ((pause)) that there are more tattoos here than in your country?
Students ((overlapping each other)): America is more free. More freedom.

Ruby then told a story, to the accompaniment of student laughter, about a tattoo experience of her own. Here, she seems to be drawing upon her identity as a long-term resident of the United States who is not yet fully acculturated, who sees US culture from outside, and is still engaged in discovery, interpretation and evaluation (Byram *et al.*, 2002). Although her attitude toward tattoos does not demonstrate openness and acceptance (rather shock and amazement), nor does she state 'explicit ethical criteria', she certainly models curiosity (Byram *et al.*, 2002).

> **Ruby:** I must say that I didn't think that there were that many tattoos, but several years ago, already, let's see, my kids were younger, [...] about 8 or 9 years ago, I went to a public swimming pool in Sacramento to a birthday party, I was completely shocked ((pause)). Because there, you could see everybody's tattoos because everybody was wearing a bathing suit or some very small, or bikinis, and I don't know if it was that particular place or what, but I would say, I think 70% of the people had tattoos ((pause)) and I was amazed, I was shocked, [...] I mean, everyone I looked at had a tattoo, but I don't, I'm not saying that 70% of American people have tattoos, it may just be, maybe it was just that one day at that pool ((laughing)).

After reiterating her amazement at the tattoos she saw that day, Ruby returned to the question of employment discrimination raised by Cecilia, asking students if they thought a US employer could refuse to hire an applicant with a tattoo, again requiring students to make an interpretation (Byram *et al.*, 2002). Students initially chorused, 'No!' but when Ruby asked them 'Why not?' she received a more nuanced reply that it would depend on the position, and the image of the company. Students from different countries shared examples of employers asking about tattoos during interviews, thus building cultural knowledge within the classroom (Byram *et al.*, 2002). When Ruby responded, 'My feeling is that in America people would consider this private information,' a number of students pointed out legitimate health concerns related to blood-borne diseases – a good example of evaluating a cultural practice based on explicit ethical criteria (Byram *et al.*, 2002). This led to a discussion of blood-testing practices around the world, before returning to the idea of tattoos as a contemporary fashion statement. At last, Ruby drew a tentative conclusion, based on a student comment:

> **Ruby:** So you're saying that people are more concerned about standing out as different, they want to make a mark ((pause)) they want to show their individuality more, and you think that that's where this is coming from.

Thus, this discussion included the most common features of the dialogically expansive cultural pedagogy in Ruby's classroom (White, 2003): encouragement to make general remarks about 'your countries' and also about personal experiences, Ruby's sharing of her own experiences, and the relation of a small issue (tattoos) from a text used in a form-focused exercise to more general cultural concerns (privacy, individuality, employment discrimination). While engaging the class in cultural discovery and interpretation (Byram *et al.*, 2002), this discussion also implicitly raised other important issues: first, in addressing discrimination against tattooed individuals, it noted the influence of societal power structures; second, it illustrated the dynamic transnational nature of many contemporary cultural practices (Risager, 2007). Ironically, when I asked Ruby about this interaction in an interview, she said this was a 'good cultural issue' (or in other words, perhaps, a discursive faultline), but worried that she did not know enough about privacy and individualism in American culture 'for a teacher to be discussing and trying to tell students' about them.

Paloma

For Paloma, teaching culture relates to her larger goal of social transformation through education. She stated both in interviews and while teaching that she saw good teachers as 'agents of change'. In her own case, studying multiculturalism in Iowa had led her to value diversity in Chile, especially the indigenous cultures, and she now had 'an agenda there, to expose students to these beliefs'.[6] At times, however, she simply tried to prepare students for transformations in education outside their control. In an interview, I mentioned that *change* seemed to be a theme in all her classes. She laughed and said, 'The idea about adjusting to new times [...] so it surfaces, huh?' She saw living abroad as influential to her ability to raise these issues. As she explained in a follow-up email, 'I was away from Chile for 18 years...I came back in 2003 with a very objective set of mind to see things that my fellow Chileans did not see.'

Paloma usually connected her class activities to a central theme, extending one theme over several lessons. Although this was officially a class on English rather than teaching methodology, her students were prospective teachers already practice-teaching in local schools. For this reason, 'pedagogy' was one theme she included. The other two themes I observed were 'the changing family' and 'terrorism' (the latter requested by students after the London subway bombing). Like Ruby, Paloma introduced cultural issues through short readings. Generally, the class went from comprehension exercises to sharing opinions about the ideas presented. Unlike Ruby, Paloma rarely asked students to compare different countries, but rather to contrast

Chile's past and present. Since contemporary cultural trends in Chile are widely seen as wholesale adoptions of 'global' culture (Moulián, 1997), interculturality can involve comparing today's 'globalized' culture (to some extent borrowed from English-speaking countries) with older Chilean practices and values. Thus, Paloma's approach focused on cultural change, emphasizing the dynamic nature of cultural practices and values (Kramsch, 1998).

In an audiotaped classroom observation dated 5 July 2005, Paloma introduced the discussion by citing her students' performance in their last round of oral presentations: some had done extremely well, while many needed improvement. She had photocopied an article titled '30 Second Success' (Demarais, 2004) their public-speaking skills and ultimately their teaching. Thus, she presented a short text from North America and asked students to interpret and perhaps evaluate it (Byram *et al.*, 2002). She began by assigning a student, Casandra, to read the first paragraph aloud, which was on eye contact and body language. There was a brief discussion of these issues, during which no substantial disagreement surfaced. Paloma then asked another student, Elena, to read further:

Elena ((reading)): Smile even when you aren't in the mood.
Paloma: Imagine. Smile even when you aren't in the mood. OK! Elena, continue.
Elena ((reading)): We actually encourage our clients to fake it.
Paloma: Oooo. Wow!
Elena ((reading)): It's a gift of social generosity, with a powerful payback. Just going through the motions of showing some teeth may make you – and others – feel better, says the research.
Paloma: How do you feel with that? ((pause)) Mmmm? ((pause)) So…good Pepsodent and start smiling. ((Students laughed)). I see three faces that are absolutely serious and I know what that means. ((pause)) What do you think about faking? ((Students laughed)). Because that's a value. Are you supposed to do it – or not? Who would like to reply to that? Some of you may say, 'I am sorry, I don't feel like smiling and I will not do it.'

As the subsequent discussion showed, Paloma was correct in assuming that not everyone agreed with the value of 'fake' smiling. In fact, she mocks the commercialization of the smile in her 'Pepsodent' remark, making an intertextual connection between teaching and the discourse of advertising. However, students were initially hesitant to voice objections. Finally,

Casandra decided to take the challenge. From her use of 'we' below, she appears to have appointed herself spokesperson:

> **Casandra:** Probably if I am working as a salesclerk, I should smile all the time, but in our own cases, we think that – I mean, I think, I've heard – that when we are in front of a teacher that is always smiling, we (feel that they are faking), and that makes us, I don't know, feel uncomfortable.

Casandra added that she hoped her own future students would not expect her to be happy all the time. Another student said that she disliked teachers smiling when they gave her a bad grade. Antonio then raised a larger issue:

> **Antonio:** I think that we will focus on the social context in which occurs this situation. Here it says 'we actually encourage our clients'. So it (tells) you that in business you have to forget your emotional moods and perhaps be smiling every time, but it is different when you are with your friends ((pause)) or with your professors. And I think that's a bit different.
>
> **Paloma:** Mmhmm.
>
> **Antonio:** The kind of image…you are working in a company etcetera, often you are with people ((pause)) with whom you feel more uncomfortable.
>
> **Paloma:** This is very interesting. I come from that model, in the past, that education, in education you do not have 'clients'. And today, that's all there is to it! Everything is selling a good product, selling a good education, with a methodology ((pause)). And also, we become clients. I become a client of [textbook publisher] if I am a good professor, and you are my students. It's interesting that in our mind we have no concept for that. A client is only – for business. But I like what she said 'It's a gift of social generosity.'

Similar to the discussion of employment discrimination in Ruby's class, there is a sub-text here regarding the societal power structures that compel or limit new cultural practices. Although neither Antonio nor Paloma says the word *neoliberalism*, the management of education 'like a business' is part of the current economic model in Chile, as in many parts of the world (Holborow, 2012a, 2012b); indeed, ULP students had recently gone on strike to protest the privatization of student loans. It was against this discursive faultline that students interpreted the text provided by Paloma (Byram *et al.*, 2002). Moreover, the social solidarity invoked by Antonio is widely seen as a traditional Chilean value now being lost to neoliberalism (Moulián, 1997). Paloma picks up these implications of Antonio's remarks, implying her willingness to entertain regrets for lost solidarity. None of her students is displaying attitudes of 'curiosity' or 'openness' to neoliberal cultural phenomena, but as in Ruby's class, critical cultural awareness (Byram *et al.*, 2002) appears through the juxtaposition of different value systems.

While Paloma's time abroad was not explicitly thematized in this interaction, I contend (and she concurs) that her view of educational change was facilitated by her experiences of teaching in different sociocultural and historical contexts. It was her intercultural attitude (Byram *et al.*, 2002), her ability to see the issue from divergent perspectives, that allowed her to understand and address her students' concerns, while still giving them a realistic picture of the current educational climate. In this way, she created a dialogically expansive space (White, 2003) between her students' preferences for emotional authenticity and the article's more calculating recommendations on how to self-present. When I interviewed her about this exchange, she expressed ambivalence toward business-oriented values, but said she had to prepare her students for the future, 'otherwise they are going to suffer in the schools'.

Telecollaboration for Intercultural Learning

In the preceding section, I explored the *biographical identities* of two teachers (Ivanic, 1998), whose life histories and current pedagogies illustrate the development of interculturality over decades. In the next section, I will examine the (apparent) development of interculturality in *discursive identities* (Ivanic, 1998) from a telecollaboration project that linked a class in Chile with a class in California during April and May of 2006 (Menard-Warwick, 2009b; Menard-Warwick *et al.*, 2013). In California, I was the instructor for Second Language Literacy and Technology, in which nine graduate students were enrolled, six from Linguistics and three from Education. At ULP, my colleague Ana Heredia (not a pseudonym) was teaching English to 30 undergraduate students in the fourth year of the English Pedagogy program. Four of my students were studying to become English teachers in a MATESOL program, while five had worked as teachers previously and were now pursuing doctoral degrees with the intent of becoming professors. In the project, each of my students served as an online tutor for a group of 3–4 of her students, using MSN Messenger to communicate synchronously 1.5 hours per week for eight weeks. Throughout the project, the graduate student tutors saved the chat transcripts and submitted them (with the permission of all participants) as data for this project. In the interests of space in this chapter, I present data from only four of the nine groups.

The groups chatted about articles on US cultural topics taken from the popular media and posted on the course website by the graduate students. As well as providing experience with learning and teaching English online, one purpose of the course was for the Chilean students to find out more about the United States, so they could teach effective cultural lessons to their future students. Although most of them had spent a lot of time consuming US media products (see Chapter 4), the information they had obtained this way was not always accurate. Conversely, the US graduate students knew almost nothing about Chile, so the Chilean students also took on a teaching role. The graduate students' selections of articles were based partly on what the Chilean students in their group had expressed interest in learning. Topics ranged from Walmart to baseball to podcasting. Articles were posted throughout the quarter, one per week, close to the time when they were discussed online.

This 'just-in-time' posting facilitated the focus on the political cultures of both countries when massive strikes and demonstrations broke out in May. In the United States, the immigrant rights movement sought a path to legalization for undocumented immigrants (Ferre et al., 2006), while in Chile the nationwide student movement demanded free bus passes and free university entrance exams (Dunn, 2006). During the sixth week of this project, the ULP was temporarily closed due to student protests. Despite the unrest, Ana and her students decided to continue with the telecollaboration project, and found computers off campus. The California university was not affected directly by the protest movement but some class members attended local demonstrations. What we could not have predicted was that the richest internet chat exchanges of the entire project would take place over the next week, during which time Ana's students and mine compared the Chilean student movement with the contemporary US immigrant rights movement. In these interactions, students not only constructed representations of cultural phenomena but actually participated in dialogue with each other on the meaning of these representations.

Below, I analyze the chat exchanges that contrasted the political cultures of both countries in order to explore the linguistic resources used to construct interculturality (Byram et al., 2002; Kramsch, 2005). In connecting students transnationally, telecollaboration projects can be seen as ideal for intercultural pedagogy, as learners have an opportunity to 'raise new questions for a foreign culture, ones that it did not raise itself; (and) seek answers to (their) own questions in it' (Bakhtin, 1986a: 7). However, it is undeniable that some exchanges are more successful than others in fostering interculturality. For example, Ware and Kramsch (2005) report on a project that paired US students of German with German students of English, but where exchanges were dominated by miscommunication and eventual disengagement. Liaw (2006), in contrast, describes telecollaboration between Taiwanese English learners and prospective teachers in Texas, where materials from the learners' culture helped both groups to develop cultural insights. Ware and Kramsch conclude that teachers should model 'an intercultural stance (which)... includes the willingness to engage with students in an exploration of difference' (Ware & Kramsch, 2005: 203).

Analyzing students' intercultural learning brings its own complexities. Belz (2002) suggests examining linguistic resources (e.g. evaluative adjectives) used to portray attitudes of curiosity and openness, affective responses to cultural phenomena and a willingness to decenter from one's own cultural perspectives. In a similar vein, Vogt looked for content in email transcripts that 'represent(ed) observable instance(s) of...the willingness to engage with others in a relationship of equality' (Vogt, 2006: 160). This can be seen, for example, when participants pose follow-up questions that indicate an interest in a partner's experience or perspective. This is important, because, as Abrams argues, some learners are 'able to develop cross-cultural awareness only when they (make) personal connections to the cultural information' (Abrams, 2002: 141). From a Bakhtinian perspective, follow-up questions show active listening, and thus genuine dialogue (Bakhtin, 1986b, Kramsch, 1993).

In order to accomplish my analysis of these discursive resources, files were thematically coded for topics of discussion (e.g. politics, education, gender) using Nvivo 7 software as discussed above. Once the thematic analysis was completed, I discursively analyzed Week 6 chat interactions that had been coded under politics, since this week was when the most intense intercultural learning seemed to occur. Specifically, I looked for linguistic evidence of intercultural attitudes, knowledge, interpretation, discovery and engagement (Byram et al., 2002). In this analysis, I focused on expressions of interpersonal engagement and affiliation (Arnold & Ducate, 2006; Vogt, 2006; Ware & Kramsch, 2005); evaluation and comparison (Belz, 2002); identity (labels for social categories) and claims of knowledge (Fairclough, 1992) and negotiation of meaning (Gass et al., 1998) regarding cultural issues. I then chose data for this chapter to illustrate the discursive realization of the components of Byram's model.

Interculturality in internet chat transcripts

In this section, I present my analysis of four brief chat excerpts that illustrate components of Byram's interculturality model. I have adjusted the chat format for ease of reading, but chat text has not been modified. US tutors' names appear in bold, while Chilean learners' names are in italics.

Intercultural attitude

In this section, the participants demonstrate an intercultural attitude of curiosity and openness in discussing the Chilean student protests. Here we see an Argentinean-American graduate student (Eugenia) and a Peruvian international student in Chile (Dalia) asking their Chilean interlocutors about the student protests at ULP:

Eugenia: Did you not have classes today?
Piera: we have had classes but only in the morning because all the riots have taken place at mid day
Eugenia: Oh, I see.
José: we usually have classes in the morning becuases the protest are in the afternoom
Dalia: but i classmate told me that this kind of fact happens during this month Is it true?
Piera: yes, it is because today is the anniversary of student who died in riot...
Eugenia: How will this affect your classes, your finals and papers?

Although this appears to be a non-evaluative exchange of information, Dalia's and Eugenia's questions show their interest in what is happening in Las Peñas even while discussing an article about the United States. This basic attitude of curiosity and openness is key to intercultural learning. In particular, Eugenia wants to know how the political unrest affects these students as human beings – note her use of the second person pronoun, which Ware and Kramsch (2005) found to be rare in an exchange dominated by miscommunication. Note also Eugenia's use of 'oh I see' to demonstrate her understanding, and Dalia's use of 'is it true' to confirm her understanding of student protest as a cultural practice. Meanwhile, Piera and José must find ways of explaining to foreigners what is common knowledge for them. In so doing, they present practices from their own country 'from an outsider's perspective' (Byram *et al.*, 2002: 12), distancing themselves from taken-for-granted cultural knowledge in order to describe it.

Intercultural knowledge

This excerpt comes toward the end of a long discussion of the Chilean student protests and shows the US tutor's knowledge of *'general* processes of societal and individual interaction' (Byram *et al.*, 2002: 12, italics added), which these authors consider to be the most necessary kind of knowledge for intercultural communication. Here, Geraldine is actively learning about her chat partners' perspectives on the protesters' tactics, while drawing on general cultural knowledge in deciding how to respond:

Claudia: maybe if cops wouldnt give that much attention maybe students wouldnt have a reason to be violent

Jacinto: It's like almost a 'performance' it's a show and every year is the same

Geraldine: ah...and are you guys sick of this 'performance'?

Jacinto: yes competely sick

Raúl: yeah i'm very sick of that very tired and in a bad mood

Geraldine: aw, i'm sorry to hear that, guys hang in there, yeah?
i wish i could make you guys feel better...
would you like me to send you guys some snacks or something?

By this point, Geraldine had become quite knowledgeable about what was happening with the Chilean protests, and had also come to understand her partners' affective stance (Arnold & Ducate, 2006; Belz, 2002), as 'completely sick', 'very tired' and 'in a bad mood'. Geraldine begins her extended turn at the end of this excerpt by sympathizing with her partners, addressing them informally and affectionately as 'guys'. However, by the end of that turn, Geraldine appears to have decided that verbal sympathy is insufficient, and the knowledge that she displays here is a generalized cross-cultural strategy of making people feel better by offering them food. Subsequent to this interaction, she in fact sent her Chilean chat partners a box of snacks through regular mail, and when I met them in Chile several months later, they expressed appreciation for this gesture.

Geraldine, who had lived in both the United States and Hong Kong, was able to make a good guess based on her own transnational experiences about an appropriate way to cheer up her Chilean partners. The next excerpt illustrates the value of having at least some specific knowledge about the world of one's interlocutors (Byram *et al.*, 2002) as a basis for intercultural interpretation.

Intercultural interpretation

In Dionne's group, their discussion of the immigrant demonstrations in the United States has brought up similar issues with immigration in Chile. Here, Graciela is explaining to Dionne (not a pseudonym) why many people in Las Peñas have negative attitudes toward Peruvian immigrants:

Graciela: so we had a lot of crimminals in my city but one day 3 peruvians were thinking of plan in which they will assault a bus they needed to steal a car before so they were to the beach and found a young couple in a car so they kidnaped them and then they prefer to have fun killing them instead of stealing the bus was horrible
Dionne: what cruel people
Graciela: yes for that reason people who lived in Las Peñas those years dont like peruvians i think it is a generalization and it is wrong but we are afraid of them i think it is the same with you and musulmans muslim?
Dionne: yes, i agree that there is a fear of people from the middle east or muslims because people are afraid of terrorism now (after 9–11).

Graciela uses the explicit evaluation 'was horrible' to conclude her narrative about the murder of the Chilean couple by Peruvian criminals. Dionne concurs in her evaluation with the comment 'what cruel people'. Thus, Dionne and Graciela construct a (non-controversial) shared view of violent crime. However, this is not really Graciela's point, and in order to make Dionne understand the perspective of people in her city, she needs to interpret an event from her own culture by relating it to an event from her partner's culture (Byram *et al.*, 2002; O'Dowd, 2003). First, however, she distances herself from inhabitants of her city who 'don't like peruvians' by stating that she thinks this dislike is 'a generalization' and 'is wrong'. Nevertheless, her pronoun *we* in 'we are afraid of them' implies that she shares her fellow citizens' fear of Peruvians if not their dislike.

Having clarified these feelings, Graciela finally draws a tentative analogy with fear-based prejudice in the United States: 'I think it is the same with you and musulmans muslim?' Interestingly, although Dionne ratifies Graciela's interpretation by stating 'I agree,' she distances herself from anti-Muslim prejudice, first with the impersonal construction 'there is a fear', and then by referring to 'people' who 'are afraid' in the third person. Like Graciela, she ties bigotry in her society to a specific incident that aroused alarm (the 9–11 attack). Thus, both participants are able to examine and compare ethnic prejudice in a dialogically expansive way (White, 2003), without fully identifying themselves or their partners with racist discourses (Menard-Warwick *et al.*, 2013).

Intercultural discovery

As Byram *et al.* point out, because it is impossible for potential intercultural communicators or their teachers to 'anticipate all their knowledge needs, it is equally important (for learners) to acquire the skills of finding out new knowledge and integrating it with what they already have' (Byram *et al.*, 2002: 13). In the following excerpt, we see an example of intercultural discovery skills in the resolution of a misunderstanding based on different political cultures.

Lori: I think mayor Antonio Villaragiosa[7] agrees with the protesters he feels the same way about the laws that are being propsed right now so he was happy that the people were protesting
Karola: is like a communist ¿
Lori: is what like a communist¿ the mayor¿ are you asking if the mayor is a communist¿
Karola: yes
Lori: i don't know anything about the mayor of los angeles but i would not expect him to be a communist communism tends not to be very popular in the us
Karola: ahhh ok no problem
Lori: no problem

Apparently, from the Chilean perspective, a mayor who agrees with protesters is likely to be a Communist (as Karola suggests), but from a contemporary US perspective (as represented by Lori), a Communist mayor would be unthinkable. Indeed, Lori does not even initially understand what Karola is asking, as shown in her request for clarification: 'is what like a Communist¿' Interestingly, they both feel the need after the negotiation of meaning (Gass *et al.*, 1998) to say 'no problem' – which implies a potential offense, an apology, and the acceptance of an apology. Thus, they are demonstrably working on their social relationship (Vogt, 2006), not just exchanging information or engaging in 'intercultural discovery'.

Critical cultural awareness

Critical cultural awareness involves 'the ability to evaluate...on the basis of explicit criteria, perspectives, practices and products in one's own and other cultures' (Byram *et al.*, 2002: 13). As this excerpt begins, Ariana is explaining her analysis of the article about the immigrant rights protests in the United States (Ferre *et al.*, 2006):

> *Ariana:* At the end of the second subtittle..Richardson[8] says......'they come to america to work, yet they're not working'...I think that it was an uggly comment that mades me think that they see (or he) imigrants as slaves.. I'm I wrong?
> **Mark:** .Hmmm...well, that's a very good point, and you could certainly interpret it that way....
> *Valeria:* AA[9]..with Ariana
> *Ines:* AA
> **Mark:** ...actually, I didn't think about this at all. Wow...a very good point...what he said......has been kind of a common argument from the opposition, saying like if you say you come here to work, why are you marching instead of working? But you're right, I think this is kind of a cruel statement, like the immigrants don't have the right to take just one day off of work...

Ariana evaluates the comment about not working as 'ugly' and compares the immigrants' situation with slavery. Mark hesitantly accepts her interpretation, but Valeria and Ines agree strongly. Then Mark thinks through Ariana's critical reading. His comment 'wow...a very good point' is strongly positive and indicates that he is personally impressed; he now evaluates Richardson's statement as 'cruel'. Here, all the participants seem to base their evaluations on some kind of unstated global human rights criteria (Byram *et al.*, 2002), rather than on the values of one particular cultural group. This excerpt also demonstrates how Mark, the tutor, is learning critical reading from his students – and is willing to learn, which is crucial in intercultural encounters.

Discussion: Intercultural Identity Development

In this final section, I discuss what these cases have in common and how they collectively illustrate processes of intercultural identity development. As Bakhtin writes, 'outsideness is a most powerful factor in understanding' (Bakhtin, 1986a: 7). This is illustrated most poignantly in Paloma's and Ruby's realizations that they had very different communication styles from close friends and family members who had grown up in different countries: 'sometimes I'm talking to (my son), I sound like a person from Las Peñas and he responds as an American'. As their multiple identities interacted within their daily lives, interculturality became central to their worldviews. Both defined their identities as split, hybrid, mixed: indeed, Paloma saw herself as having two umbilical cords, one tied to Las Peñas and the other to Cedarville, Iowa. These transnational teachers' life histories show how experiences of crossing borders, making friends and living long term in more than one country can facilitate intercultural understanding, as when Ruby guided her students to an understanding of tattooing as a manifestation of conflicting values. Both women displayed not only intercultural identities, but also 'metacognitive awareness of their competence' (Byram, 1997: 20) as they 'mediate(d) between a number of cultural perspectives' (Risager, 2007: 114).

Nevertheless, if intercultural identity development is defined as a growing awareness of how the world looks through the eyes of others (Kramsch, 1993; McKay, 2002), there is evidence of this not only in Paloma's and Ruby's narratives and classroom comments, but also in the chat transcripts, as when Mark accepts Ariana's critique of US attitudes that view immigrants 'like slaves'. As Kramsch writes, dialogue occurs where 'speakers of different languages...struggle to keep the channels of communication open in spite or because of the ideological differences they recognize and maintain between them' (Kramsch, 1993: 23). In these case studies, it was crucial that teachers and learners were temporarily able to stand outside their own cultural assumptions, while at the same time making an effort to elucidate their perspectives (Byram *et al.*, 2002). Though participants did not appear to change their own views in any significant way, they did observably have to distance themselves in order to explain cultural perspectives, as when Dionne admitted that in the United States 'there is fear' of Muslims, while not identifying herself with that fear. Cross-cultural engagement was made easier because to some extent all participants were able to construct joint evaluations of practices and perspectives based on global humanitarian criteria (Byram *et al.*, 2002), as well as to indicate their 'willingness to engage with others in a relationship of equality' (Vogt, 2006: 160). Geraldine's decision to send snacks to her chat partners reinforced this sense of each other as individuals with affective relationships, as did Eugenia's questions about how the strike would affect her interlocutors' exams.

However, as Ruby and Paloma had discovered over the course of their transnational life experiences, it was not inevitable that successful intercultural communication would result from crossing boundaries. Throughout most of the project, Mark's group interacted smoothly, but goodwill and negotiation of meaning broke down shortly after the last excerpt above, with Ariana and Valeria beginning to suspect Mark himself of holding the anti-immigrant attitudes that he was attempting to explain. Latin Americans' common historical memory of US economic and political exploitation presents a significant discursive faultline that many naïve North Americans only discover when the interactional ground starts to shake beneath them. While Mark was able to clarify his own views after several minutes, Valeria characterized their communication as 'a mess'.

Indeed, intercultural dialogue can be messy, and often the most that educators can hope is to draw some renewed understanding out of the miscommunication (Ware & Kramsch, 2005). Discursive faultlines often become manifest through unexpected conflict – and they can lead to new understandings through further dialogue in the aftermath of the conflicts that reveal them, 'creat(ing) a special space and time at the boundaries between two views of the world' (Kramsch, 1993: 30). In the next chapter, I will look at how these processes took place across the range of classrooms that I observed in my research.

Notes

(1) This chapter draws on data and analysis that first appeared in Menard-Warwick (2008, 2009b, 2011b) and Menard-Warwick et al. (2013).

(2) In a few cases, cultural and linguistic content was inextricably interwoven.

(3) Ruby told me that she actually talked about culture to her students more when I was not there.

(4) As discussed in Chapter 1, Chile was under military rule from 1973 to 1990.

(5) Paloma and Alán also identified these as Latin American values, see Chapter 4.

(6) Some Chilean teachers have come to similar commitments through contact with the Pan-Andean indigenous education movement in South America, but Paloma attributes her interest in multiculturalism to her education in the United States.

(7) Antonio Villaraigosa (Lori has spelled his name wrong) was the mayor of Los Angeles at the time of this interaction. His political affiliation was Democrat.

(8) At that time, Bill Richardson was the governor of the US state of New Mexico. Of mixed Anglo-Latino heritage, he often appeared in the media as a spokesman for Latino political issues, but he had chosen to distance himself from the 2006 immigrant rights protests.

(9) A = Agree, AA = Agree strongly.

6 Cultural Pedagogies[1]

> **Sachiko:** I have a question.
> **Cherie:** Yeah⸮
> **Sachiko:** I am going to have a birthday party for my son on Saturday. The time is 4–6⸮
> **Cherie:** That's *very* good.
> **Sachiko:** I was wondering cause…should I serve pizza⸮ or just cake⸮ ((laughs)).
> **Cherie:** You should serve pizza. And I…how old is your son⸮
> **Sachiko:** He's going to be 8.
> **Cherie:** I would recommend that you have some kind of vegetable ((pause)) available also. This is a dietary suggestion. If you ask the children, they will say 'no, no, I don't want that.' ((Sachiko laughs)) But if you put it on the table, it disappears. ((pause)) Especially if they have something like ranch dressing[2] to dip it in or some kind of a dip to dip it in, it disappears! And you feel much better than having just fed them pizza.
> […] ((pause))
> **Minoru:** I have a question about her question. So if I were the host of the birthday party, do I need to ask the parents about religious things, or allergy, food I mean, in advance⸮

Culture is dynamic, contested within cultural contexts. However, the aspects of culture that are actively contested are going to vary between one context and another. At first glance, the excerpt from Cherie's California adult-school class (audiotaped on 6 April 2005) looks like a classic example of an ESL teacher imposing dominant cultural norms on hapless 'foreigners' like Sachiko: 'you feel much better [if you serve vegetables with ranch dressing].'

However, a closer look at the transcribed observation shows more complexity. Cherie is responding to Sachiko's question about a specific cultural practice that Sachiko has already decided to carry out, and about which she wants more details. Then Minoru's question complicates things further, showing his recognition that Cherie's dietary advice about party cuisine has skirted issues that are important in California. For reasons of space, I have neither quoted Cherie's lengthy response, in which she explains that her own children do not eat pork (they are Muslim, like her Tunisian husband, see Chapter 4), and then adds that some children could go into anaphylactic shock from merely smelling a peanut butter sandwich. Nor have I quoted the next question, in which a Korean woman, Jung Hee, asks what kind of party she should hold for her 15-year-old son and his US classmates, after which Cherie recommends serving bulgogi (a Korean beef dish), and calling it 'Korean barbecue' because 'Boys 15 [years old] love meat.' Thus, Cherie represents America, or at least California, as a place where party hosts are supposed to accommodate Muslim (or other religious) diets and a wide variety of health concerns, but where at the same time teenage boys are happy to eat meat in any form, regardless of the national origin of the recipe. Jung Hee replied, 'Sounds great.'

Since, as Kubota argues, 'images of culture (in language education) are produced by discourses that reflect, legitimate or contest unequal relations of power' (Kubota, 2003: 16), I initially set out to examine how 'culture' is discursively represented by English language teachers in different contexts. However, in analyzing my data, it became clear that most of the time in the classrooms I was observing, 'images of culture' were co-constructed by teachers and students across a wide variety of classroom activities, most of them focused on language skills rather than cultural knowledge. The interaction above is one in which the teacher does a lot of the work of cultural representation – but with support for this work from Sachiko, Minoru and Jung Hee, who ask complicated questions and express appreciation for Cherie's answers.

In a majority of cases, this co-construction appeared to be a harmonious, consensual process, resulting in at least a semblance of intersubjectivity (Kramsch, 1993) on cultural issues, as in the case above. (Apparent) intersubjectivity makes for a comfortable classroom; however, this chapter eventually comes to focus on moments when this intersubjectivity was temporarily suspended, as teachers and students contested each other's cultural representations, moments when discursive faultlines became activated, when tectonic plates of difference collided in classroom discussion.

Given that cultural content must be discursively constructed (i.e. represented) in order for it to become a topic of discussion in the classroom, in this chapter, I explore discursive faultlines as areas of cultural difference or misunderstanding that become manifest in classroom talk. In the rest of this chapter, I review recommendations on cultural pedagogy from the foreign language and second language research literatures, describe my process of collecting and analyzing observation and interview data, detail teachers' comments on culture in the classroom, and analyze three interactions that manifested discursive faultlines around cultural issues (previously discussed in Menard-Warwick, 2009c). I conclude by discussing the extent to which the exploration of discursive faultlines seemed to lead toward interculturality.

Constructing Images of Culture

In the National Standards for foreign language learning in the United States, students are expected to analyze the relationships among practices, perspectives and products of the cultures studied (Phillips, 2003: 164). 'Culture', in this framework, can be inferred to mean either a group of people who share practices, perspectives and products, or else the shared practices, perspectives and products themselves. This implies a view of culture as stable, harmonious and normative. However, there has been a shift in recent years toward seeing culture(s) as heterogeneous, dynamic, loosely bounded and subjectively experienced, depending upon the social position of participants (Kramsch, 1998; Turiel, 1999). As discussed in Chapter 5, a number of recent authors have stressed the importance of teaching not just cultural knowledge, but *interculturality*, which along with knowledge involves attitudes of curiosity and openness, skills in discovery and interpretation, and critical awareness of conflicting value systems (Byram *et al.*, 2002). Encounters with people from other cultural groups can help to facilitate this, but so can critical reflection on texts (Kramsch, 1993, 2005).

The language teaching profession has long distinguished between second language teaching, in which the language being taught is widely used in the learners' place of residence, as in California, and foreign language teaching, in which the target language has restricted uses in the learners' society, as in Chile.[3] Learners' degree of access to the target culture is likely to be greater within second language settings, and such learners are often under greater pressure to acculturate to target culture norms. For these reasons, literature on the teaching of culture in language classes has tended to focus on either foreign language or second language settings, but not both together; much of this literature is prescriptive, offering pedagogical advice.

Culture in foreign language teaching

Foreign language teaching contexts vary widely, of course, depending on the relations between the learners' country and the countr(ies) where the target language is used, as well as by the goals and levels of the learners. Thus, much of the pedagogical literature on teaching culture in foreign language settings is aimed at helping teachers find pedagogical approaches that are appropriate to their own students.

McKay (2002) gives an overview of issues involved in teaching culture when English is seen as an international language (EIL). She writes that international speakers of English do not need to internalize the cultural norms of traditionally English-speaking countries, rather, one of EIL's 'main uses is to allow speakers to tell others about their ideas and culture' (McKay, 2002: 12). Thus, teachers and educational programs may choose English language materials reflecting local realities (Cortazzi & Jin, 1999; Ramanathan, 2005) rather than, for example, scenes of London. For McKay, a key goal of language and culture instruction is to 'establish a sphere of interculturality... (which) requires that an individual consider his or her own culture in relation to another' (McKay, 2002: 82). However, as Cortazzi and Jin point out, learners often need to consider cultural materials from other groups in order to comprehend their own backgrounds.

Thus, dialogue is seen as key to developing intercultural understanding in foreign language learners (Guilherme, 2002; Kramsch, 1993, 2005; Savignon & Sysoyev, 2002; Zarate, 1997). Since members of target language cultures are not always available in foreign language settings, this can often mean dialogue in response to texts that contain culturally divergent viewpoints. However, in Kramsch's observations of classrooms, she found that too often discussion activities left 'students in their native cultural mindsets and failed to engage them in making sense of a reality other than their own' (Kramsch, 1993: 27). As mentioned in Chapter 2, she conceptualizes dialogue as occurring when language learners 'struggle to keep the channels of communication open' despite ideological differences (Kramsch, 1993: 23), while teachers facilitate further exploration of 'the historical and political context' of L2 materials (Kramsch, 1993: 27). In keeping with Bakhtin's emphasis on response and anticipation of response in dialogue (1981, 1986b), Kramsch argues that the goal for cultural pedagogy should be 'not only to exchange words with people who speak that language but actually to understand what they mean' (Kramsch, 1993: 34).

Although Kramsch found that teachers tended to 'shy away from too conflictual a clash of opinions' (Kramsch, 1993: 85), other observational and survey studies illustrate teachers and learners actively grappling with dilemmas around cultural content. In a Mexican EFL study, Ryan (1998) portrays a North American teacher, a long-time resident of Mexico, comfortably drawing out 'students' cultural background knowledge about Latin American folk music while at the same time contrasting music customs in Mexico with those in the US' (Ryan, 1998: 143). However, the Mexican EFL teachers she observed and surveyed often felt uncomfortable talking about North American culture, and reported that their students negatively stereotyped the United States, based on Hollywood movies (Ryan, 1998, 2003). In Canagarajah's ethnographic studies of English teaching in Sri Lanka (1993, 1999), he found the cultural content of Western-produced textbooks to be deeply alienating for many students, who reacted with resistance. In Japan, Duff and Uchida (1997) observed teachers avoiding what they saw as 'cultural' topics, fearing to privilege one culture over another. Despite this avoidance, the authors noted that the teachers were inevitably 'very much involved in the transmission of culture' (Duff & Uchida, 1997: 476) as they selected and presented certain materials and not others.

Culture in second language teaching

Less has been written about cultural pedagogies in second language teaching, perhaps due to the belief that it is relatively easy in these contexts for students to access target language culture. However, as Paige *et al.* point out, students in L2 classrooms may 'fear assimilation into the target culture...compounded by the fact that these students are experiencing cultural dislocations and culture shock in their own daily lives' (Paige *et al.*, 2003: 190). Thus, Kubota advocates 'critical multiculturalism' that views culture 'as a site of political and ideological struggles over meaning' (Kubota, 1999: 30). She suggests that ESL teachers and students problematize representations of culture, with the aim of 'transforming the status quo' (Kubota, 1999: 28). Similarly, Auerbach (1992) recommends a 'problem-posing' approach to L2 instruction, inspired by the work of Brazilian educator Paulo Freire (1999). Whereas Bakhtin was a literary scholar with an elastic concept of dialogue in society (see Chapter 2), Freire's conception of dialogue provides for more concrete educational applications. In language and literacy teaching, his approach involves discussion of problematic themes that are relevant in the local context. For example, language loss in immigrant communities can be represented as a cartoon of a mother speaking Spanish to her daughter, who replies in English (Auerbach, 1992: 71). In dialogue, students can share personal experiences, look for root causes to the problem, and collectively define appropriate actions to be taken in response.

While Freire's approach depends on the identification of themes relevant to learners, observational studies in ESL classrooms have tended to depict teachers making incorrect assumptions about students. Such misunderstandings have primarily been described in classes serving Generation 1.5 immigrant students, who are asked by their teachers to explain the customs of 'their countries', which many of them left as small children (Duff, 2002; Harklau, 1999; Talmy, 2004). While adult immigrants tend to maintain closer relationships with their countries of origin, teachers may still misunderstand their backgrounds and language learning goals. In such cases, Harklau writes that researchers can 'see the miscues between teacher and student intent and goals, and the missed opportunities to channel the intellectual and emotional energy that students have invested in cultural identity issues' (Harklau, 1999: 122).

Problematizing cultural representations

Thus, the pedagogical literature recommends that teachers and students, in dialogue, problematize cultural representations. To some extent, the EFL literature sets forth interculturality as a goal, but that has been less prominent in ESL. In any case, what researchers have often observed are teachers imposing cultural representations on students, who are not given space in the classroom to construct their own. Although several authors describe students appropriating linguistic and cultural materials for their own purposes (e.g. Canagarajah, 1999), research in cultural pedagogy needs more attention to how teachers and students jointly construct and contest cultural representations, even in classes largely focused on linguistic issues. Moreover, the literature provides few examples of what problematization, dialogue or interculturality look like in actual practice. In this chapter, I address how teachers describe their approaches to cultural pedagogy, as well as the approaches to teaching and learning culture that I observed in their classrooms.

Analyzing Cultural Pedagogies

Data for this chapter come from interviews with Chilean EFL teachers and Californian ESL instructors, and from audiotaped classroom observations. In each observed classroom I spent eight hours over several weeks focusing on how teachers talked about cultural issues. At ULP, I requested permission from the three instructors then teaching the highest level of general English classes in the foreign language department (Paloma, Genaro, Alán),[4] and they all agreed to let me observe their classes and interview them. In California, I drew on personal contacts to find instructors teaching classes at a similar level in local adult schools (Cherie & Ruby) and community colleges (Susanna, Melinda & Eric).

While observing, I wrote detailed notes, and expanded these into full ethnographic field notes immediately after each observation (Watson-Gegeo, 1998). Transcription of classroom observation audiotapes was done selectively following thematic coding of the field notes (see below). I interviewed each observed instructor twice (see sample interview protocols in Appendix 3). The first interviews covered their history of language study and use, their experiences as English teachers, their cross-cultural experiences and their perspectives on culture in language teaching. During my second interviews, I shared my field notes with the teachers, in order to learn their views of the cultural issues I had observed in their classes. Interviews lasted approximately 1.5 hours; all were audiotaped and transcribed. Aside from the observed teachers, I additionally interviewed 13 other Chilean teachers and 6 other Californian teachers for approximately one hour each.[5] A limitation of this study is that I did not interview students for their perspectives on the observed interactions. However, some of the observed students I also interviewed as prospective teachers, so I have a general idea of student perspectives.

Following transcription of the interviews, my first step was a thematic analysis of both interview and classroom field note data using NVivo 7 qualitative data analysis software. I coded data as having cultural content when it concerned practices, perspectives and resulting products (e.g. works of art) that are shared among groups of people (Phillips, 2003). For example, the data from Cherie's class above involves an explanation of cultural practices around children's birthday parties in Farmington, California, along with dietary perspectives connected to those practices. A raw vegetable slice dipped in ranch dressing can be seen as a cultural product that exemplifies these dietary perspectives. Thus, this discussion was coded as having cultural content. In analyzing interview data on cultural pedagogy, I additionally categorized teachers' comments as referring to culture where they described their own priorities for teaching culture in the classroom, or mentioned successful lessons that they had taught as illustrations of their cultural pedagogy. The interview data below were selected to illustrate the range of perspectives of all the teachers interviewed, not only those whose classes I observed.

I also coded classroom observations for approaches toward culture taken by participants. The excerpt from Cherie's class that opens this chapter was coded as *cultural orientation* – an approach that was almost absent in my Chilean data. The principal approaches discussed in this chapter are cultural change, cultural comparison and cultural values. I selected the first of these to illustrate another clear difference between cultural pedagogies in EFL and ESL contexts: *cultural change*, discussion of how contemporary practices differ from those of the recent past, was a common approach for all three Chilean teachers, but extremely rare in my California data. *Cultural comparison*, the approach to pedagogy most widely discussed in the literature (McKay, 2002), was common in both contexts. I define this approach as discussion of how practices of one group differ from or are similar to practices of another group. Finally, an approach common in both contexts and often associated with discursive faultlines was *cultural values*, discussion of what particular groups believe or should believe about what is right and wrong, good and bad, valuable or worthless – for example, the importance of serving vegetables at children's birthday parties in California.

Finally, I coded culture data from classroom observations to see whether it exhibited *tension*, that is misunderstandings or disagreements about substantive issues between students, between teacher and student(s), or between student(s) and their perceptions of target language culture. To select specific interactions for this chapter, I made a log of all the interactions from each classroom that exhibited tension. From this log, I selected three interactions so as to illustrate the range of cultural approaches that I had decided to compare: a Chilean example of cultural change; a Chilean example of cultural comparison; and a US example of cultural values.

Findings on Cultural Pedagogy

In this section, I first present interview data that illustrate teachers' perspectives on cultural pedagogy. Second, I examine classroom observation data, to illustrate the trends that I actually saw in Chilean and Californian classrooms (Menard-Warwick, 2009c). It was while analyzing these data in 2007 that I began to use the term 'discursive faultlines' to describe my study and the tensions I was noticing.

Interviews

First of all, teachers in both California and Chile portrayed themselves practicing the most mainstream and traditional form of cultural pedagogy: introducing students to what are usually considered 'safe' cultural topics like food and celebrations (Sercu, 2006). Of course, the excerpt from Cherie's class above shows that even 'safe' topics get complicated very quickly, as Veronica's comments about her California high school class (see Chapter 1) also illustrate:

> **Veronica**: Because I'm Jewish too, there is discussion in the classroom just about holidays, ( ) during this Christmas time, 'Let's have a Christmas party,' [...] and I, you know, 'We're not all Christian in this room,' [...] and (we had) Muslim kids, and then Christian and Catholic kids, and (that was nice), and then that came up, and then the discussion was, 'Well, if we can't have Christmas (then), we have to have a party,' because Mexican kids love a party, I mean, and I'm always happy to have a party, but then we have to have food, and then it becomes 'Okay, but we have to be careful with food,' because I don't eat pork, I don't eat shrimp, and Muslim(s), [don't either] [...]. So ((pause)) that, religion became part of it only on that level, the kind of practical aspects of how you deal with a mixed community and not bring something that someone can't eat, or would eat and then kind of react to in a bad way. So that still comes up, (with) food, I always, 'I don't want you bringing any pork in this room, (and no) shrimp.'

Moreover, religious beliefs kept many students in both California and Chile from celebrating Halloween. As Melinda commented about her community college students, 'the very, very religious in the classroom think that it is a manifestation of Satanism.' As a partial remedy, she encouraged in her California classroom a 'lighthearted' approach to holidays, drawing on symbols such as reindeer and snowmen for Christmas (and presumably pumpkins for Halloween). In Chile, Azucena (university instructor) complained that for many grammar-oriented English teachers, 'the only thing about culture that they teach is about Halloween,' implying that this is boring and humdrum; prospective teacher Maritza, however, like Melinda in California, ran into trouble with religiously conservative students, whose 'parents said that [Halloween] is something of the devil'. Dialogically voicing this conflict in narrative, she portrays herself employing a discourse of cultural difference to defuse religious concerns in her practicum placement at a working-class elementary school (see Chapter 4):

> **Maritza**: 'Here in Chile, we have another culture, and we associate Halloween with monsters and something like that,' and (they) said, 'Yes, you have to wear also masks, and the devil,' [...] and I said, 'No, because

in the United States, they don't wear all these things about devils, they wear costumes of angels and something like that.'

Probably the most successful holiday celebration described to me was Alicia's party in honor of United States Independence Day at a Chilean high school:

Alicia: I make them to cook traditional American food. Each group has to have one person dress in a typical American dress, like Indian, cowboy, Mickey Mouse ((laughter)). [...] They made mashed potatoes, hamburgers, hot dogs ((laughter)), things like that. They investigated it on the Internet, they made popcorn too, I think. [...] Oh! They made apple pie too! [...] So I said okay, 'Music, it has to be country music,' and I couldn't remember any other singer of country music. I gave them two names like Shania Twain. [...] And the other, the blonde one with the big hair...
Julia: They all have blonde big hair. Dolly Parton?
Alicia: Yeah! Exactly. And I said, 'Dolly Parton and Shania Twain.'

Although celebrating a patriotic holiday from a country considered imperialist by some Chileans is a potential source of tension (Menard-Warwick, 2009d, and see Alicia's Chapter 2 narrative), the only complaints that Alicia mentioned in this case came from teachers who did not get invited! Moreover, the use of country music to celebrate a US holiday illustrates how popular culture materials can enliven the English classroom, which also happened occasionally in California.

Indeed, a number of Chilean teachers told me that popular culture is perhaps the best way to promote Chilean students' interest in English (see Chapters 3 and 4). Genaro, who worked with teacher training and professional development, told me that teachers should 'look for the world that students might be interested in [...], so probably good approach could be music, another approach could be movies, they are more inclined to music than anything else'. As an example, Diego (see Chapter 1) mentioned a recent high school classroom discussion of the song 'Zombie' by the Irish rock band The Cranberries:

Diego: We were talking in my class, 'why "Zombie"?' I started reading the lyrics, and it seems to me that they were ((pause)) too many people were killed, see? And the kids were walking without mommies or daddies. They were walking like zombies.

In this case, the pedagogical value of using popular culture goes beyond motivating or entertaining students: the song's war imagery requires interpretation, which potentially leads students into critical thinking and a deeper level of comprehension.

However, the use of music could occasionally backfire, as when the Ministry of Education included an outdated hit tune in a high school English textbook:

Sofía: There are certain songs in the books too, you see? Britney Spears, I don't like, but I have to teach.
Julia: Really?
Sofía: Anyway, that's right, and the song appears in the book, and the biography...
Julia: Wow, Britney Spears. ((laughing))
Sofía: Britney Spears, so I have to teach Britney Spears songs.
Julia: 'Oops, I did it again!' ((laughing))
Sofía: 'Oops, I did it again!' ((laughing)). That's right.
Julia: ((laughing)) Oh, that's amazing.
Sofía: But some students don't like her...
Julia: No.
Sofía: No, they don't, 'I'm so sorry, just for the sake of English, listen to the English language, okay? Forget about the lyrics.'

Here, Sofía and I dialogically draw in the voice of pop star Britney Spears ('oops I did it again') to refract our own intentions (Bakhtin 1981) of ridiculing the educational authorities' decision to inflict her turn-of-the-millennium hit on Chilean youth. Whereas popular music is supposed to 'motivate' adolescents to learn English, here Sofía must invoke English as motivation for listening to Britney Spears!

Many teachers stressed the importance of using popular culture materials chosen by students:

Azucena: I (had) never seen the 'The Simpsons' before, because I thought that it was gross and rude, I didn't like (it), but then I decided if they liked (them) so much, we should see it together. [...] And we talked about [...] during the chapter in which Bart Simpson goes to Japan, and he laughs about all these cultural aspects, so it was good for them to realize the respect that they have to do.

Having catered to her university students' tastes, Azucena found, paradoxically, that the rudeness of cartoon character Bart Simpson impressed students with the importance of cultural sensitivity. Indeed, the inspiration of cross-cultural respect was an objective cited by many teachers in both national contexts. As Melinda described the approach she took at her California community college:

Melinda: My job is not so much to acculturate or to teach directly about culture, but to bring students to an understanding that cultural experience is just one point on a continuum, and that different isn't bad, that different is different, [...] and for those students who come from a monoculture, that's a really, really big reach, and their reaction to this very diverse society is that there's a lot of evil out there. And I feel that that is in some way handicapping for their ability to become comfortable in our cultural context. So I try to expose them gently to things that make their skin crawl.
Julia: Uh-huh. Could you give me an example of that?
Melinda: Gay marriage ((laughing)).

Whereas Azucena's Chilean students were unlikely to confront Japanese customs like bowing, same-sex couples are part of the social scene on California campuses. To pursue their educational goals, religiously conservative immigrants must learn how to interact civilly with students whose gender identities or sexual orientations violate their sense of propriety, as Melinda points out. Discussion of varying gender norms remains an active discursive faultline in classrooms such as hers.

While the discussion of controversial issues was a valued approach to cultural pedagogy across contexts (see observation excerpts below), at the same time, Melinda and other teachers recognized that cultural maintenance was important to students in both contexts: immigrants in the United States felt pressure to 'Americanize' whereas Chileans found themselves in a context rapidly 'globalizing'. Along with her efforts to make immigrant students more tolerant of other cultures, Melinda said she also stressed that their 'first culture is precious'. As one way to make this sentiment concrete, she asked students to share folk tales and proverbs. For example, she quotes her Russian students telling her, 'Nobody's rich enough to buy cheap shoes.' As she explains:

Melinda: Those sorts of things lead into long discussions about 'Well, what do you mean?' ( ) 'Well, there's certain things that you can't scrimp on, that they'll affect your quality of life, and it's much better to bite the bullet and take the hard punch the first time.' [...] And then there's another one that sticks in my mind, that made a really interesting discussion in the classroom, and that was, 'The flower of a pumpkin is still a flower.' And that was Korean. And the meaning that we found in that was that 'you can't discount a woman because she's not beautiful'.

In this way, Melinda tried to balance her efforts 'to expose [learners] gently to things that make their skin crawl' with classroom activities that allowed them to apply traditional wisdom to new contexts.

Finally, in both California and Chile, there was a recognition by many teachers of the importance of helping students overcome stereotypes. After a discussion in Susanna's community college class that focused on negative images held against each other by Latin and North Americans (including the stereotype that 'Americans are racist'), she explained her approach to me:

Susanna: I think I was trying to get them to think about, 'Okay, could we really say this? Or am I really thinking about just my experience with five people, and now I've generalized it to everybody?' [...] And so I was hoping that they would see, 'Okay, well this is a smaller group, but it may not be fair to say for the whole, for all Americans in general.'

Norma also said she emphasized the avoidance of stereotypes with her Chilean university students:

Norma: I always try to tell them that 'stereotypes are not... that we all have stereotypes, and even us, about Chileans who live down the South, or up in the mountains, and that's what they are, stereotypes,' and that what they see in the movies [about English-speaking countries] is not what it is.

Describing a year she spent in Pennsylvania, she quoted herself sharing with US students of Spanish the Chilean stereotypes about them:

Norma: 'Look, there is one thing that probably you're not gonna like, which is the idea that Chileans think that [whenever] you date an American girl, there's always sex,' and there were two girls that really got mad, I mean, and I said, 'Look, that is because of the movies, that's simply because of the movies,' and I told them there, right there, I always began my Spanish classes in the States with stereotypes, and I also do that when I teach here.

However, along with similarities, there were differences in cultural pedagogies between Chile and California. Although US teachers told their students to avoid stereotypes, almost all my Californian interviewees described at length their process of learning to teach particular national groups[6] over the course of their career – a process which inevitably involved stereotyping. The following narrative in which Cherie dialogically voices nationalities could have been told by almost any of the California teachers. As a long-time ESL instructor myself, I feel a queasy sense of deja vu at Cherie's conflation of national and cultural identities. At the same time, I recognize that her effort to make students see their own practices as cultural rather than normative in fact takes them in the direction of interculturality, as do Norma's and Susanna's efforts to build awareness of stereotyping (Byram et al., 2002).

> **Cherie**: We talked a lot about culture because, the South Americans would say to the Koreans, and the Koreans say to the South Americans... The South Americans talked about how all the Koreans stank like kim chi.[7] And the Koreans talked about how the South Americans were so impolite, and shouting out and interrupting, and not really listening to the teacher, and coming late to class. That's- and, and, and, and, and, and, and.
> **Julia**: So what would you say? ((pause)) [...]
> **Cherie**: I would laugh. ((laughs)) I would laugh. I would say, 'You know, these are so much the cultural differences between your groups.' It's like, you are here, and they are here, and Americans are in the middle. And, so, we look at both of you, and we say, 'Both of you are a little bit odd. In opposite ways.' ((laughs)) Yeah, it was fun. [...] And we did a lot of talking about classroom behavior in America as compared to South America and the Arab countries where there was a lot more of very active and loud participation. And compare that to the Japanese, and the Koreans, and... ((laugh)) [...], and, so, what's considered polite in one culture is different from what's considered polite in the other. And they'd look at each other and say, 'Oh. You're trying to be polite?'

None of the Chileans told stories like this one, where the art of language teaching involves handling clashes between nationalities.

Rather, in contrast to US teachers, Chileans were far more likely to teach history in English class, and to mention historical issues in interviews as important to cultural pedagogy. For example, Alicia portrayed her follow-up to the Independence Day party at her high school as follows:

> **Alicia**: I put on the blackboard the flag, they draw the flag and everything, they were very excited about it, and then I asked some other things

like, 'First president of the United States,' 'George Washington,' and things like that. 'The ship that they were traveling in from England to United States,' 'Mayflower,' and everything.

This was in a beginning high school English class, and Alicia apologized for leaving out the details. Azucena felt obligated to teach the Mayflower Compact to her second-year university English majors, even though she personally considered the topic 'boring'. In my interviews with Chilean teachers, nine of them talked about presenting history as part of culture in English class, or of having learned history while studying English. In contrast, of all the California teachers, only Charles (MATESOL student) briefly mentioned US history as a topic for cultural pedagogy. Melinda remarked that she did not 'like to talk a lot about politics or specific historical things' in teaching culture. I now regret not asking why.

None of the teachers mentioned concepts from the literature such as *problematization, dialogue* or *interculturality*. Thus, my use of these terms when I analyze the observations below should be seen as etic (reflecting the perspective of scholars in the field) rather than emic (reflecting the perspective of participants) (Watson-Gegeo, 1988). Rather than following the dictates of the contemporary research literature, teachers in both contexts had two primary goals in teaching culture: to motivate students and to provide cultural knowledge (Byram *et al.*, 2002). Teachers were aware that cultural content is not motivating in itself (McKay, 2002), unless it is tailored toward the interests of students. However, they felt responsible to make students aware of 'typical' target language practices, such as listening to country music while eating apple pie. This remained an important goal even when target language cultural practices were offensive to some students, as noted by Melinda. Teachers additionally believed it important to provide students explicit knowledge about their own national cultures, so they could stop taking their own practices as the unexamined norm, and thus potentially become more accepting of other people. As Byram *et al.* point out (2002), such cultural knowledge is one of the components of intercultural competence.

Classroom observations

The data below compare cultural pedagogy based on classroom observations in northern California and northern Chile (most of the data and some of the discussion that I present here first appeared in Menard-Warwick, 2009c). In general, although I observed teachers in two national contexts, I did not see great diversity of teaching practice; other educators may have contrasting approaches to cultural pedagogy. All the teachers I observed were highly skilled and experienced; all had good rapport with most students most of the time; all occasionally made space for wide-ranging discussions on issues of interest to students; all found the need at times to curtail discussion in order to pursue other pedagogical goals. Rather than evaluating teachers, the purpose of this section is to suggest the range of cultural pedagogies that I actually observed, and additionally to explore cultural tensions in classrooms.

To this end, I present analysis of three observations, two from Chile and one from California. More information about the observed teachers appears in Chapter 3 and especially Chapter 4, and in Paloma's case, Chapter 5. In the US segment, I mention students' nationalities, if I know them, or otherwise the region of the world from which they come.[8] All but one of the students in the Chilean segments are in fact Chilean (to the best of my knowledge), so I only note nationality for that one student.

Cultural change: Genaro's class, Chile

This was a professional development class for practicing Chilean English teachers to improve their communication skills. Out of 13 students, ranging in age from perhaps 25 to 65, only two were men. In this lesson, observed on 9 July 2005, Genaro played a commercially produced (British) ESL audiotape on gender differences in mathematical performance, then asked the class for other gender differences they had noticed. One of the younger teachers, Tania, suggested that women were better at multitasking than men because they had to balance motherhood with paid employment; an older man, Marco, disagreed:

Marco: I think that the situation has changed now. Maybe uh 20, 30, 50 years ago men are... were more machist. Can you say machist?[9]
Genaro: You mean like more chauvinist? ((overlapping))

**Several
students:** ((overlapping)) Chauvinist?
Marco: Since 10 years ago, I think the situation has changed, maybe. Now men are looking after the children very very well, they are cooking very very well. What is the difference that you have the child, you know, in your body, that's it.

Genaro: That's it!
Marco: The only different ((overlapping))
Genaro: ((overlapping)) In your bellies...
Marco: Bellies. That's it, the only different. And now women are more conservative... You know what I mean, conservative?
Renate: Traditional.
Marco: Traditional. Women are more conservative.
Tania: I don't agree.
Marco: Yes. In some ways. In some ways.
Tania: I disagree. There is an image that men are cooking and cleaning but in spite of the fact they say that, there are some of them that take care of children, there are some who like to help in cooking, some. An image.
[After several more turns of argument, and considerable laughter, Genaro called on Renate, a woman in her 50s (for more about Renate, see Chapters 2 and 4).]
Renate: Yeah. I should say that women, we as women (are blamed for the production) of this chauvinism. Because we raise our boys traditionally in that way. We make everything for them instead of the girls. The girls are supposed to help their mother at home and the boys...
Genaro: The boys...
Renate: are supposed to...
Marco: Play football.
Renate: Play football, yeah, or take care of the garden. You have to be outside. Mostly I did that...
Genaro: Yeah!
Renate: I have tried to change this with my son.
Genaro: Okay...
Renate: Because as Marco said, times change today. And ((pause)) maybe 100 years ago, 50 years ago men were the supporters... of the
Genaro: Providers. Providers.
Renate: Yeah. Provi...? Providers. Yeah. Of the house, you know, and women were supposed to be at home, supporting the children, and do the cooking and do cleaning and everything, but now with just one wage, a family cannot live ((overlapping))
Genaro: ((overlapping)) Survive
Renate: with only one wage, and they work, they have to work both of them...
Genaro: Both of them!

> **Renate:** Both of them, and that's why both of them have to help in
> the house and with the children ( ) and that's why we have to change,
> we have to change our concept of life now.
> **Genaro:** All right. The goals and concepts are changing because
> society itself has changed a lot.

Here, the issue of societal change was introduced by students rather than the teacher. Indeed, in my follow-up interview, Genaro expressed having met other pedagogical goals. He felt that discussing a controversial issue caused students to speak more freely, without worrying about grammar, an important objective for this class where the students themselves taught English grammar rules five days a week. Nevertheless, when students discussed the audiorecording, their priority became representing their own experiences accurately. In order to do this, they drew on discourses of gender, economics and social change that are prevalent in contemporary Chilean society. Thus, the discussion has strong 'dialogic overtones' (Bakhtin, 1986b: 92): Marco asked the women in the class to acknowledge that men have become more involved in housework; Tania problematized this representation, arguing that men's involvement is more discursive than practical; then Renate presented an alternative analysis in which women as well as men had to change their gendered practices due to widely recognized economic changes in society. When Genaro summarized at the end, he seized on the only point that most seemed to accept: 'society itself has changed a lot'.

In this discussion about Chile, speakers represented their shared national culture as torn between different groups: men versus women, traditional versus non-traditional thinkers. Talk of transformations in families triggered discursive faultlines, as students with different social positions drew on varied discourses to represent the changes from their own viewpoints. Utterances tended to be dialogically contractive, as each interlocutor presented his or her opinion about contemporary Chile as the only one possible (White, 2003). For example, Renate's comment that 'with just one wage, a family cannot live' forecloses the possibility of families surviving on one worker's earnings. Nevertheless, there are glimmerings of dialogical expansiveness, as when Marco mitigates his assertion that men have changed with the word 'maybe', or when Tania concedes that some men do take care of children.

Moreover, the participants in this interaction are clearly listening to each other, 'struggl(ing) to keep the channels of communication open in spite or because of the ideological differences they recognize and maintain between them' (Kramsch, 1993: 23). Marco's first comment about how men have changed responds directly to Tania's assertion about women's unique involvement in paid and domestic work. Tania takes his remark into account in her statement, conceding that some men *have* changed, in order to formulate her argument that most of this change is illusory ('an image'). Renate's extended remarks about contemporary family life directly cite Marco's ideas (both that times have changed and that boys are expected to play football), while expanding upon the unspoken point of agreement between Tania and Marco: the desirability of men's involvement in domestic chores.

As is common in my Chilean data, a teacher (Renate) provides historical analysis to support a particular viewpoint, in this case that men are changing even though the change is incomplete. She constructs intersubjectivity among men and women on these issues by referring to traditional Chilean men with the positive term 'supporters'; while blaming women for reproducing male chauvinism; and finally reminding everyone of the economic difficulties that men and women collectively face. She gives herself authority on these issues by talking about her own efforts to raise her son non-traditionally.

Renate could not have mediated the gender conflicts in the classroom without having first listened to both Marco and Tania. That is, she is 'not only exchang(ing) words with people (from different social positions) but actually ... understand(ing) what they mean' (Kramsch, 1993: 34). Generally, this classroom discussion can be seen to exemplify dialogue, in many senses of the word. However, it is less clear that interculturality is being constructed here.

Cultural comparison: Paloma's class, Chile

This was an advanced English class for fifth-year undergraduates. Of the approximately 20 people in attendance, a majority were female and in their twenties; all but one were Chilean, the exception being Ming, a young man from Taiwan. All the students were prospective English teachers. In this lesson, audiotaped on 26 July 2005, they were discussing in pairs how to prevent classroom violence. When Paloma asked students to report back, Eliza summarized her partner's comments:

Eliza: He was telling me about ... on the TV it said there are students, young students who bring those type of weapons, although they are an exception, I mean they are not like in the States [...] [Paloma reminded the class that they had discussed this topic last month]

Paloma: I remember we said that not all kids do that in the States, but many do. But why is it that many do in the States?
Ming: They (perceive) that somebody just bothers them, you know, and they feel kind of unfair ((pause)) and then they hold just some offense ((truck noise)) and nobody...and maybe they ask the teacher to help them, and then they believe the teacher didn't help them, and so they just find the final solution ((truck noise))
Paloma: Sometimes you are afraid of giving a bad grade!
Ming: And they just kill...
Paloma: Anyway, yes, thank you, Ming.
Eliza: I don't know about this, but Cesar was telling me, in the States you can find stores where they sell guns.
Paloma: Stores! That's what we said last month. That's exactly the...access to buying, the access to buying! And many argue against that in the States, so I don't want you to think that's the culture of everybody, you know, supporting guns. Many do hunting and that's why, you know, you have guns at home.
Cristóbal: I have an idea. [...] Because last month I was watching a...report. If you go to Canada there is also availability of guns but people they do not kill each other. (Michael Moore) went around opening doors of people's houses and nobody[10]...And if he did that in the States maybe he would be shot. [...]
Paloma: Excellent point, excellent point, because if you have two neighboring countries that have access to guns, and you have one that reacts violently, you wonder what's behind that. Then you have to go back and study the culture, and how they arrived in the United States...You know, there's a whole history there to understand the violence.

In this excerpt, tension exists between students and their perceptions of US culture. Discursive faultlines become apparent as students bring up and discuss a controversial topic based on sources outside the classroom, in this case media reports about the United States. The teacher did not have the goal of making cultural comparisons in this lesson: Paloma wanted her students to focus on violence prevention strategies for Chilean classrooms. Nevertheless, she is willing to entertain the topic of US gun violence when it is introduced by Eliza. Together, the class problematizes this cultural phenomenon, while Paloma individually problematizes media representations of the issue.

Employing a common international discourse about US violence, the students are participating in a worldwide evaluative dialogue. Eliza's is probably the most dialogically contractive utterance (White, 2003). When she states that Chilean teenagers who bring weapons to school are 'an exception. . . .not like in the States', she presupposes the normality of gun-toting students in America. Cristóbal draws on the same discourses and perceptions, bolstered by the documentary film *Bowling for Columbine*, when he says that if film-maker Michael Moore opened the doors of US rather than Canadian homes, 'maybe he would be shot', with the word *maybe* adding a hint of expansiveness to the dialogue.

Paloma uses the occasion to caution her students against seeing the United States as a homogeneous collection of 'gun nuts'. Having lived in Iowa for many years (see Chapter 5), she brings to the dialogue her understanding of the complexity of US opinions, and she stresses that carrying weapons to school is not a universal US custom. Although her statements are not dialogically expansive in themselves – she presents her remarks as cultural knowledge that is factually accurate, not up for debate (White, 2003) – she is offering her students a more expansive view of US culture than what they see in the media. Nevertheless, in an interview, she said she pursued the topic of violence with her students because 'if there is anything that I can say, not favorable, for the US, at this point would be this war'. Thus, it was her concern about the Iraq war that led her to speak against US violence, though it was not the lesson topic.

Additionally, it can be noted that Paloma connects violence in the United States to US history, in keeping with the greater emphasis on history in Chilean cultural pedagogy. In making this connection, she is engaged in a pedagogical practice that Kramsch claims rarely to have observed (in the United States), 'explor(ing) . . . further . . . the historical and political context' of student utterances (Kramsch, 1993: 27). Nevertheless, when Paloma exclaims, 'Sometimes you are afraid of giving a bad grade!' she is identifying with US educators who fear students' violent propensities. She thus demonstrates her own conflicting opinions: on the one hand, she implies that US schools are less dangerous than Chilean students believe; on the other hand, she reveals her own fear as a teacher. These multiple viewpoints bring expansiveness to the dialogue.

While Paloma attempts to explain US opinions to her students, only Ming takes on the more challenging task of comprehending the mindset of school shooters. A trilingual Taiwanese immigrant to Chile, he perhaps exemplifies how transnational experience aids the development of interculturality (see Chapter 5). In this excerpt, stepping outside both his 'native' and adoptive 'cultural mindsets' (Kramsch, 1993: 27), he spontaneously 'engage(d)...in making sense of a reality other than his own' (Kramsch, 1993), presumably based on clues that he had picked up from the same media reports that the other students were citing. His imaginative empathy for school shooters represents a feat of intercultural understanding much deeper than the literature has generally advocated. In cutting him off with a thank you, Paloma perhaps demonstrates discomfort with this level of interculturality in her classroom.

The conversation between Paloma and her students, and between the class and the global media, has elements of both contractive and expansive dialogism. Missing from the exchange is much dialogue between students, although Eliza's citation of Cesar's comments means that she was at least listening to him during pairwork. In thanking Ming rather than inviting students to respond to him directly, Paloma reinforced the common framework in which classroom dialogue (if any) is mediated by teacher questions.

Cultural values: Susanna's class, California

This was an advanced ESL reading class at an urban community college, attended by about 30 adult immigrants, a majority of whom were women younger than 40 years. Students came from Eastern Europe, East and Southeast Asia, the Middle East and Latin America. Of the students who participate in the discussion excerpt below, Viviana is a young woman from Mexico, Hassan is a young Afghani man, Yakov is a middle-aged man from Eastern Europe and Anet is a young woman from Armenia. For this lesson, audiotaped on 21 September 2005, they had read several articles on the topic of education, and had then been asked to discuss related questions in small groups. As the groups reported to the class, Susanna found that everyone had agreed on the first question: that all children had a right to an education. When she asked for reasons to support this argument, Hassan argued that education would reduce discrimination. Viviana disagreed:

Viviana: You know in Texas [they] made a law to deny education to different people who come from another place.[11] So all the educated people (didn't stop this).
Susanna: OK, so Viviana just made a point that right now in Texas, is it the governor that's doing this? [...] Yeah, that's what I thought. OK, so he's making a law that says that education in the United States should not be available to illegal immigrants.
Viviana: Mmhmm.

Susanna: Any idea what his reasoning would be? And then what's the idea that we just said, it should be provided to everyone, how would you respond?
José: Discrimination.
Susanna: ((overlapping)) What do you think the governor sees in this? ((pause))
Viviana: Maybe money.
[Susanna talked briefly about the economics of education, and then asked again why education would be denied specifically to illegal immigrants]
Hassan: To get the vote and the support of the people that they are against immigrants.
Susanna: OK, so maybe he's doing it for political reasons. [. . .] OK. . .Any. . .What kind of logical argument can the governor use? ((pause))
Yakov: Maybe some reason that. . .because the government wants to help poor immigrants with law that (they be) legal. But somebody no for. . .
Susanna: The law?
Yakov: Yeah.
Susanna: Right. Because an illegal immigrant ((pause while she writes 'illegal immigrant' on the board)) is someone who is in the United States without a legal document, or a legal reason, so I am sure the governor is using the argument that 'hey, they are not here legally, so why should they benefit?' From. . .O.K.
Viviana: ((overlapping)) But children doesn't have. . .
Susanna: ((overlapping)) But. . .Go ahead Viviana.
Viviana: But children doesn't have a fault (that the parents come. . .)
Susanna: So it's not the child's fault that the parents came here illegally. So that's a good counterargument. [. . .] But think about this idea that they are here illegally, the governor maybe has good reasons, they're not here legally, it costs money, taxpayer dollars to educate people, but we just said all children should be provided with an education. So how would you respond to the governor? One is that it's not the child's fault, but are there any other ways you could respond?
Hassan: Yeah! There is a United Nations human rights declaration that says that every children has the right of education, it doesn't matter if they are illegal or legal, you can say that ( ).
Susanna: OK.

Hassan: And America is one of ten countries that signed that declaration.
Susanna: OK! And I think that's a very good argument also.
Anet: And I think most of...some of the countries, children they don't have opportunity to go to school but America, it provides more opportunity for children to go to school. [...] Because I wanted to get a good education there but it was too expensive, and I didn't have more opportunity. But here the government helps you to get to your goal. And I think children um...some of the students, that's why they come here to get their goal.
Susanna: OK, so that is a great strength of the United States. [She then asked the next discussion question from the textbook].

In this event, tension as well as dialogism lies in the juxtaposition of competing discourses (Holquist, 1990). Susanna told me that she was unconcerned about the substance of her students' opinions: 'I usually don't try to weigh in on one side, I usually [...] try to play a little bit more of the devil's advocate, where I get them to think about a lot of different things.' Thus, her response to controversy is similar to Genaro's. Just as his students represent Chile as fraught with gender divisions, Susanna's class discussion references a number of contemporary US controversies. In this short inter-action, faultlines appear repeatedly: between the students' agreed-upon values and those of US politicians; between legal and illegal immigrants; between undocumented immigrant children and their parents; between the values of the United States and the United Nations; and finally between students able and unable to take advantage of US opportunities. As Kubota writes, 'images of culture (in language education) are produced by dis-courses that reflect, legitimate or contest unequal relations of power' (Kubota, 2003: 16).

In this discussion, a striking feature is how the discourses employed by particular individuals tend to represent their national origins, and especially the ways that people from similar origins have been positioned in the United States. Viviana's and José's concerns arise from the contemporary struggle of undocumented Mexicans to achieve legal status in the United States; the human rights of Middle Easterners like Hassan are threatened by US anti-terrorism policies; Yakov and Anet come from former Soviet nations whose citizens can often access governmental assistance as legal refugees in the United States. Thus, this entire interaction represents the discursive faultlines between immigrants and the larger US society, as well as between groups of immigrants from different national origins. None of these tensions were resolved, although Susanna let Anet's comment about educational opportunity stand as the last word.

There is no evidence of interculturality in this discussion: no one seemed to be making an effort to see issues from other cultural viewpoints, or to comprehend how their own values are seen by others. Moreover, as in Paloma's class, the dialogue is primarily carried on between the teacher and individual students. In the beginning, Viviana is responding to Hassan, but only to problematize his cultural representation (Kubota, 1999) about the power of education. None of the other students respond directly to her or to each other, but only to Susanna's questions.

Although Viviana's refutation of Hassan leaves little room for his point of view, and is thus dialogically contractive, the concrete example she gives of the discriminatory Texas law grounds the discussion in the US sociohistorical context (Kramsch, 1993). Although neither she nor Susanna is historically accurate in the strict sense, Viviana raises and Susanna entertains the possibility that political factors in the United States militate against equal opportunity for all children, a point seconded by José. This creates space for Hassan to address the contemporary context, where politicians may be observed passing discriminatory legislation for short-term gain. ('To get the vote and the support of the people that they are against immigrants.') In noting the signature of the United States on a UN human rights declaration violated by the purported Texas law, Hassan also references US hypocrisy on human rights. Although he is responding to Susanna's questions rather than to Viviana directly, it seems that he has heeded Viviana's refutation of his earlier argument, and that he is thus to some extent in dialogue with her.

In contrast, Yakov's contribution is primarily based on Susanna's remarks about legality and economics rather than the concrete situation that Viviana has raised. Moreover, Anet's comments show little awareness of her classmates' arguments about discriminatory practices: she simply shares her own positive experience without reference to political complexities. Her statements are dialogic in referencing a common discourse about the United States as land of opportunity. However, they are dialogically contractive (White, 2003) both for constructing her own experience as a universal fact, and for not taking other students' comments into account.

Throughout the discussion, Susanna has been carefully listening to student contributions, paraphrasing them and inviting responses, while additionally ventriloquating (Bakhtin, 1981) what she supposes to be the discourse of the Texas governor so that students can respond to him. She puts considerable effort into constructing pedagogical dialogue. However, her final ratification of Anet's remark leaves this unproblematized representation of US society as the monologic (or dialogically contractive) last word.

Thus, a dialogue about cultural values that discursively contested 'unequal relations of power' (Kubota, 2003: 16) ended by reflecting discourses that ignore and thus normalize these unequal relations.

Discussion

My interviews with Californian and Chilean teachers showed more commonality than difference in teachers' beliefs about cultural pedagogy. In both contexts, teachers reported planning activities around food and holiday celebrations, asking students to debate controversial issues, promoting cross-cultural respect, bringing in popular culture materials like songs, and warning their classes to avoid stereotyping. Chileans mentioned historical issues when teaching on cultural topics; Californians did not. For Chileans, teaching culture meant enabling students to understand differences and similarities between their homeland and the major English-speaking nations, and to compare the remembered Chilean past with the globalized present. For Californians, teaching culture involved helping students from different parts of the world get along, and they drew on their own learning experiences with stereotypically shy Asians and boisterous Arabs to help all students 'understand each other better'.

Spending eight hours in each classroom did not allow me to observe the full range of cultural pedagogies practiced by individual teachers. However, in the lessons I observed, there were a number of interesting trends and approaches aside from those mentioned by teachers in interviews, and it is these trends that I have reviewed in the second part of this chapter. In choosing observation data to present, I deliberately chose discussions that were illustrative of tensions in the classroom. I did so because I believe that uncovering misunderstandings and disagreements (discursive faultlines) is necessary in order for intercultural understanding to develop.

In my observations, I observed tensions most commonly in cases where students were presenting their own knowledge of particular issues (often based on electronic media); where teachers' agendas for the activity were different from those of the students; where participants from different social positions had different stakes in the issues under discussion; and finally, where students were trying to come to terms with the threats and promises that the United States represents. Under these conditions of tension, images of particular cultures were often constructed out of remarks from several individuals, each drawing from different discourses: they thus tended to be contradictory rather than coherent (Kramsch, 1998). Although the literature suggests that the English language itself could be a source of discursive tension (e.g. Canagarajah, 1999; Menard-Warwick, 2009d), this was not a faultline that I observed in these classrooms.

The cultural representations I observed were generally of national cultures; the two national cultures discussed at greatest length, and with greatest heat, were Chile (in Chile) and the United States (in both Chile and the United States). Much less common was talk about the other countries where students came from. In my observations, the only US teacher who made much effort to ask students in depth about 'your countries' was Ruby (see Chapter 5).[12] Melinda's college held a diversity fair in which some of her students created exhibits about their countries; she led an enthusiastic class discussion about this, and also about a visit to the college from Guatemalan human rights activist Rigoberta Menchú (see Chapter 3). Eric's students read a book that took place in England. Paloma's class discussed the 2005 London subway bombings. The textbook used in Alán's class had information about tourism in Europe. Cherie's students took a field trip to a nearby Chinese restaurant. However, in terms of creating cultural representations, the Chilean classes spent a lot of time debating life in Chile, and both Chileans and US immigrants thrashed out images of life in the United States.

It was in the co-constructions of images of these two countries that discursive faultlines became most apparent. Although some authors have recommended that students discuss the role of English in their societies (e.g. Pennycook, 1994), it seemed to be the cultural practices and perspectives connected to the language, rather than the language itself, that students wanted to debate. I saw little evidence that students were afraid 'of being assimilated into the target culture' (Paige et al., 2003: 29). Rather, in constructing and then debating cultural representations, students seemed primarily concerned with convincing others that their own representations and evaluations were more correct than those of their classmates.

While Chileans generally agreed that their country was heading toward ever greater involvement in globalization (while evaluating this direction in strikingly different ways), representations of the United States were more contradictory: it was seen as a land of violence, greed, discrimination, wealth and opportunity, as well as a principal source of electronic media. Whether or not this was the goal of the teacher, images of contemporary Chile and the United States were often problematized by students with divergent viewpoints (Auerbach, 1992; Harklau, 1999). The main difference is that immigrants in California had some chance to sort out the media images from their own experiences; students in Chile had very little (cf Ryan, 2003) – in Norma's words: 'what (you) see in the movies is not what it is.' However, even though Chilean students could never be sure how media images differed from lived reality, they could (and did) evaluate the media images based on their own values.

How were these representations constructed? From discourses, as Kubota writes (1999, cf Vitanova, 2005). Multiple, contradictory discourses are semiotic resources (Blommaert, 2005) available in contemporary societies as raw materials for speakers to fracture and intermingle. Students and teachers drew upon available discourses in constructing images of the world that made sense to them (Bakhtin, 1981; Blommaert, 2005; Vitanova, 2005); the resulting classroom representations of culture were often collage-like and heteroglossic.

In this way, the classes I observed came to exemplify Kubota's contention that culture should be seen as 'a site of political and ideological struggles over meaning' (Kubota, 1999: 30). In Chile, as in many countries, a discourse of family breakdown and dysfunction competes with a discourse of feminism and women's rights. There is a worldwide discourse about violence in the United States, fed by images of war in Iraq and Afghanistan, as well as by Hollywood movies where guns provide, in Ming's words, 'a final solution'. There is also a worldwide discourse about discrimination and human rights, that Hassan and Viviana drew upon in discussing the US immigration system. And there is additionally a discourse of the American Dream, of America as 'the land of opportunity', which Anet and Susanna employed in the same discussion. In my observations, outspoken students were able to problematize these discourses (Auerbach, 1992; Harklau, 1999) when they conflicted with their own experiences.

Teachers handled cultural representations in a variety of ways, at times entertaining alternate positions and voices in a dialogically expansive way, at times contracting opportunities for dialogue by presenting only one position as correct (White, 2003). Teaching 'culture' was not a central curricular objective in any of the classes I observed: I knew that as I began this project, and I am not arguing now that it should have been. As authors involved in EFL survey research point out (e.g. Sercu, 2006), a major difficulty in focusing on culture in language classes is that there are always other priorities, and there is never enough time. Of course, as Cortazzi and Jin point out (1999), all teaching materials contain cultural content, but when this is straightforward, familiar and non-controversial, it is easy for teachers and students to take cultural representations for granted.

In any case, how teachers handled discursive faultlines tended to depend on their agenda for the activity they were conducting. If giving students speaking practice was the goal, they were more likely to accept whatever they said. They would also at times use their power as teachers to make short authoritative statements, as Paloma did about gun violence. Nevertheless, a fair number of students continued promoting their own views of the world, and could not easily be silenced. It was not so much that teachers empowered students, but that certain students already felt entitled to express their own views. Thus, 'the teaching of culture as a dialogic process of coming to terms with the often conflictive encounter between two or more cultures' (Kramsch, 1993: 21) certainly happened in the classes I observed, but was no one's first priority.

In fact, as the resolutions to these discussions above illustrate, the creation of intersubjectivity, the sense of 'everyone being on the same page', was far more common in these classes than the development of interculturality, of truly understanding differences (Byram, 1997; Kramsch, 2005). All the teachers valued a cooperative, collaborative class atmosphere, in which people, as individuals, were 'free to disagree', and they would thus try to conclude discussions on a note of commonality before going on to the next activity. When dialogue began to erupt along discursive faultlines, teachers rarely prioritized 'explor(ing)...further the ideological content of the students' utterances or...the historical and political context' (Kramsch, 2005: 27). Rather, as Kramsch also found, discussion activities often left 'the students in their native cultural mindsets and failed to engage them in making sense of a reality other than their own' (Kramsch, 2005). Playing 'devil's advocate' as Susanna did above tended to encourage students to bolster their own positions rather than re-think them.

Finally, the setting of the classes, ESL versus EFL, affected the kinds of representations that students could construct. Because Chile was a major topic of discussion, the Chilean students had a better chance to articulate understandings of their own culture; in contrast, the US immigrants had a better opportunity to see their culture through the eyes of another (Kramsch, 2005) through interacting with students from a range of nations. Thus, students in both contexts had some chance to develop interculturality, to view the world through multiple perspectives. This was exemplified in Ming's attempt to understand the factors that lead US youth to bring guns to school, a phenomenon baffling to his Chilean classmates. In any case, at least some students in each class were demonstrably able to appropriate English to represent their own realities (Canagarajah, 1999), and to construct their own voices (Blommaert, 2005). Whether these debates along cultural faultlines helped anyone to understand realities other than their own (Kramsch, 2005; McKay, 2002) was harder to observe. I will discuss the implications of this phenomenon in the following chapter.

Notes

(1)   This chapter draws on data and analysis that first appeared in Menard-Warwick (2009c, 2011a).
(2)   Ranch dressing is a salty creamy US salad topping.

(3) This distinction does not easily apply, of course, to multilingual societies in which English is an official language (e.g. India), but does accurately capture the difference between the classic ESL context (California) and EFL context (Chile) described in this study.

(4) I also observed Azucena's class on culture for second-year English majors at ULP, which was taught mostly in Spanish. We discussed my observation during my interview with her, but I decided not to use the observation field notes as part of my data for this research.

(5) Given that observed teachers were interviewed twice, this means that I conducted 16 interviews with Californian teachers and 19 interviews with Chilean teachers.

(6) This was sometimes expressed in terms of regions of the world, such as 'Middle Eastern students'.

(7) *Kim chi* is spicy pickled cabbage, an iconic feature of Korean cuisine.

(8) I did not survey students for their nationalities, but these were sometimes mentioned in the classroom.

(9) The Spanish word is *machista*, from *macho*, meaning 'male'. *Machista* is an adjective referring to the practices and ideologies of male dominance.

(10) In the popular documentary film on US gun violence, *Bowling for Columbine* (2002), filmmaker Michael Moore walks along a block of middle-class homes in Toronto, Canada, throwing open front doors, and confronting startled homeowners. He did this to demonstrate that Canadians do not feel the need to lock their doors, and that they do not respond with violence to intrusive strangers. Cristóbal draws the expected implication that US homeowners lock their doors at all times and pull guns when threatened.

(11) To the best of my knowledge, Viviana was not referring to a current Texas law, but to one overturned by the US Supreme Court in 1982 (Tallman, 2005). This law was in the news in 2005 because John Roberts, then a nominee for the Supreme Court, had supported the overturned Texas law.

(12) This comparative lack of attention to students' homelands contrasts with the findings of authors such as Harklau (1999).

7   Teaching on the Faultlines[1]

> *Truth is not born nor is it to be found inside the head of an individual person, it is born between people collectively searching for truth, in the process of their dialogic interaction. Socrates called himself a 'pander': he brought people together and made them collide in a quarrel, and as a result truth was born; with respect to this emerging truth Socrates called himself a midwife, since he assisted at the birth.*
> Bakhtin, 1984: 110

> *Capitalism, similar to that 'pander' Socrates on the market square of Athens, brings together people and ideas.*
> Bakhtin, 1984: 167

The year 1929, when Bakhtin first published the book in which these quotes appeared, also happened to be the year he was arrested (possibly for practicing Christianity), and was exiled to Kazakhstan (Emerson, 1984). In that same year, global capitalism went soaring high – and then came crashing down. Similar ups and downs were apparent in the 1980s at the time Bakhtin's works were appearing in English and Pinochet was drastically privatizing the Chilean economy. And we have seen similar 'market turbulence' also in the last several years, between the time I collected most of my data (2005–2006) and the time I realized I had better get serious about turning it into a book (2010–2012). Indeed, the recent vagaries of capitalism have seriously affected ELT in both my contexts of research, as I shall explain below.

In this final chapter, I will bring the historical context up to date (as of 2012), summarize my research findings, then discuss how this work has influenced my pedagogy as a teacher educator – and from that perspective I will offer implications for teacher education in ELT. First, however, both historically and pedagogically, it is worth examining Bakhtin's claim that capitalism creates conditions for dialogue by bringing together people and ideas. I will illustrate this through field notes from an observation audio-taped on 1 July 2005 in Alán's Chilean university classroom.

Holding up the pictures he'd brought for his oral presentation on Dallas, Texas, Reuel said, 'This is Dallas and this is the rodeo.' Seeing a cowboy hat in one of the pictures, Alán said, 'It is important to remember that people wear cowboy hats, is that common?' Reuel said yes, adding, 'And there are a lot of horses.' Alán asked the class, 'Did you ever watch on TV the series *Dallas*? [...] Dallas is in Texas, right? There was a drama series in the past that was famous not only in the States but I think worldwide.' [...]

Tomás commented, 'I didn't like it. Because it was too...sorry...' he looked at me, 'Yankee, too Yankee for me.' I said, 'I don't like it either.' Alán said, 'It's OK, she can handle things like that. You mean it was too far from your reality.' I added [feeling clever], 'It is too Texas for me.' Alán told Tomás, 'Remember that each state has its own reality.'

To the rest of the class, Alán said, 'But the main character used to wear a cowboy hat in that, and his name was Larry Hagman, and in the series he was...' A number of students chimed in 'Jota Erre (*J.R.*).' Alán repeated, 'Jota Erre. He was on TV for a long, long time.'

Dallas was a show that exemplified the 1980s love affair with capitalism around the world, glamorizing rapacious behavior in business and personal life. This was not the kind of show that would have had trouble making it past Pinochet's censors into the Chilean television market. For thoughtful young Chileans like Tomás, the show exemplifies all the negative stereotypes about US greed that can be contained in the derogatory term 'Yankee/ *Yanquí*'. For a 'film buff' like Alán, however, *Dallas* is both great TV, and also a way to help his students picture the foreign setting that Reuel is exploring in his oral presentation. Reuel, it is important to note, did not bring up greedy oilmen. In his oral presentation, the city of Dallas (as portrayed on the internet) was home to Stetson hats, bull riders, barbecue and beer. In an interview a week later, he told me about his interest in cowboys, stemming from childhood cartoon-watching days, especially an episode from the *Tom and Jerry* series in which 'the cat was a cowboy'. For me, the world of cowboys *and* oil barons is remote enough to seem exotic, distant from my reality, as Alán quickly understands.

For Tomás, the television show *Dallas* about rich Texans is 'too Yankee', or in other words, exemplifies all that he finds wrong with US culture, to the extent that he must apologize to a US visitor in his classroom. Alán and I try to explain that the show is not really about America, rather about a small part of America. I attempt to dissociate myself entirely from *Dallas*'s cultural milieu ('it's too Texas for me'), whereupon Alán vouches for my ... what? My toughness, intrepidity and dispassion as a researcher who can 'handle' anti-American sentiment? In any case, looking back at my notes on Tomás, I realize that he already knew there was more to the United States than rich Texans. He was an avid consumer of alternative rock, such as the Los Angeles band Tool whose lyrics expressed what Tomás viewed as Mayan cosmology. Moreover, Tomás had just given an enthusiastic presentation on tourist attractions in Detroit, such as the Motown (music) and Ford (automobile) museums. Unlike Dallas, Detroit was apparently *not* a 'Yankee' city in Tomás's eyes, or at least not 'too Yankee'. Besides, it is Alán, the Chilean instructor, who has brought up the show *Dallas* precisely because he thinks it will be culturally familiar to his Chilean students: the show was 'on TV for a long, long time'.

Those of us present in this Chilean classroom in 2005 are able to orient to these same media images across generations, languages, geographies, histories – even while remembering the national stereotypes, discordant ideologies and painful histories that divide us. Our collective memory of this global product allows a brief moment of dialogue between Tomás, Alán and I precisely *about* the shared faultlines that divide us. 'Capitalism, similar to that "pander" Socrates on the market square of Athens' (Bakhtin, 1984: 167) brings us together here.

Historicity, Revisited

The last time I was in Chile, it was 2010. The country was riding a copper bubble, so in many ways doing better economically than California, which was still suffering from the 2008 collapse of our housing bubble. Chile's unemployment rate that year was 7.1% (Index Mundi, 2012); California's hit a high of 12.4% (Bureau of Labor Statistics, 2011), not outrageously high by global standards but in conflict with our collective self-image as a land of opportunity. Meanwhile, despite economic growth in Chile, most Chilean students and their families were struggling. Not only were public universities costly compared to family income, many students from poorer families could not get into public universities at all due to a competitive admissions process. Neoliberal education policies in recent decades have encouraged privatization of higher education: rather than provide increased access to public universities to meet rising demand, the government has touted the expansion of for-profit colleges. Low-income students in the burgeoning for-profit sector have found themselves forced into high debt while receiving sub-standard educations (Economist, 2012).

Despite the comparatively good economy in 2010, tensions were mounting. At the end of that year, Sebastián Piñera was elected the first avowedly right-wing president of Chile since Pinochet; by early 2011, the nationwide perception of intensifying privatization led to student strikes that shut down universities and high schools throughout the country for most of the year (Economist, 2012; Goldstein, 2012).

My MA student, Whitney Whitener, a California teacher married to a Chilean, went to Santiago in 2011 to collect data for her thesis regarding teachers' views of language policy, and found the task more challenging than anticipated. As she reported:

At the time of my arrival in Santiago, August 2011, Chile had been in the midst of protests regarding the country's education system for several months. The students of the main public university, Universidad de Chile, Santiago, had begun to protest the high cost of public university-level education, among other things.[2] The University went on strike and many public and semi-private high schools participated in the strikes as well, suspending classes until their demands were adequately responded to by the government. Thus, the priorities of many teachers and the students were different, not all schools were in session, and not many teachers responded to my request to meet. (Whitener, 2012: 8)

At the same time, even in a city wracked with protest over the government's neoliberal economic policies, Whitener was struck by 'the inroads English was making into the culture, which seemed to be more extensive from the time (when she) had lived in Chile from 2007–2008' (Whitener, 2012). In exploring this phenomenon, she analyzed an advertisement in a middle-class shopping mall, showing 'a young, light skinned girl with long light-brown hair, smiling off camera' surrounded by 'a montage of images in the background depict(ing) summer scenarios' such as 'a man surfing' (Whitener, 2012: 17). As Whitener emphasizes, the written text of the ad was entirely in English, stating 'summer attitude' and 'give me liberty'. As she notes, this advertisement continues to associate English with people of European ancestry via the girl's appearance, as well as with globalized discourses of fashion and consumption. However, in 2011, Chileans who could decipher the words 'liberty' and 'attitude' (perhaps through the Spanish cognates 'libertad' and 'actitud') could also connect English to the ongoing and popular street protests, in which young people with 'attitude' were demanding 'liberty'.

One of the teachers whom Whitener managed to interview drew the same connection between English and political empowerment more explicitly in an email:

> in the education aspect is necessary to build a communication bridge, and English is the bridge, thanks to it we can express our political, social and education plans as a country to the rest of the world,... the most representatives students leader have had to present their suggestions in France and UN, they speak English, so now the English not only is a language is a 'powerful gun' to help for students and ordinary people. (Whitener, 2012: 29)

As Whitener clarifies, her interviewee is referring to super-star student leader Camila Vallejo's speaking tour through Europe where she presented her ideas on educational reform. Given that Vallejo self-identifies as Communist (Goldstein, 2012), the next generation of leftist youth will have a harder time making the argument that English is irrelevant to their political identities (see Chapters 2 and 3) – despite the powerful discursive connections that remain between the language and the neoliberal global marketplace. Camila Vallejo, Communist student leader, is visibly using English as an International Language, just as US scholar Sandra McKay recommends: 'to tell others about (her) ideas and culture' (McKay, 2002: 12). With resistance commodified in advertisements, and English now recognized as a legitimate language of protest, the complexities along these discursive faultlines have recently become – more complex.

Meanwhile, in California, the collapse in home prices beginning in 2008 led to budget crisis, as we collectively came to the realization that a lot of the state's wealth was in fact virtual, and built on speculation. One of the casualties of the crisis has been state-funded English as a Second Language instruction. In summer 2009, the family literacy funds that had paid for Cherie's class dried up, and she stopped teaching adult ESL. This was only the beginning of a massive transfer of funding from adult classes to the hard-hit K-12 public education system. Ruby's state-funded adult school class went from 10 hours per week to 4. However, she has increasingly found herself working with international students who pay to study English at a university extension program.

While Whitener was conducting her MA thesis research in strike-torn Chile, another of my MA students, Kate Caslin, an adult-school ESL instructor, was investigating the effects of drastic budget cuts on adult English learners. As she explains:

> The California State Education Code requires that funds budgeted for adult education, ... be spent only on adult education ... However, in

2009, in response to a worsening budget crisis, the state lifted this requirement, allowing school districts to spend money allocated for adult education on k-12 programs. As a result, adult education budgets throughout the state were decimated, forcing the reduction of classes, laying off of teachers, and elimination of adult education programs altogether in some districts. In Sacramento County, there were 14,437 adults enrolled in ESL classes in the 2007–2008 school year. In 2010–2011, there were only 6410, a 56% decrease (CASAS.org). These are the most current statistics available, but the downward trend is sure to continue as at least two entire adult schools in Sacramento County closed their doors after the 2010–2011 school year. (Caslin, 2012: 10–11)

As Caslin goes on to illustrate (and this is the focus of her MA thesis), students shut out of adult schools often try to register in community college classes, even when the academic curriculum of these classes does not meet their needs. Moreover, as Caslin explains, community colleges not only face severe cuts in their own budgets but also a contraction of their traditional mission to serve a wide range of adult educational goals, with two high-level statewide reports recommending greater efficiency in moving students through educational programs:

> Both reports cite the need for students to be able to remediate any basic skills needs quickly and to make measurable progress toward specific goals in educational plans...What is not made clear is how this might apply to a student who is only taking ESL classes, which would not be considered a program of study since most of the ESL classes are not degree-applicable. (Caslin, 2012: 13–14)

In this educational climate of shrinking resources, public colleges in California are beginning to implement privatization measures reminiscent of those that have sparked strikes in neo-liberal Chile. While steep tuition hikes have become commonplace around the state and have led to widespread protests, the most radically neo-liberal budget solution was adopted in early 2012 at Santa Monica College: that is, to offer some sections of popular classes at much higher fees to students who can afford them, thus 'creating a two-tiered system of wealthier students who can afford classes and struggling working-class and low-income students competing for the scraps of what's left', as one student leader commented (Rivera, 2012). In an eerie parallel with Chile, 'trustee Louise Jaffe dismissed fears that the plan would shut out low-income students, arguing that they already are being driven to expensive for-profit institutions where they are amassing huge debt' (Rivera,

2012). Moreover, as in Chile (Goldstein, 2012), and as increasingly common in California, Santa Monica protesters were sprayed with noxious chemicals, two of them ending up in hospital (Rivera, 2012).

In both California and Chile, education across the board, and thus English language education, is increasingly more commodified, more for those who can pay. This is a powerful historical trend, with potentially profound effects on teacher identities and pedagogies that must unfortunately remain unanalyzed in this book. Nevertheless, in my next section, I summarize findings from my study, emphasizing themes that I believe still remain relevant across the economic, political and educational changes of recent years.

Connecting Identities and Pedagogies

In this section, I compare the tensions around ELT that I found in my two contexts of research. More specifically, I compare how teachers' identities influenced their approaches to English teaching in these two very different settings: Las Peñas, Chile, home to a small public university in a small city on the sea coast, at the edge of the driest desert in the world; Farmington, California, with its diverse array of schools and colleges, its farmland, freeways and shopping malls. I set out to make comparisons not with the aim of establishing deterministic cause-and-effect relationships between having a certain cultural identity and practicing a certain kind of cultural pedagogy, but rather to bring all these teachers' lived experiences together, based on common trends across many interviews.

In both Farmington, California and Las Peñas, Chile (as elsewhere around the world), English teachers' identities and pedagogies are shaped in response to the status of the language and its role in society. On the one hand, authoritative discourses (Bakhtin, 1981) insist on the prestige and economic value of English, and teachers in both contexts cannot help but be influenced by these discourses – even when the purported economic rewards of English are neither immediate nor clearcut. On the other hand, one clear difference between Farmington and Las Peñas is the extent to which English is used for communication and daily life activities. Although both Californian and Chilean teachers think of the language as enabling learners to talk to people from around the world, this is a concrete reality in Californian but not in Chilean classrooms.

Indeed, while both California and Chile are socially stratified and economically inequitable, the discourses that shape residents' perspectives on social division vary considerably between the two locations. In my interviews, Chilean teachers tended to focus on social class, whereas Californians paid far more attention to ethnic or national identities. In both contexts,

English is considered to be a powerful language, but the Chilean focus on social class contributes to English being seen as an *elite* language, a language that potentially confers prestige. As Diego reconstructed the typical dialogue between himself and his private high school students, 'I told them if you are going to study in the university, medicine or architecture, you need to speak English. You need to know the language. "Oh sure, I know that, I know I want to be a doctor..."' (see Chapter 3). While teachers held the hope that working-class students might attain successful futures through studying English, their students themselves often argued against this idea. California teachers, in contrast, tended to conceptualize English not as 'elite' but rather as 'mainstream', and to see immigrant communities as isolated from the larger society. As Susanna said about her community college students (see Chapter 3), 'they're learning English that will help them participate more in the community, that will help them get a better job, that will help them, you know, sometimes just even communicate with their family members'. Thus, in both locations, the English language is seen as a force that can either reproduce or transform the social structure.

In constructing identities for themselves and their students, teachers drew upon these typical ways of conceptualizing the world – discourses of social class in Chile and discourses of ethnicity in California. While the teachers I interviewed were mostly from middle-class backgrounds, one important career decision described by Chilean teachers was whether to teach in working-class public schools or more elite institutions. Sofía, near the end of her career, and Maritza, just beginning, both stated preferences for teaching students from impoverished backgrounds. Recalling the badly behaved children from her first student-teaching assignment, Maritza said 'I think that they loved me a lot.' Other teachers shied away from the challenges that Sofía and Maritza embraced, with Alán even 'kind of blam(ing him)self, because (he) wasn't the right person for [working-class students]' when he switched from high school to university teaching (see Chapter 4).

While Chileans occasionally mentioned ethnicity, for example, when noting indigenous Aymara students as educationally disadvantaged, or in talking about their own family heritage, Californians had very little to say about social class. Usually when it arose at all, it surfaced briefly along with ethnicity: for example, Melinda described herself as 'white and middle-class'; Charles depicted his hometown as 'middle class and mostly white'. California teachers were far more likely to describe their own ethnic origins than their social class origins, some in passing (Cherie mentioned Norwegian ancestry), some in detail: Eric talked at length about the German heritage of his family, which like Renate's father had maintained the custom of singing 'O Tannenbaum' on Christmas Eve (see Chapter 4).

Moreover, when asked to describe their students, national or regional origin was almost always the first thing that California teachers mentioned. This almost inevitably led to essentialization and stereotyping: South Americans and Middle Easterners as loud and eager, Asians as shy and withdrawn (see Cherie's Chapter 6 narrative). Typical narratives about learning to teach in California recounted trial-and-error strategies for managing these cultural trends. Whereas Eric said that he had initially found Russian students to be 'kind of rough and harsh', he now depicted himself as having adapted his own style to theirs: 'you know [they say], "Oh, you know this was a hard test, too hard." [I say] "Yeah?"' (see Chapter 4). In describing how they taught these different groups of students, teachers often quoted themselves proclaiming diversity: 'different isn't better or worse, it's just different.'

Indeed, the discourse of diversity had become internally persuasive (Bakhtin, 1981) for the California teachers. Although they could not always see economic success as a result of learning English, they perceived signs of interculturality in themselves and their students. Ruby, from Brazil (see Chapter 5), drew on discourses of cultural difference to articulate US practices from an outsiders' perspective that made it easier for her adult-school students to understand. Describing her students' growth in this area, she said, 'It was just learning and the friendships that they made with people [...], and they say, "you know, I've never in my whole life met a Japanese person."' Molly, a young teacher from a small California town, expressed similar excitement about cultural exchange (see Chapter 4). When given a chance to design a class for international students, she gave it the theme of California travel and recreation based on her own background – but she also talked at length to me about having learned music, politics and Spanish conversation from a Colombian in her class.

This kind of international friendship through English was not as easily available to the Chilean teachers, many of whom had never been able to travel abroad, and all of whom lived in an area where most immigrants were Spanish-speaking laborers from Peru or Bolivia. At the same time, like the Californians, they often found economic success through English to be illusory. To explain their work to themselves and their students, they drew upon discourses about global culture, which were made internally persuasive through their own participation in English-language popular media, often via the internet. Alicia's Chapter 2 narrative about introducing her 'Communist' high school student to the music of Rage Against the Machine provides an illustration, as does Tomas's Chapter 3 account of sharing his popular culture interests in film and music with his imagined future students: 'I want to say to my students that "the world … doesn't end in the corner of their street.'" He mentioned the Holocaust film *Schindler's List* as an example of what he would like to watch with them. In fact, many Chileans talked about using English-language popular culture in their classes (see Chapter 6), especially songs whose images had helped them make sense of their own experiences, such as Pink Floyd's *The Wall* (banned by Pinochet's censors, see Chapter 1).

Thus, teachers in both California and Chile situated their work in terms of their distinct experiences of globalization. Chile's national economy is often described as 'export oriented', with English teaching discursively connected to this orientation. As department director Norma noted, 'Ever since they started with this free trade treaty, there was an awareness of a need of improving the levels of English.' At the same time, Chile is an importer of cultural products, as in the Hollywood film *Schindler's List* mentioned by Tomás, and the internet has made this importation easier than ever before. In contrast, California teachers rarely mentioned their state's strong engagement in international trade, nor its worldwide role as a cultural exporter. Instead Californians described globalization in terms of personal relations with students from many countries, and in their own opportunities to travel and live abroad – including in Chile. These experiences affected their teaching, as when Veronica expressed her preference for immersion language teaching, based on her own learning in France (see Chapter 1). Moreover, while international trade provided a predominant orientation for Chilean globalization, some of the Las Peñas teachers additionally had taken part in foreign travel opportunities that had connected them to the larger world and informed their pedagogy, as in Paloma's Chapter 5 narratives. Francesca, after a year in Denmark, perceived herself as more outspoken than the 'typical Chilean girl' (see Chapter 4); while teaching students she asked her pupils to take stands on social issues (see below).

As well as being part of these larger social and historical trends, teachers also brought a range of personal interests into the classroom. For example, Melinda's history with American Sign Language had given her an interest in formal linguistics, thus a fascination with the languages of her community college ESL students, thus a commitment to encourage the use of L1 knowledge while learning English. Her native-speaker discourse, appropriated in part from Chomskyan linguistics, led her to value her own California accent in ESL teaching – but it *also* helped her to see her students' native-speaker capabilities as 'precious' resources. Alán, a lover of art, film and literature, carried those enthusiasms into his teaching, one day drawing on his students' knowledge of *Dallas,* another day the film *Chicago,* another day Michelangelo's David statue. Indeed, this research highlights the wide range of resources that teachers appropriate and then bring into their teaching, from Pink Floyd to the Haitian poem in Chapter 2, all part of the larger transcultural flows currently eroding the boundaries between the global and the local (Pennycook, 2010). Thus, although there are vast historical, linguistic, political, social, economic and cultural differences between California and Chile, English language teaching nevertheless has some commonalities across the contexts – as teachers assimilate their own consciousness to the (globalized) world (Bakhtin, 1981). For Bakhtin, the conflicting languages and discourses that exist in *heteroglossia* provide resources for identity development – but also sharpen the need to construct personal and collective coherence in times of change and contradiction. Around the world, English language teacher identities develop through the ongoing struggle between 'helping one's students achieve their aspirations (while) supporting the linguistic, cultural, commercial and increasingly military dominance of the USA and its allies' (Edge, 2006, xiii) – or in California, through the endless tension between helping diverse students achieve diverse aspirations while simultaneously furthering the continued dominance of English within the state.

Along these discursive faultlines, new ways of using language and interpreting social phenomena provide resources for teacher identity development. As Vitanova puts it, 'the opportunity for re-evaluation and the creation of new meanings become two of the core features of the Bakhtinian agentive self' (Vitanova, 2010: 16). The need for teachers, and eventually their students, to create new meanings in English and about English is a strong point of commonality in Chile and California. In both places, English language teaching remains a site where authoritative discourses about English as the language of social and economic power are reconciled with internally persuasive discourses about English as a path to personal growth (Bakhtin, 1981). Teachers' own cultural and intercultural identities are a resource for this reconciliation. Francesca, for example, student teaching in a Las Peñas high school, recounted a recent experience of using a popular song (by Canadian Avril Lavigne) 'to talk more about values', and in particular to make her students think critically about gender concerns:

Francesca: The music was about a girl, she didn't like the boy that was in love with her, she was very famous, she had many friends, and she was really ( ) shy, you know, and things like that, and she was really pretty, and after, eh 'Tell me, what do you, how do you think she is?' 'She's pretty,' ( ). I told them, 'Do you think she's intelligent?' 'No,' they, some girls say. 'Why don't, you don't think she's pretty? She's pretty but she cannot be intelligent?' you know, like prejudice, like, 'Oh, you (look) good, so you can't be intelligent,' you know, 'Do you think ( ), so if it's a good looking guy, he must be a stupid guy?'. (Menard-Warwick, 2011a)

In sharing this example, I recognize my own desire 'to talk more about values', as something that Francesca and I have in common. Teachers I interviewed in both California and Chile shared with me their hopes that their classes could offer students important life lessons beyond linguistic competence. While my journey as a transnational researcher has made me ever more aware that transcultural flows are too often uni-directional from places like Hollywood, California, I continue to find the idealism and commitment of teachers inspiring. Moreover, in presenting the thoughts and experiences of Chilean as well as California teachers, I hope this book can represent a small dialogic ebb against the powerful one-way flow in this globalizing world. In the rest of this chapter, I will offer ideas, in a spirit of dialogue, for using this research to inform pedagogy.

Implications for Cultural Pedagogy in Teacher Education

In this section, I address the implications of my findings for teacher education in the area of cultural pedagogy, based on my own experiences of putting this research into practice as a teacher educator in both Chile and California. I begin by summarizing the perspectives on culture that I bring to the teacher education classroom, and then present two case studies of cultural pedagogy at the MA level that illustrate my own approaches to language teacher education that have emerged from this research: first, I discuss the workshop on language and cultural identity that I offered in Chile in July 2006, and second, I highlight data from the action research that my student Dennis Mahler conducted in his California classroom for his 2012 MA thesis. I offer these examples not as a way to present a lot of new data on cultural dialogue at the last possible spot in the book, but rather as a way to share with readers my own pedagogical practice as a teacher educator, as I strive to incorporate the insights I have gained from conducting this research into my work with graduate students.

As Mahler wrote in his thesis:

> While culture has long been a subject within ESL education, the exact conception of culture that the teacher imparts and that students come with is still under debate. However, [one major theme in the literature] ... is that the teacher should create a space for students to question and confront previous stereotypes of culture... This suggests that students come into a foreign language classroom with a set of preconceived notions, assumedly many of which are in need of further adjustment. (Mahler, 2012: 4)

Mahler explores in his thesis the varied concepts of culture that international students brought to his ESL classroom. In doing so, he critiques tendencies in previous research to look upon language students (and teachers) as cultural neophytes in need of 'adjustment'. His research explicitly builds upon and responds to research described in this book (Menard-Warwick, 2009c), and in this way illustrates Bakhtin's concept of dialogue. I will return to the specifics of Mahler's work below, but throughout this section I will attempt to keep his critique in mind, and approach the following discussion, as I try to approach my teaching, as a person whose own best learning comes through dialogue with other human beings.

Therefore, along with other authors in the field of cultural pedagogy (see Chapter 6), my first recommendation is inevitably for dialogue between teachers, students and texts. Specifically, I call for dialogue that is aimed at problematizing cultural content (Kubota, 1999) with the goal of developing interculturality, the ability to see cultural issues from multiple perspectives (Byram et al., 2002). While teachers may fear that their students will share with each other simplistic or wrong-headed notions of cultural groups and practices, it is important to keep in mind that the process of problematization necessarily involves the construction of cultural representations (Risager, 2007): *multiple* images of groups and their practices. These can be seen, for example, in the classroom discussions of tattoos and 'fake' smiling in Chapter 5 – or of Chilean gender relations, US gun violence, and access to education for US immigrants in Chapter 6. In these examples, ongoing dialogue led to the complexifying of the provisional representations that had been put forth initially. In some circumstances (from extreme political unrest to administrative pressure to cover grammar points), the kind of problematization illustrated by these examples may be too risky to explore in classrooms. Nevertheless, when pedagogically possible, it is valuable to confront difficult issues in order to prepare learners for communication with people from other cultural groups.

In classes with outspoken students, teachers themselves may not have to problematize representations of cultures and cultural issues: it may be enough to leave space for students to do so. In such classes, the teacher can ask students to elaborate or provide evidence for their views, while making sure students with unpopular viewpoints get heard, and finding places for shy students to share their ideas (perhaps in their L1 or in writing). However, in other contexts, teachers may need to pay attention to subtle cues of student discomfort or resistance in order to determine unresolved cultural tensions (Harklau, 1999). Upon noting areas of tension, teachers can then hold up for scrutiny certain aspects of representations, for example assertions in texts. As students note contradictions between their own experiences and the assertions of others, the teacher can highlight these contradictions, with the aim of helping students to see all representations as partial and provisional. While heated discussions are often valued in language classrooms as occasions for speaking practice, cultural learning needs to go further than the simple sharing of strongly held opinions. That is, since dialogue is the goal, the process of problematization needs to go beyond critique. In order for students to recognize their own experiences and opinions as valid but necessarily partial, it is essential that cultural discussions provide not just an occasion for speaking practice, but also for listening and comprehending (Kramsch, 1993). For this reason, strong teacher facilitation may be necessary for thoughtful exchanges to occur. To ensure dialogue, teachers should require that learners respond to previous comments that have been made in the class or in the text, and not simply present pre-existing views. The teacher can encourage this by paraphrasing statements that have been made and inviting comment, keeping in mind that interculturality does not imply *agreement* but rather understanding.

If this kind of classroom dialogue is seen as essential for cultural pedagogy, then one goal of teacher education should be to prepare new teachers for their role as cultural facilitators. This will be easier if they are used to thinking of culture in terms of tension and change rather than as the static traditions of tightly bounded groups. Indeed, teachers who can comprehend and articulate their own experiences of exploring cultural boundaries should be better able to help their L2 students do likewise. In talking about these questions with my own TESOL students, I have found it important to ask them to share specific experiences, and to be explicit in interpreting how these experiences can inform teaching. As students interact in this way with TESOL classmates, they find that their collective cultural narratives are far more complex than any one student's individual experience. Learning interculturality from each other, they gain a clearer understanding of how to explore in L2 classrooms the variety of cultural differences that inevitably arise, while avoiding simplistic stereotyping (Kumaravadivelu, 2008). In this way, even teachers with minimal intercultural experience can develop *metacognitive awareness* (Byram, 1997) of their own social and cultural identities, and the constraints and resources these provide for their teaching. As new teachers compare the subjective experiences that have shaped them, they can begin to 'distance (themselves) from (their) own cultural assumptions and see (themselves) as . . . possessing a learned culture' (Wesche, 2004: 279).

In such activities, teacher educators should question static notions of national or ethnic cultures (Kramsch, 1998); elucidate power relations between different groups (Kubota, 1999); juxtapose divergent value systems (Byram, 1997); and facilitate explorations of culture based on the diversity of students' backgrounds (Harklau, 1999). At the same time, they should never assume that prospective teachers are naïve in these areas (Mahler, 2012). Discussions of cultural identities will be far more powerful when teacher educators demonstrate clear willingness to learn from their students, and continue to develop new cultural understandings as well as to impart them.

One rich experience in my own lifelong cultural learning has involved leading a workshop on Language and Cultural Identity at University of Las Peñas. This workshop counts as a course toward the Masters in Teaching English at ULP, in a program which offers courses during winter and summer breaks for practicing English teachers. I first co-taught (and videotaped) this course over 25 hours in July 2006, along with a Chilean colleague, Jaime Gómez (not a pseudonym), then taught it again in 2008 and 2010 without collecting further data. The program is currently suspended until at least 2014 due to the 2011 strikes, as well as new accreditation requirements for Chilean universities.[3] Jaime co-taught once more in 2008 but not in 2010, and in all three years, I was primarily responsible for preparing the syllabus and course reader.

As well as providing research findings, the workshop curriculum also *resulted* from the research I had conducted in 2005, and I refined the curriculum in subsequent years based on my ongoing data analysis. For this workshop, I bring in some readings to provide students an international perspective on issues such as resistance to English (e.g. Canagarajah, 1993; Lin, 1999), but I primarily facilitate the exchange of ideas between teachers on how to approach cultural and ideological issues in the classroom. In comparing syllabi from 2006 and 2010, I notice that the language I used to talk about the course changed little; however, in 2010, we discussed fewer readings in more depth, and the readings were far more focused on Chile. This Chilean focus has been facilitated by the fact that between 2006 and 2010, I had published (or had in press) several research articles devoted to the same topics as the seminar (Menard-Warwick, 2009c, 2009d, 2011a).

To provide an overview of the weeklong workshops, we begin with a discussion of language and identity, in which we examine how learning and speaking particular languages or language varieties affects our sense of who we are (Canagarajah, 1993; Dorfman, 1998). We go on to consider how linguistic and cultural identities intersect with other social identities, such as those based on class, ethnicity and nationality (Canagarajah, 1993; Lin, 1999; Niño-Murcia, 2003). Specifically, we explore the contemporary state of Chilean culture and cultural identity (Moulián, 1997),[4] and especially the effects of English as an International Language on Chilean cultural identities (McKay, 2003; Niño-Murcia, 2003).[5] As the week goes on, we begin to review ways of bringing cultural and intercultural perspectives into the language classroom (Byram *et al.*, 2002; McKay, 2002; Ros i Solé, 2003), especially in the contemporary Chilean context (Menard-Warwick, 2009c). To this end, we discuss how to use learners' interest in popular media both to encourage the acquisition of English and to develop a critical perspective on contemporary cultural trends (Menard-Warwick, 2009d, 2011a).

Along with these seminar-style discussions, time is built in for the participants to work more actively on cultural lessons that they can use in their own classrooms. First, we take an hour a day over three days to analyze three kinds of teaching materials: a page or two from a Chilean English textbook (see below); a popular song in English (ranging from The Black Eyed Peas to Miley Cyrus); a film or television clip (from *Crash* to *Eat Pray Love*) – with all materials provided by participants in the workshop. In our analysis, we explore the identities and cultural values represented in the materials, and suggest ways to use the materials in the classroom. The highlight of the workshop is the group teaching demonstrations on the last day (Menard-Warwick, 2013), based on the following prompt: 'given our discussions, how would *you* teach cultural issues in your classroom?' Students are also required to write a paper on this topic individually, due via email several weeks after the workshop is over.

I have already included in Chapter 3 data on language ideologies from the 2006 workshop, the only year in which the class was videotaped. To illustrate my own challenges and learning as a teacher educator, I briefly analyze here part of the discussion I led that year on the excerpt from the Chilean English textbook. To prepare for this discussion activity, my co-teacher Jaime and I had asked students to lend us textbooks they used to teach, and the two of us each picked out a passage. He chose one from a high school textbook on the Woodstock music festival in 1969, and I chose one from an elementary school book about two Chilean children, Martín and Ana, who have a British pen pal named Simon. The discussion analyzed below, on the pen-pal passage, came immediately after our conversation about the Woodstock passage, which had been facilitated by Jaime. The page had been photocopied, but I read over some highlights aloud at the beginning of the discussion, as captured on videotape:

Julia: And Simon sends them a letter and some pictures, and Simon writes, 'Hello Martín and Ana. Here are some photos from England. There's London, the Tower of London, some big red buses, Big Ben, the Houses of Parliament, and the river Thames. Love, Simon.' [...] And apparently when Ana and Martín got this letter from Simon, they decided to write him a letter. And they wrote, 'Hello Simon. S.O.S!!', exclamation point, exclamation point, 'What are the capital cities of these countries? New Zealand, the United States, the U.K., Australia, Canada, Jamaica. We need to know for our English home-work. Thank you. Ana and Martín.' And Simon very kindly sent back this information about the capitals of English speaking countries. ((pause)) The end. ((chuckling)) Um, so what kinds of identities are being presented here?

In choosing this excerpt, I had been struck by the narrow view of British culture as tourist attractions, and the even more impoverished view of Chilean culture as not worth mentioning. Attempting not to editorialize and especially not to impose my views on the workshop, I was nonetheless tempted into monologue – pointing out (without explicitly evaluating) the parts of the passage that I found objectionable. Although I spoke at length, I was hoping paradoxically to get quickly to dialogue about what was wrong with this textbook without imposing my own views. Like the teachers cri-tiqued by my student Dennis Mahler in his MA thesis quoted above, I had the idea that my job was to 'create a space for students to question and con-front previous stereotypes of culture'.

However, in my remarks I had 'created' perhaps *too much* 'space' and not sufficient explicit direction. Perhaps, due to their discomfort with unfamiliar vocabulary like 'identities', workshop participants initially responded very superficially to my questions, commenting that Ana and Martín were ele-mentary school children, that they seemed lazy (wanting Simon to do their homework for them), that they looked like typical Chileans with black hair and brown eyes, that probably Chilean children would identify with them. When we began brainstorming cultural values, participants said laziness, friendship, the internet, cultural exchange, cooperative learning and the use of English. This set me off again.

Julia: Right, so Simon isn't writing in Spanish, the Chilean kids are writ-ing in English. Uh-huh. So, um, if it's a cultural exchange, why are, why aren't the Chilean kids saying anything about Chile? Why aren't they sending pictures of Chile?
Vicente (university instructor): Because they think that Chile not as important as uh UK, (maybe) ( ).
Julia: So is this a value that's being promoted by this textbook that the UK is more important and Chile is not worth sending pictures (of)?

The more I thought about this text, the more indignant I was becoming, and Vicente's comment reinforced my feeling. Having a vision of cultural exchange as dialogue, I did not want to settle for travelogue, and it surprised me that so few participants had the desire to problematize this. Rather, several responded by saying no, it was valuable for children to learn about other cultures. I accepted their comments, but several turns later was drawn to remark:

> **Julia**: It's not an exchange. [...] All the information is coming from Simon. There's no information coming from Ana and Martín. Okay.
> **Jaime**: (That's) a very colonial message.
> **Students**: ((chuckling)) Mmhmm.
> **Male**: Yes it is.

Now that I was making my objections more explicit, my co-teacher Jaime was able to translate my concern into historical discourses more familiar to Chileans. Although it quickly became clear that several teachers agreed with Jaime that 'colonialism' provided a valid way to describe the relationship between these Chilean children and their British pen pal (as evidenced by the chuckling), many of their colleagues had strong personal investments in English as an International Language which precluded their desire to see this textbook through an anti-imperialist discursive lens.

After several turns of agreement and disagreement about whether this text represented 'colonialism', another student brought up Chile's geographically remote location. Trying to tie the ideas together, I inquired whether the textbook might be implying that 'Chile is so far away from the rest of the world that the rest of the world is just not interested'? upon which Jaime chimed in, 'What a terrible message.' Rita, however, had been trying to break into the discussion for some time (readers may recall her as the adult-school teacher who featured prominently in Chapter 3), and I finally called on her. Looking back, it was at this moment that dialogue actually began, especially when her colleague Francisco, a high school teacher, supported her point of view.

> **Rita**: I think that the message is the opposite, that it doesn't matter that the children are so far away from the rest of the world, there is still a possibility to communicate with people from the UK or from wherever, right?
> **Francisco**:We're part of, anyway, although we are far away in a little corner, we are part of the world...uh using English, (as a medium).

I see these comments as particularly dialogic in that both teachers are responding concretely to earlier comments as they construct their own perspectives. Further, elaborating Rita's and Francisco's defense of the textbook, Alán (university instructor quoted above) pointed out that Santiago had been included as a capital in the geography matching exercise, 'so that's important

I think.' Then, Rita reinforced her argument by pointing out the important role of the teacher in using these materials:

Rita: Because maybe it's not here in the book, but you as a teacher can make your students, I mean, like write the letter to sign, right?, telling him about...what we have here.

Hector (see Chapter 3) then shared his experience of actually teaching this unit in an elementary school classroom using Google Earth:

Hector: For example I was traveling around the world with the capitals. I wrote in the Google Earth search toolbar, for example, Wellington, [...] and then I wrote 'Santiago de Chile,' ((gestures a globe)), and after that, I made my students to make oral and most of my students choose Chile. And they made their presentation on Chile, but in English. So if, in the way you take the unit, is the way that you are going to eh....
Julia: This is very true....
Hector: So, the, eh MINEDUC[6] gives us this, but we can...
Everly (university instructor): Adapt it.
Hector: ...do whatever we want with it. We just (take it).
Julia: Right, yeah, no, so Rita, you [Hector], and Everly are all making the same point, you get this and then you adapt it. And there's different positive ways you could adapt this.

Thus, although discourses and ideologies clashed in this dialogue, we were able to construct intersubjectivity around this passage: perhaps it represented colonialist attitudes, but it was possible for creative teachers to transform it into a way for students to reflect on their own realities. What I learned from this, I think, as a North American teacher educator, is that many Chileans in fact share my 'critical perspective' on international politics and economics – so I do not need to insist that everyone notice every instance of cultural imposition. Rather, I need to stand back and let participants share their own ways of handling these issues. Or, better than standing back, I can facilitate their conversations to make sure that as many people as possible get a chance to speak; I can raise important questions about teaching practice; and I can occasionally contribute my own perspective as an applied linguist or a North American – but all this as part of the dialogue.

While heading into the workshop I had perhaps feared that participants would arrive with 'a set of preconceived notions, assumedly many of which are in need of further adjustment' (Mahler, 2012: 4). However, I found that in dialogue, all of our views were adjusting. Looking back I can say that the learning we did together provides a good illustration of Bakhtin's contention that 'truth is not born nor is it to be found inside the head of an individual person, it is born *between people* collectively searching for truth, in the process of their dialogic interaction' (Bakhtin, 1984: 110, italics in the original).

A more recent learning experience for me as a teacher educator has come out of the action research projects of MA student Dennis Mahler at my home university in California. Although I was not officially on Mahler's 2012 thesis committee, he carried out the pilot study for his research as the final project for a class I taught in 2011, and his assumptions, questions and methodologies were partly drawn from the research I report in Chapter 6 of this book (Menard-Warwick, 2009c). Thus, through Mahler's work, I gain new perspectives on how educators can apply the ideas I promote to concrete contexts of language teaching.

Mahler carried out his thesis research in a university ESL conversation class, focused on the theme of health. As he explains, 'attention was purposefully moved away from the topic of culture. This was done so that any discussions concerning culture that ensued were from students' own impetus and thus reflected their concerns' (Mahler, 2012: 22). Focusing on student conceptualizations of culture and the links between culture and nationality, Mahler collected data through student journals, audiorecorded classroom interactions and interviews. As he had hypothesized, some but not all participants conflated culture and nationality, and students voiced conflicting views on the meaning of 'culture'. Below, I share some of Mahler's data that explicitly follows up on my own research (see Chapter 6) regarding student tendencies to challenge cultural representations that they believe to be inaccurate or misguided. In Mahler's class, the seemingly innocuous topic of 'leisure time' presented significant discursive faultlines. In discussions of this theme, a Chilean student, to whom he refers by her initials as PP, played a prominent role.

Mahler first noted tension around this topic during a discussion of an article on Third Places, defined as a location that is not one's home or work, for example, a coffee shop. In response to the article, PP commented in class:

> **PP**: Personally, when I read the...the article I...I tried to think in my country and in my...my (university¿). Well, well, in Chile it is expensive to drink coffee you know¿ ((Inaudible)). So, only article is only thinking of persons who have the, enough money to spend EVERY day, I don't know, five dollars in the cofEEE. But this real...this reality is very different in another country. Like in Chile maybe only once per month I went out to coffee. (Mahler, 2012: 34)

PP's comments about the article sparked the following reflection in Mahler's thesis:

Here, we see a case where a student brings in nationality for a reason very different than we have previously encountered. The student here is making not only a critique of the article but by appealing to nationality is saying something very clear about the perceptions of me as a teacher and the culture of academia within the United States: namely that, while sympathetic to those with lower socio-economic status, I (and probably other academics like me) have failed to keep in mind the social realities facing some of our students. (Mahler, 2012: 34)

Although a goal of Mahler's research from the beginning had been to question simplistic equations of nationality and culture, PP's brief remark on coffee in Chile here pushes Mahler to expand his own perspective on the meaning of nationality. Previously interested in the extent to which students associated national identities with cultural practices, he now realizes that nationality indexes relative economic status in the global marketplace. When I read this data excerpt in Mahler's thesis, my first impulse was to write a comment to the effect that 'talking about social class is part of Chilean culture', presupposing the centrality of PP's national identity, as well as the idiosyncrasy of her attention to social class. Reflection on this impulse in turn made me recognize my own continued tendency to conflate culture and nationality, even while reading a thesis problematizing this connection!

In the same discussion of the Third Places article, Mahler brought up the response of his previous class to the topic, sparking more disagreement:

Mahler: Umm so last time I taught this class there were a couple of students who said that in their country there is no third places I think some of them were from China. Umm I think actually the Chinese students were the ones who were most you know 'There is no third place we don't do it ((LY laughs)) we just go to work and home, go to school and home.' [...]
LY: (I think) there are a lot of third places in China I think the problem is that they don't even bother to go there. ((Laughter)) They're just so used to studying all the time (Mahler, 2012: 36).

Mahler welcomed LY's refutation of his own former students. In analyzing this excerpt, he wrote, 'in this case the cultural attribute is dislodged from being combined with nationality and is instead posited within the culture of "busy students" or perhaps the individual' (Mahler, 2012). Like PP,

LY was speaking from a particular national identity, but also clarifying the complexity of life in her homeland, where not everyone's lifestyle permits the same leisure practices. Moreover, PP was clearly interested in the topic of leisure time because she returned to it in her final presentation several weeks later, again prompting argument from LY:

> **PP**: Yeah I've heard that the Americans who been there [Europe] say that the Americans work like robots. [...] The reports say Americans work more than Europeans because hard work is associated with, with success in America.
> **Mahler**: Ok good, good. Any other thoughts
> **LY**: You should go to Asia [...] Cause, cause for me I can't find the empathy for it. Because China represents cheap labor. People have to work really hard to make ends meet. And like ... I don't know other companies but in my high school we don't get week. Only get half day off every week and we have to study on Saturday and Monday, Sunday morning. [...] (Mahler, 2012: 35).

Mahler notes this as a classroom interaction in which national and cultural traits are conflated: 'Here students are representing Americans, Chinese and [...] other Asian groups as being wholes. Americans work hard and have no vacation or Chinese work hard and have no vacation' (Mahler, 2012: 36). Although he is unhappy with this conflation and the way it reinforces stereotypes, this exchange could also be seen as dialogic: LY is clearly listening to PP in order to contest her representations of different societies. In the conclusion to his thesis, Mahler emphasizes the complexity of student views:

> Comments made in class discussions often appear to take the link between culture and nationality for granted; however, interviews showed that students were at least aware that this might not be the case.... This project has also suggested to me that there is still room for further investigation into the ways in which students conceptualize such taken for granted concepts as culture and nationality. (Mahler, 2012: 50)

Agreeing with Mahler that there is room for further investigation on this topic, I was also challenged to bring his findings to my next cohort of MA students. When Mahler was a beginning MA student in my introductory class on Language Pedagogy in 2010, he offered a teaching demonstration on the topic of 'culture in the ESL classroom' by presenting a powerpoint of Japanese youth cultures. His own time teaching at a Japanese middle school,

along with his BA in anthropology, had made it clear to him that the monolithic conception of Japanese Culture long common among TESOL professionals is misleading at best (Kubota, 1999), and he wanted to share this
insight with his MATESOL classmates.

However, six months later, discussing some readings on cultural pedagogy with Mahler and his classmates in a more advanced graduate seminar,[7]
it was clear that most members of his cohort were only just beginning to
question simplistic equations between nationality and culture (Risager,
2007). In the seminar, Mahler's classmates were particularly interested in
Harklau's (1999) and Talmy's (2004) data on immigrant youth rejecting the
national identities of their former homelands. However, during those inter-
vening six months, they had all been teaching conversation classes, similar
to the one described by Mahler above, in which (they were now embarrassed
to realize), they had repeatedly made monolithic pronouncements on
'American Culture' or asked their students to hold forth on 'Chinese Culture'.
Why hadn't I stopped them sooner?!? they wanted to know. In response, a
Russian immigrant PhD student in the seminar argued convincingly for the
centrality and specificity of both Russian history and Russian literature to
the cultural identities of people in her community. Her thoughts on this issue
reminded me of the value of national identities for combating the homoge-
nizing forms of globalization that are most akin to imperialism (Risager,
2007), an insight which has helped me to better understand Chileans' conflicted reactions toward English teaching.

In Fall 2012, I brought Mahler's data into my MATESOL Language
Pedagogy course, for which about half the students were teaching the same
conversation class practicum. That week we had read Kumaravadivelu's 2003
article about stereotyping by TESOL professionals, and I had also assigned
my 2008 article about Ruby and Paloma (see Chapter 5), so that we could go
over the definitions of some technical terms (e.g. *culture*) and talk about how
our identities affect our teaching.

We had a lively discussion, but I saw that my students had difficulty
distinguishing between cultural and social identities, or between identities
assigned by society and identities actively developed by individuals.
Moreover, I found myself saddened that many of these prospective teachers
described themselves negatively, dwelling on whatever identity or personal
quality seemed to delegitimize them as an educator; for example, a young
woman who had grown up trilingual confessed to a lack of academic
vocabulary in English, and several Linguistics graduate students admitted
to anxiety when students asked them complex grammar questions. As a
teacher educator, I felt the need to affirm each one of them, to point out the
experiences that would help them connect with their students. I nodded

along with everyone in the room when an international student, the last person to speak, emphasized how her struggles learning English gave her empathy.

It was at this point that I handed over Mahler's data on the connections and disconnections between nationality and culture in the ESL conversation class, and asked my MA students to analyze it in small groups using the vocabulary from course readings, like *interculturality*. They seemed to enjoy the activity and to be interested in the data. However, as I walked around the room, I noticed them joining in with Mahler's students' discussions rather than standing back and analyzing them: Is coffee really more expensive in Chile than in the United States? Do you think Chinese people work all the time, or is that just a stereotype? Realizing again how complicated and slippery remain the definitions I explore in this book (identity, interculturality, etc.), I had to remind myself that regardless of whether my graduate students can apply theoretical concepts with precision, their participation in classroom conversations about varied cultural practices will allow them to connect to *their* students. I ended the activity by pointing out Mahler's title, 'Learning to listen', and suggested they cultivate this active listening with their own students. This they seemed happy to try.

As Brazilian educational theorist Paulo Freire defines dialogue, 'at the point of encounter, there are neither utter ignoramuses nor true sages; there are only people who are attempting together to learn more than they now know' (Freire, 1999: 71). Year by year, my experiences of teacher education on the discursive faultlines continue to reinforce the importance of this insight. However, in promoting dialogue, I cannot discount the responsibility that I have as an educator for my graduate students' learning as well as my own. Aware that I cannot truly participate in dialogue from a position of expertise but only as a co-learner, I am likewise aware that new discourses can provide significant resources for teacher identity development. For example, in my spring 2011 class described above, it was helpful for my students to learn how to distinguish national identities from cultural identities (Risager, 2007). An important part of my work as teacher educator is to offer such discursive resources (through course readings and discussions) to new teachers, as they begin to come to terms with basic ideological conflicts in the field of language education.

Above all, however, this research, my teaching, my experiences leading workshops for Chilean teachers, as well as my reflections on Mahler's research, have together strengthened my conviction that the most important thing I can do as a teacher is to try to ensure *listening*: to listen carefully to my students, to encourage them to listen to their classmates and to their own students, to cultivate their ability to learn culture from each other.

Conclusion

> What we have in mind here is not an abstract linguistic minimum of a common language, in the sense of a system of elementary forms (linguistic symbols) guaranteeing a *minimum* level of comprehension in practical communication. We are taking language not as a system of abstract grammatical categories, but rather language conceived as ideologically saturated, language as a world view, even as a concrete opinion, insuring a *maximum* of mutual understanding in all spheres of ideological life. (Bakhtin, 1981: 271, italics in original)

Language education has often focused on providing learners with 'an abstract linguistic minimum of a common language' in order to facilitate 'a *minimum* level of comprehension in practical communication'. However, in this book, I promote an alternative goal of cultural pedagogy, whether in the foreign language classroom or in teacher education. That is, teachers and students, co-learners together, should work toward a 'maximum of mutual understanding' through going beyond 'abstract grammatical categories' and into 'all spheres of ideological life'. From this perspective, language education needs to go beyond what is usually taught as 'culture' (e.g. coffee shops) to explore more dangerous areas such as Chinese labor practices or colonialism in English textbooks. In arguing for attention to cultural pedagogy, I am not contending that grammar instruction or communicative practice are useless, but rather that they are in themselves insufficient to bring about dialogue between individuals, communities, and nations, a dialogue that becomes every year more necessary in this inequitable, conflicted, imperilled planet.

In this book, I contend that dialogue across social and national boundaries is indispensable for maximal understanding; I also recognize that even partial understanding and nascent dialogue have the potential to regenerate each other in the chain of speech communication (Bakhtin, 1986b), as new truths are 'born *between people* collectively searching for truth' (Bakhtin, 1984: 110, italics in the original). Thus, by means of this book, as I carry Bakhtin's ideas into further dialogue with teachers on the faultlines, I hope to contribute to mutual understanding in all spheres of ideological life.

Notes

(1) This chapter offers some pedagogical recommendations that first appeared in Menard-Warwick (2008, 2009c).

(2) The new accreditation requirements have been imposed due to concerns about declining academic quality in the wake of privatization (Economist, 2012).

(3) In 2010, we compared contemporary Chile with Chile in the 1990 s as described by Moulián.
(4) Niño-Murcia writes about English in Peru, so we compare Chile to Peru. In 2010, one teacher attending the workshop was Peruvian, and she gave a presentation on changes in English education in Peru since the time Niño-Murcia collected her data.
(5) MINEDUC is the Ministry of Education for Chile.
(6) It was as a project for this class that Mahler conducted the pilot study for his thesis (Mahler, 2012).

Appendix 1: Transcription Conventions

In the interests of space and readability, I leave out most questions, back-channeling, false starts and repetitions. Below are the symbols I use.

text	Field notes from classroom observation, or classroom observation transcript
...	Trailing intonation
[...]	Text omitted
[text]	Author's paraphrase or background information
( )	Transcriptionist doubt
(( ))	Comment on voice quality or paralinguistic features (e.g. laughter, gestures, pause)

Appendix 2: Teacher Information and Schedule of Data Collection (Chronological Order by First Interview Date)

Pseudonym	Teaching/ learning context*	Level of education*	Birth decade, approximate	Year of research	Interview dates	Observation dates (8 hours per teacher total)
Cherie	Farmington Adult School (instructor)	US Masters degree	1950s	2005	14 April, 12 May	6 April, 13 April, 18 April, 25 April
Ruby	Farmington Adult School (instructor)	US Masters degree	1950s	2005	6 June, 13 June	9 May, 11 May, 16 May, 18 May
Alán	University of Las Peñas (instructor)	In progress Chilean Masters degree	1970s	2005	4 July, 27 July	22 June, 28 June, 1 July, 5 July, 8 July
Paloma	University of Las Peñas (professor)	US Masters degree	1940s	2005	6 July, 29 July	21 June, 28 June, 5 July, 7 July, 12 July, 14 July, 26 July

Pseudonym	Teaching/ learning context*	Level of education*	Birth decade, approximate	Year of research	Interview dates	Observation dates (8 hours per teacher total)
Genaro	University of Las Peñas (professor)	US doctoral degree	1940s	2005	7 July, 26 July	25 June, 2 July, 9 July, 20 August
Francesca	University of Las Peñas (student)	In progress Chilean university degree	1980s	2005	5 July	
Reuel	University of Las Peñas (student)	In progress Chilean university degree	1980s	2005	7 July	
Lydia	University of Las Peñas (student)	In progress Chilean university degree	1980s	2005	8 July	
Renate	High school in Las Peñas (teacher)	Chilean university degree	1950s	2005	14 July	
Sofía	High school in Las Peñas (teacher)	Chilean university degree	1940s	2005	14 July	
Edith	University of Las Peñas (student)	In progress Chilean university degree	1980s	2005	14 July	
Maritza	University of Las Peñas (student)	In progress Chilean university degree	1980s	2005	14 July	
Tomás	University of Las Peñas (student)	In progress Chilean university degree	1980s	2005	15 July	

(Continued)

Pseudonym	Teaching/ learning context*	Level of education*	Birth decade, approximate	Year of research	Interview dates	Observation dates (8 hours per teacher total)
Javier	University of Las Peñas (professor)	US doctoral degree	1940s	2005	25 July	
Norma	University of Las Peñas (professor, director)	US Masters degree	1940s	2005	22 August	
Azucena	University of Las Peñas (instructor)	In progress online US Masters degree	1950s	2005	25 August	
Susanna	Farmington Community College (instructor)	US Masters degree	1960s	2005	23 September, 21 November	12 September, 14 September, 21 September, 23 September, 30 September, 3 October
Melinda	Farmington Community College (instructor)	US Masters degree	1950s	2005	9 November, 30 November	12 October, 21 October, 4 November, 18 November.
Veronica	High school in Farmington (teacher)	US teaching credential	1950s	2006	6 January	
Eric	Farmington Community College (instructor)	US Masters degree	1970s	2006	24 March, 31 March	6 February, 13 February, 27 February, 6 March
Alicia	High school in Las Peñas (teacher)	Chilean university degree	1980s	2006	10 July	
Diego	University of Las Peñas (instructor, student)	In progress Chilean Masters degree	1950s	2006	13 July	

Pseudonym	Teaching/ learning context*	Level of education*	Birth decade, approximate	Year of research	Interview dates	Observation dates (8 hours per teacher total)
Molly	University of California Davis (student)	In progress US Masters degree	1980s	2010	16 February, 30 July	
Charles	University of California Davis (student)	In progress US Masters degree	1980s	2010	17 February	
Martin	University of California Davis (student)	In progress US Masters degree	1980s	2010	3 March	
Linnea	University of California Davis (recent graduate)	US Masters degree	1980s	2010	8 April	
Jokwon	University of California Davis (student)	In progress US Masters degree	1980s	2010	15 April	

*At the time of interview.

Appendix 3: Interview Protocols

I rewrote protocols depending on the interview context, depending on whether I was conducting a first or second interview and depending on whether the interviewee was actively teaching at the time. By 2010, I had changed my interview questions to reflect my evolving research interests. Here are four sample protocols, edited only to replace names with pseudonyms.

(a) Questions for Chilean prospective teachers, University of Las Peñas, 2005
(b) Questions for my first interview with Susanna, Farmington Community College, 2005
(c) Questions for my second interview with Genaro, University of Las Peñas, 2005
(d) Questions for my interviews with prospective teachers at University of California Davis, 2010

Questions for Chilean Students

(1) Could you tell me about the language history of your family? What languages did/do your parents/grandparents speak? Did you have any experiences with languages other than your first language when you were a child? What attitudes about other languages and cultures did your parents or grandparents have? What did they tell you?

Me puede describir la historia de lenguas – que lenguas hablan sus padres o abuelos? Tenías alguna experiencia con idiomas o dialectos cuando era niño/a? Qué actitudes sobre otras lenguas y culturas tenían sus padres y abuelos? Qué te decían sobre otras lenguas y culturas?

(2) Could you tell me about your experiences of learning English? At what age did you begin learning? Why did you begin learning? How did you

feel about language learning? What were the classes like? What kinds of activities did you do in class? What do you remember about your teachers? What do you remember about your classmates and how they reacted to learning English? Did you learn British or North American English? What do you remember learning about the culture of English speaking countries?

Me puede describir tus experiencias de aprender inglés? A qué edad empezaste a aprender? Por qué? Cómo te sentías sobre la experiencia de aprender inglés? Cómo eran las clases? Qué tipo de actividades hacían en clase? Qúe recuerdas de tus maestros y compañeros de clase? Aprendiste el inglés británico o norteamericano? Qué recuerdas aprender sobre la cultura de países anglo-parlante?

(3)   What other experiences have you had with other cultures? Travel? Music? Literature or films? Television/radio? Internet? Food? Friends and acquaintances? How have these experiences affected your life? How have these experiences affected your attitude toward other cultures? In your cross-cultural experiences, what aspects of other cultures have most impressed you, either positively or negatively?

Qué otras experiencias tienes con otras culturas? Viajes? Música? Literatura? Películas? Televisión? Internet? Comida? Amigos o conocidos? Cómo te han afectado tu vida estas experiencias? En estas experiencias que aspectos de otras culturas más te han impresionado, en manera positiva o negativa?

(4)   What aspects of Chilean or Latin American culture do you particularly value? Have you traveled in Chile or other Latin American countries? What kind of cultural activities do you participate in in Spanish? What Spanish-language media do you watch, listen to, or read?

Para tí qué aspectos de la cultura chilena o latinoamericana tiene más valor? Has viajado en Chile o en otros paises Latinoamericanos? En que clase de actividades culturales participas en español? Qué música escuchas en español? Qué programas de televisión miras? Qué peliculas? Qué lees en español? Cómo usas el internet en español?

(5)   What is your understanding of the political, cultural and economic relations between Chile and English-speaking countries? How has your language learning experience been affected by these relations between countries?

Cómo me explicarías las relaciones politicas, culturales, y económicas entre Chile y los países anglo-parlantes? Cómo han afectado sus experiencias de aprender inglés, estas relaciones entre paises?

(6)   How would you define your own cultural identity? How has your cultural identity been affected by language learning?

Cómo te definirías tu propia identidad cultural? Cómo ha sido afectado por la experiencia de aprender idiomas?

(7) Why did you decide to major in English at the university? Describe your decision-making process. What are your professional goals? How have your family and friends reacted to your career decisions?

Por qué decidiste de especializar en inglés en la universidad? Me puedes describir tu proceso de tomar la decisión? Cuáles son tus metas profesionales? Cómo han reaccionado tu familia y amigos a tus decisiones de carrera?

(8) What do you see as the value of the English language teaching in Chile – why is it worthwhile/important/meaningful to be an English teacher in Chile?

Cómo me describirías el valor de la enseñanza de inglés en Chile? Por qué es importante o significante de ser maestro de inglés en Chile? Por qué tiene valor esta profesión?

(9) Is there a pseudonym that you would prefer?

Hay un pseudónimo que preferirías?

Questions for Susanna 23 September 2005 (First Interview)

Linguistic and Cultural Identities of English Language Teachers in Chile and California (first interview)

(1) Could you tell me about your linguistic background? What languages did/do your parents/grandparents speak? What language(s) was/were spoken in your home when you were a child? What experiences did you have with languages other than your first language when you were a child? What attitudes about other languages and cultures did your parents or grandparents have? What messages did they give you about learning and using other languages? What messages did they give you about other cultures?

(2) Could you tell me about your experiences of learning second languages? At what age did you begin learning? Why did you begin learning? How did you feel about language learning? If you were in a formal school setting, what were the classes like? What kinds of activities did you do in class? What do you remember about your teachers? What do you remember learning about the target language culture? If you were learning in an informal setting, describe the setting and how you learned in that setting. What aspects of the target language culture

really impressed you, either positively or negatively? How has language learning affected your life?

(3) What other experiences have you had with other cultures? Travel? Music? Literature or films? Television/radio? Internet? Food? Friends and acquaintances? How have these experiences affected your life? How have these experiences affected your attitude toward other cultures? In these cross-cultural experiences, what aspects of other cultures have most impressed you, either positively or negatively?

(4) What is your understanding of the political, cultural and economic relations between your country and the countr(ies) whose language(s) you have studied? How has your language learning experience been affected by these relations between countries?

(5) Why did you decide to become a language teacher? Describe your decision-making process. How did your family and friends react to your decision?

(6) Could you tell me about your language teaching experiences? Where have you taught, what kinds of classes? Describe the kinds of students you have had, and their attitudes toward the target language and culture. What are some of your favorite classroom activities, and why do you find these activities particularly useful? What are your goals as a language teacher? What are the central goals of the program in which you teach? What do you like about teaching in this program? What do you not like?

(7) What do you see as the value of your profession – why is it worthwhile/ important/meaningful to be an ESL teacher? Do you have any regrets about your decision to teach ESL?

(8) Under what circumstances do you considerate it appropriate for second language teachers to use their students' first language in the classroom? Please describe your experiences communicating with students in their first language(s) and in their second language(s). How do you handle communication difficulties? When have your students seemed to prefer to communicate with you in their first language? In their second language?

(9) How do you teach about the target language culture? How do you define culture? What aspects of the target language culture do you consider particularly important to include? Do you ask your students to compare their own culture with the target language culture? Why or why not? What aspects of the target language culture have particularly impressed your students positively or negatively? What kinds of experiences have your students had with the target language culture outside the classroom? In what way, if any, do you discuss these experiences in the classroom?

(10) How would you define your own cultural identity? How has your cultural identity been affected by language learning and teaching?

Questions for Genaro 26 July 2005
(Second Interview)

(1)   What experiences have you had with other cultures? Travel? Music? Literature or films? Television/radio? Internet? Food? Friends and acquaintances? How have these experiences affected your life? How have these experiences affected your attitude toward other cultures? In these cross-cultural experiences, what aspects of other cultures have most impressed you, either positively or negatively?

(2)   What aspects of Chilean or Latin American culture do you particularly value? Have you traveled in Chile or other Latin American countries? What kind of cultural activities do you participate in in Spanish? What Spanish-language media do you watch, listen to, or read?

(3)   How would you describe the political, cultural and economic relations between Chile and English-speaking countries? How has your language learning experience been affected by these relations between countries?

(4)   What do you see as the value of your profession – why is it worthwhile/ important/meaningful to be an English teacher in Chile? Do you have any regrets about your decision to teach English?

(5)   Under what circumstances do you considerate it appropriate for second language teachers to use their students' first language in the classroom? Please describe your experiences communicating with students in their first language(s) and in their second language(s).

(6)   In the following excerpts from my notes, how would you describe what is going on, from your perspective, in terms of teaching and learning about culture?

A. Marcela is a new student [in the professional development class]. She teaches English in _____, an Aymara village high in the altiplano. She said she has problems to come to classes here, she has worked there 6 years. It is a special experience, the weather is very hard. She apologized for not coming to classes before.

Genaro asked, 'how do you manage the weather in _____?'
Marcela replied, 'lots of clothes.'
Marco, I think, said 'drink.' This led to laughter.

Marcela added that she takes vitamins, natural vitamins. She said the houses are built using special metal things, it is warm in the house. Most of the houses are made of adobe.

Genaro asked me how do you say adobe in English, and I said 'adobe.' He said something about learning new vocabulary.

Marcela said, 'I don't have problems with cold except when I go to class early in the morning, the nights too. It's not advisable to go in this season, better to go in September. The days are sunny, better to enjoy the landscape.'

B. Genaro said, 'So when you have a short vacation what do you do?'

Marcela said, 'I like to work out at the gym. And I love reading also.'

Carlos said, 'I am going to receive some visitors from Santiago. So I am going to do some tourism...'

Genaro said, 'Some asados....'

Carlos agreed, 'A barbecue, a city tour, go to Tacna, we are going to have a good barbecue too.'

Genaro said, 'You are going to enjoy it.

C. The students were reading two examples of British letters of apology, one formal and one informal. Genaro asked, 'And what is the purpose of the second one?'

The students said, 'To apologize for being late to an appointment.'

Genaro asked, 'And the first one?'

A student replied, 'The same.'

Genaro asked, 'An appointment? Is it an appointment or a date?'

The student replied, 'date.'

Genaro asked, 'What is the relationship?'

One of the men replied, 'Very close. Because he says love.'

Genaro asked, 'What is the relationship in the second letter?'

Several students replied, 'Business, probably business.'

Genaro asked the rest of the class, 'Do you agree?'

They said yes.

Genaro reiterated, 'Business is the area.' He asked, 'How are the 2 letters different?'

A student replied, 'Specially in vocabulary, the first one is more informal and the second one he uses special words

D. Genaro next called on Renate, Marcela, and Sofía, and they got some paper to cover the transparency as the earlier students did. Their first letter read as follows:

Hi, Bob,

Please come and join us at Sally's birthday, so don't have a bit, 'cos we're going to have a barbecue. Try not to be hold up at work, and please, text this message to Peter and Mark.

Stay at my place at 7:00 sharp.

Love you,

And the second one said:

Dear Mr. Kent,

I would like to invite you to celebrate my birthday, Therefore, do not have a snack, because we will have a special dinner. Please, attempt not to be delayed at work.
Would you be so kind as to send a text message to inform Peter and Mark.
Come to my house at 7 o'clock next Friday.
Yours sincerely,

Genaro said, 'Let's look at the resources you used.' The students pointed out the contrast between 'I would like to invite you' and 'come and join us.' Also between 'don't have a snack because' and 'don't have a bite 'cos.' And between 'try not to be hold up at work' and 'please attempt not to be delayed.' Genaro commented that it was good use of vocabulary.

E. Genaro then said, 'We are going to do a different activity but closely linked. You will stay in the same groups, and the groups are going to hire teachers. Let's suppose you are principals or sostenedores, you are going to decide who is going to have a job and who is going to lose it. Find out what are your main topics of interest. If you are a sostenedor in a Catholic school you might want to know about his confession of faith or his position regarding controversial topics nowadays, lesbians, gays.'

A student added, 'Abortion.'

Genaro said, 'Yes, but I would like you to build up 5 different topics that you would be interested in. The second step is that you will interview someone. You will play the role of interviewers and interviewees.'

Marco said he would ask about politics.

Genaro said, 'OK, you could ask if he is enrolled in a political party.'

F. Then Genaro asked the class, 'Are you done? O.K. Now the second part. Try to think, try not to write down the questions. Think of them, discuss with your partner. For example, on the topic of religion I would like to know whether he would accept other people's beliefs on religious matters. Afterwards you will write the questions that you would ask the prospective candidate. For example, what I would like to find out is if he is enrolled in any political party, why would you want to ask this? Because it is better for his management of the students? I don't think so, but just in case.

G. Genaro said, 'Now Marco and Catalina, you are going to interview Renate and Carlos. Let's suppose that they want to get the job, so you are going to interview them. Ladies first, Renate it is your turn.'

Marco said, 'I am the headmaster here, I am interested in a person to teach our children. What do you think about divorce?'

Renate said, 'I believe in the family living together, both mother and father living together. But nowadays life has changed a lot, and everyday we see more and more people divorced and that affect our children very much, and I think there is nothing we can do to avoid it, we have to work and do our best with those children.'

[During the break Renate told me that she was a divorced single mother of teenagers].

H. The class had been talking about differences between men and women. Genaro asked, 'What do you think, Marcela?'

Marcela said, 'Women take a longer time to decide. Sometimes women are afraid to take a risk.'

Genaro asked, 'Why do you take a longer time to decide something?'

Sara replied, 'Yes, I agree with that. In some cases we are more passive and more quiet.'

Genaro asked, 'You are quieter than men?'

Sara said, 'In thinking, sometimes we take more time to reflect on those problems. We are more mature than men so we take more time.'

Genaro half-jokingly pointed out, 'I am not involved in the discussion, I am just posing questions. It is safer.'

Tania said, 'Sometimes we take longer because we have to think of the consequences.'

Genaro asked, 'We don't? They don't?'

I. Marco said, 'I think this has changed now. Maybe 20 or 30 years ago men were more machist. Is that the word?'

Several people including Genaro suggested 'chauvinist.'

Marco continued, 'Since 10 years ago, men are looking after children very very well, they are cooking very very well. The only difference is that you have the child in your bellies, that's the only different. Women are more conservative...'

Several students said, 'Traditional? I don't agree.'

Tania said, 'That's an image, but I don't agree, there are *some* that take care of children, some that clean, *some*.' [She was implying that most do not].

Marco said, 'Excuse me, listen to me. Conservative is not a bad word for me. Men are conservative as well, but women are naturally conservative, like in putting pictures, in painting.'

Genaro said, 'In such an activity, painting your house, men go straightforward, women think a little more.'

Luciana was agreeing

Genaro asked, 'Renate you want to add?'

Renate said, 'We as women are blamed for this chauvinism. Because we raise our boys in that way. We make everything for them instead of the girls. The girls are supposed to help their mother at home and the boys are supposed to...'

Marco suggested, 'Play football.'

Renate continued, 'Or take care of the garden. They are supposed to be outside. I have tried to change this with my son because as Marco said times change today. Maybe 100 years ago, 50 years ago men were supporters...'

Genaro corrected this as 'providers.'

Renate continued, 'Of the house, and women were supposed to be at home, but now with just one wage, a family cannot live, and they work both of them, and that's why both of them have to help in the house and with the children and that's why we have to change our concept of life.'

Genaro agreed, 'The goals and concepts are changing because society has changed.'

J. Marco said, 'I think women are stronger than we are because women can bear a child, we can't, women have better health and they live longer.'

Genaro said, 'That's a fact they live longer, you live longer.'

Carlos said, 'women are more _____.' [I couldn't hear the adjective].

A number of students shouted, 'no!'

Carlos said, 'They mislead men.'

Genaro repeated, 'So we are misled by girls. There are many explanations, but the fact is we need each other, we don't have any choice, we get to a sort of unity, that's a fact. But we must admit that the role of women and men has changed a lot these days, you can see men taking care of babies, changing diapers, but nevertheless, but why do men do that? Because they are forced, they have to provide the necessities because the wife is attending to business in order to help the family, so probably in the future we are going to die at more or less the same age. OK, let's continue.'

Interview Protocol (2010)

(1) Could you tell me about your linguistic background? What languages did/do your parents/grandparents speak? What language(s) was/were

spoken in your home when you were a child? What experiences did you have with languages other than your first language when you were a child? What attitudes about other languages and cultures did your parents or grandparents have? What messages did they give you about learning and using other languages? What messages did they give you about other cultures?

(2) Could you tell me about your experiences of bilingual development? At what age did you begin learning your second language (or have you always been bilingual)? Why did you begin learning? How did you feel about language learning? If you were in a formal school setting, what were the classes like? What kinds of activities did you do in class? What do you remember about your teachers? What do you remember learning about the target language culture? If you were learning in an informal setting, describe the setting and how you learned in that setting. What aspects of the target language culture really impressed you, either positively or negatively? How has language learning affected your life?

(3) What experiences have you had with cultures other than your own? In your neighborhood or workplace? In school when you were a student? Travel? Music? Literature or films? Television/radio? Internet? Food? Friends and acquaintances? How have these experiences affected your life? How have these experiences affected your attitude toward other cultures?

(4) Why did you decide to become an English teacher? Describe your decision-making process. How did your family and friends react to your decision?

(5) How would you describe the value of learning English as a Second Language in California today?

(6) How do you define bilingualism? Biculturalism? Biliteracy? Do you see yourself as a bilingual bicultural and/or biliterate person? Why or why not? Do you see bilingualism/biculturalism/ biliteracy as realistic goals for your students OR future students? Why or why not?

(7) Could you tell me about your language teaching experiences, if any? Where have you taught, what kinds of classes? Describe the kinds of students you have had, and their attitudes toward English. What are some of your favorite classroom activities, and why do you find these activities particularly useful for reaching your goals with your students?

(8) Under what circumstances do you considerate it appropriate for second language teachers to use their students' first language in the classroom? Please describe your experiences communicating with your own second

language teachers in your first and second languages. Please describe your experiences, if any, communicating with students in their first language(s) and in their second language(s).

(9)   For as long as you feel comfortable, up to several minutes, speak in your best second language – describe what you did last weekend.

Appendix 4: Quotes from TESOL Website 2012

TESOL's Mission (2012)

To advance professional expertise in English language teaching and learning for speakers of other languages worldwide

TESOL's Credo

Ideals we believe in as a professional community:

- Professionalism in language education
- Interaction of research and practice for educational improvement
- Accessible, high-quality instruction
- Respect for diversity, multilingualism and multiculturalism
- Respect for individual language rights
- Collaboration in a global community

TESOL's Core Values

- **Responsiveness:** A service orientation enabled by respectful listening and accountability to mission
- **Quality:** High standards and excellence characteristic of innovation and creativity in an academically rigorous environment
- **Collaboration:** Cooperation for the common good within a diverse, inclusive and culturally sensitive global community
- **Integrity:** Reputation as a trusted resource earned by ethical, honest, fair and transparent action http://www.tesol.org/s_tesol/sec_document. asp?CID = 218&DID = 220. Accessed 10 April 2012.

References

Abrams, Z.I. (2002) Surfing to cross-cultural awareness: Using internet-mediated projects to explore cultural stereotypes. *Foreign Language Annals* 35 (2), 141–160.

Achugar, M. (2008) Counter-hegemonic language practices and ideologies: Creating a new space and value for Spanish in Southwest Texas. *Spanish in Context* 5 (1), 1–19.

Allswang, J.M. (2000) *The Initiative and Referendum in California, 1898–1998*. Stanford, CA: Stanford University Press.

Alsup, J. (2006) *Teacher Identity Discourses: Negotiating Personal and Professional Spaces*. Mahwah, NJ: Lawrence Erlbaum.

Arnold, N. and Ducate, L. (2006) Future foreign language teachers' social and cognitive collaboration in an online environment. *Language Learning and Technology* 10 (1), 42–66.

Arrate, J. and Rojas, E. (2003) Las izquierdas en los gobiernos de transición: del primer gobierno de Concertación a la elección presidencial de Lagos. Capítulo 9 en *Memoria de la izquierda chilena, 1970–2000, Tomo II*. Santiago de Chile: Ediciones, 441–528.

Assaf, L.C. (2005) Exploring identities in a reading specialization program. *Journal of Literacy Research* 37 (2), 201–236.

Auerbach, E. (1992) *Making Meaning, Making Change: Participatory Curriculum Development for Adult ESL Literacy*. Washington, DC: Center for Applied Linguistics.

Baker-González, J. and Blau, E.K. (eds) (1995) *Building Understanding: A Thematic Approach to Reading Comprehension*. Boston: Addison-Wesley Longman.

Bakhtin, M. (1981) Discourse in the novel. In M. Holquist (ed.) and trans. C. Emerson and M. Holquist *The Dialogic Imagination: Four Essays by M.M. Bakhtin* (pp. 259–422). Austin: University of Texas Press.

Bakhtin, M. (1984) C. Emerson (ed. and trans.) *Problems of Dostoevsky's Poetics*. Minneapolis: University of Minnesota Press.

Bakhtin, M. (1986a) Response to a question from the *Novy Mir* editorial staff. In C. Emerson and M. Holquist (eds) and trans. V.W. McGee *The Problem of Speech Genres and Other Late Essays* (pp. 1–9). Austin: University of Texas Press.

Bakhtin, M. (1986b) The problem of speech genres. In C. Emerson and M. Holquist (eds) and trans. V.W. McGee *The Problem of Speech Genres and Other Late Essays* (pp. 60–102). Austin: University of Texas Press.

Bakhtin, M. (1990) M. Holquist and V. Liapunov (eds) and trans. and notes V. Liapunov *Art and Answerability: Early Philosophical Essays by M.M. Bakhtin*. Austin: University of Texas Press.

Bakhtin, M.M. (1993) M. Holquist and V. Liapunov (eds) and trans. and notes V. Liapunov *Toward a Philosophy of the Act*. Austin: University of Texas Press.

Bauman, R. and Briggs, C.L. (2003) *Voices of Modernity: Language Ideologies and the Politics of Inequality.* United Kingdom: Cambridge University Press.

Bell Lara, J. and López, D.L. (2007) The harvest of neoliberalism in Latin America. In R.A. Dello Buono and J. Bell Lara (eds) *Imperialism, Neoliberalism, and Social Struggles in Latin America* (pp. 17–35). Leiden and Boston: Brill.

Belz, J.A. (2002) Linguistic perspectives on the development of intercultural competence in tellecollaboration. *Language Learning and Technology* 7 (2), 68–99.

Blackledge, A. and Pavlenko, A. (2001) Negotiation of identities in multilingual contexts. *The International Journal of Bilingualism* 5 (3), 243–257.

Block, D. and Cameron, D. (eds) (2002) *Globalization and Language Teaching.* New York: Routledge.

Blommaert, J. (ed) (1999) *Language Ideological Debates.* Berlin and New York: Mouton de Goyer.

Blommaert, J. (2005) *Discourse.* Cambridge: Cambridge University Press.

Braine, G. (ed) (1999) *Non-Native Educators in English Language Teaching.* Mahwah, NJ: Lawrence Erlbaum.

Bronckart, J.-P. and Bota, C. (2011) *Bakhtine démasqué: histoire d'un menteur, d'une escroquerie et d'un délire collectif.* Geneve: Librairie Droz.

Bucholtz, M. and Hall, K. (2004) Language and identity. In A. Duranti (ed.) *A Companion to Linguistic Anthropology* (pp. 369–374). Oxford: Blackwell Publishing.

Bucholtz, M., Bermudez, N., Fung, V., Vargas, R. and Edwards, L. (2008) The normative North and the stigmatized South: Ideology and methodology in the perceptual dialectology of California. *Journal of English Linguistics* 36 (1), 62–87.

Buckley, L.C. (2000) A framework for understanding crosscultural issues in the English as a second language classroom. *The CATESOL Journal* 12 (1), 53–72.

Bureau of Labor Statistics (2011) State unemployment rates in 2010. www.bls.gov/opub/ted/2011/ted_20110301.htm (accessed 5 October 2012).

Byram, M. (1997) The intercultural dimension in 'language learning for European citizenship.' In M. Byram and G. Zarate (eds) *The Sociocultural and Intercultural Dimension of Language Learning and Teaching* (pp. 17–20). Strasbourg: Council of Europe Publishing.

Byram, M., Gribkova, B. and Starkey, H. (2002) Developing the intercultural dimension in language teaching. www.coe.int/t/dg4/linguistic/source/guide_dimintercult_en.pdf (accessed 5 October 2012).

California Department of Finance Demographic Research Unit (2007) Revised race/ethnic population estimates: Components of change for California counties – July 1970 to July 1990 /www.dof.ca.gov/research/demographic/reports/estimates/race-ethnic_1970–90/ (accessed 26 July 2011).

California Department of Finance Demographic Research Unit (2011) Census 2010 redistricting data: Table 3A – Total population by race (Hispanic exclusive) and Hispanic or Latino: 2010. www.dof.ca.gov/research/demographic/state_census_data_center/census_2010/view.php#DP (accessed 26 July 2011).

Canagarajah, A.S. (1993) Critical ethnography of a Sri Lankan classroom: Ambiguities in student opposition to reproduction through ESOL. *TESOL Quarterly* 27 (4), 601–626.

Canagarajah, A.S. (1999) *Resisting Linguistic Imperialism in English Teaching.* Oxford: Oxford University Press.

Caslin, K. (2012) 'I need more to learn': The effects of budget cuts on the English language learning opportunities of adult immigrants in Sacramento. Unpublished paper, University of California Davis.

Castro, P., Sercu, L. and Méndez García, M.C. (2004) Integrating language-and-culture teaching: an investigation of Spanish teachers' perceptions of the objectives of foreign language education. *Intercultural Education* 15 (1), 91–104.

Choi, P.K. (2003) 'The best students will learn English': Ultra-utilitarianism and linguistic imperialism in education in post-1997 Hong Kong. *Journal of Education Policy* 18 (6), 673–694.

Clarke, M. (2008) *Language Teacher Identities: Co-Constructing Discourse and Community*. Clevedon: Multilingual Matters.

Colimon, M.T. (1992) 'Encounter', translated by B. White. *The Literary Review* 35, 4.

Colimon, M.T. (2005) 'Encounter', translated by B. White. In S. Brown and M. McWatt (eds) *The Oxford Book of Caribbean Verse* (p. 59). Oxford: Oxford University Press.

Colimon Hall, M.T. (1995) 'Encounter'. In J. Baker-González and E.K. Blau (eds) *Building Understanding: A Thematic Approach to Reading Comprehension* (p. 26). Boston: Addison-Wesley Longman.

Cortazzi, M. and Jin, L. (1999) Cultural mirrors: Materials and methods in the EFL classroom. In Eli Hinkel (ed.) *Culture in Second Language Teaching and Learning* (pp. 196–219). Cambridge: Cambridge University Press.

Dalmau, M.S. (2009) Ideologies on multilingual practices at a rural Catalan school. *Sociolinguistic Studies* 3 (1), 37–60.

De Fina, A. (2003) *Identity in Narrative: A Study of Immigrant Discourse*. Amsterdam and Philadelphia: John Benjamins.

Demarais, A. (2004) 30-second success. *Reader's Digest*. www.rd.com/content/openContent.do?contentId = 27636. Available at www.ywca.org/atf/cf/%7BB037E5E8-5FE2-485D-94A5-0DA952A018C4%7D/FIRST_IMPRESSIONS.pdf (accessed 7 February 2012).

Dorfman, A. (1998) *Heading South, Looking North: A Bilingual Journey*. New York: Farrar, Straus, and Giroux.

Drake, P. and Jaksic, I. (1999) *El modelo chileno: Democracia y desarrollo en los noventa*. Santiago de Chile: Editorial LOM-ARCIS.

Duff, P. (2002) The discursive co-construction of knowledge, identity, and difference: An ethnography of communication in the high school mainstream. *Applied Linguistics* 23 (3), 289–322.

Duff, P.A. and Uchida, Y. (1997) The negotiation of teachers' sociocultural identities and practices in postsecondary EFL classrooms. *TESOL Quarterly* 31 (3), 451–486.

Dunn, C. (2006) Chile students continue challenging Bachelet government. *Santiag Times*, May 23. http://www.santiagotimes.cl/chile/politics/9170-CHILE-STUDENTS-CONTINUE-CHALLENGING-BACHELET-GOVERNMENT (accessed 8 September 2013).

Economist (2012) Progress and its discontents. *The Economist* 402 (8780), 45–47. www.search.ebscohost.com/login.aspx?direct=true&db=a9 h&AN=74287564&site=ehost-live (accessed 19 April 2012).

Edge, J. (2006) Background and overview. In J. Edge (ed.), *(Re-)Locating TESOL in an Age of Empire* (pp. xii–xix). Houndmills: Palgrave Macmillan.

Emerson, C. (1984) Editor's preface. In C. Emerson (ed. and trans.) *Problems of Dostoevsky's Poetics* (pp. xxix–xliii). Minneapolis: University of Minnesota Press.

Erickson, F. (1986) Qualitative methods in research on teaching. In M.C. Wittrock (ed.) *Handbook of Research on Teaching* (pp. 119–161). New York: Macmillan Publishing.

Eriksen, T.H. (1997) The nation as a human being—A metaphor in mid-life crisis? In K.F. Olwig and K. Hastrup (eds) *Siting Culture: The Shifting Anthropological Object* (pp. 103–122). London and New York: Routledge.

Fairclough, N. (1992) *Discourse and Social Change*. Cambridge: Polity Press.

Ferre, I., Garlikov, L., Oppenheim, K., Spoerry, S., Keck, K. and Whitbeck, H. (2006) Thousands march for immigrant rights: Schools, businesses feel impact as students, workers walk out. CNN, May 1. http://www.cnn.com/2006/US/05/01/immigrant.day/ (accessed 8 September 2013).

Foucault, M. (1984) The order of discourse [L'ordre du discours, 1971]. Reproduced in M. Shapiro (ed.) *Language and Politics* (pp. 108–138). New York: New York Press.

Freire, P. (1999) Trans. M.B. Ramos *Pedagogy of the Oppressed* (20th Anniversary edn). New York: Continuum Publishing.

Gal, S. (2005) Language ideologies compared: Metaphors of public/private. *Journal of Linguistic Anthropology* 15 (1) 23–37.

Galindo, R. and Olguín, M. (1996) Reclaiming bilingual educators' cultural resources: An autobiographical approach. *Urban Education* 31 (1), 29–56.

Gass, S., Mackey, A. and Pica, T. (1998) The role of input and interaction in second language acquisition. *Modern Language Journal* 82 (3), 299–307.

Godley, A.J., Carpenter, B.D. and Werner, C.A. (2007) 'I'll speak in proper slang': Language ideologies in a daily editing activity. *Reading Research Quarterly* 42 (1), 100–131.

Goldstein, F. (2012) Camila Vallejo: The world's most glamorous revolutionary. *New York Times*. www.nytimes.com/2012/04/08/magazine/camila-vallejo-the-worlds-most-glamorous-revolutionary.html?_r = 1&pagewanted = all%3Fsrc%3Dtp&smid = fb-share (accessed 12 September 2012).

Gómez-Barris, M. (2009) *Where Memory Dwells: Culture and State Violence in Chile*. Berkeley: University of California Press.

Guardado, M. (2009) Speaking Spanish like a boy scout: Language socialization, resistance, and reproduction in a heritage language scout troop. *The Canadian Modern Language Review* 66 (1), 101–129.

Guilherme, M. (2002) *Critical Citizens for an Intercultural World: Foreign Language Education as Cultural Politics*. Clevedon: Multilingual Matters.

Harklau, L. (1999) Representing culture in the ESL writing classroom. In E. Hinkel (ed.) *Culture in Second Language Teaching and Learning* (pp. 109–130). Cambridge: Cambridge University Press.

Hastrup, K. and Olwig, K.F. (1997) Introduction. In K.F. Olwig and K. Hastrup (eds) *Siting Culture: The Shifting Anthropological Object* (pp. 1–14). London and New York: Routledge.

Hawkins, S. (2008) Non-national Englishes and their alternatives: Academics and the internet in Tunisia. *International Journal of Multilingualism* 5 (4), 357–374.

Hershberg, E. and Rosen, F. (2006) Turning the tide? In E. Hershberg and F. Rosen (eds) *Latin America after Neoliberalism: Turning the Tide in the 21st Century?* (pp. 1–25). New York: New Press.

HoSang, D.M. (2009) *Racial Propositions: Ballot Initiatives and the Making of Postwar California*. Berkeley: University of California Press.

Hojman, D.E. (1992) *Chile: The Political Economy of Development and Democracy in the 1990s*. Pittsburgh, PA: University of Pittsburgh Press.

Holborow, M. (2012a) What is neoliberalism? Discourse, ideology, and the real world. In D. Block, J. Gray and M. Holborow (eds) *Neoliberalism and Applied Linguistics* (pp. 14–32). New York: Routledge.

Holborow, M. (2012b) Neoliberal keywords and the contradictions of an ideology. In D. Block, J. Gray and M. Holborow (eds) *Neoliberalism and Applied Linguistics* (pp. 33–55). New York: Routledge.

Holquist, M. (1981) Introduction. In M. Holquist (ed.) and trans. C. Emerson and M. Holquist *The Dialogic Imagination: Four Essays by M.M. Bakhtin* (pp. xv–xxxiii). Austin: University of Texas Press.

Holquist, M. (1986) Introduction. In C. Emerson and M. Holquist (eds) and trans. V.W. McGee *The Problem of Speech Genres and Other Late Essays* (pp. ix–xxiii). Austin: University of Texas Press.

Holquist, M. (1990) *Dialogism: Bakhtin and His World*. London and New York: Routledge.

Index Mundi (2012) Chile unemployment rate. www.indexmundi.com/chile/unemployment_rate.html (accessed 5 October 2012).

Irvine, J.T. and Gal, S. (2000) Language ideology and linguistic differentiation. In P. Kroskrity (ed.) *Regimes of Language: Ideologies, Polities, and Identities* (pp. 35–83). Santa Fe, NM: School of American Research Press.

Ivanic, R. (1998) *Writing and Identity: The Discoursal Construction of Identity in Academic Writing*. Amsterdam: John Benjamins Publishing Company.

Jacobson, R.D. (2008) *The New Nativism: Proposition 187 and the Debate Over Immigration*. University of Minnesota Press: Minneapolis.

Jeon, M. (2008) Korean heritage language maintenance and language ideology. *Heritage Language Journal* 6 (2), 54–71.

Kanno, Y. and Norton, B. (2003) Imagined communities and educational possibilities: Introduction. *Journal of Language, Identity, and Education* 2 (4), 241–249.

Katz, M.L.S. (1999) Discursive fault lines at work: A comparative ethnographic study of three workplace literacy programs serving immigrant women in the United States. Unpublished PhD dissertation, Graduate School of Education, University of California, Berkeley.

Koven, M. (2001) Comparing bilinguals' quoted performances of self and others in tellings of the same experience in two languages. *Language in Society* 30 (4), 513–558.

Kramsch, C. (1993) *Context and Culture in Language Teaching*. Oxford: Oxford University Press.

Kramsch, C. (1998) *Language and Culture*. Oxford: Oxford University Press.

Kramsch, C. (2005) Post 9/11: Foreign languages between knowledge and power. *Applied Linguistics* 26 (4), 545–567.

Kristeva, J. (1986) Trans. M. Waller with an introduction by L.S. Roudiez *Revolution in Poetic Language*. New York: Columbia University Press.

Kroskrity, P.V. (2000) Regimenting languages: Language ideological perspectives. In P. Kroskrity (ed.) *Regimes of Language: Ideologies, Polities, and Identities* (pp. 1–34). Santa Fe, NM: School of American Research Press.

Kroskrity, P. (2004) Language ideologies. In A. Duranti (ed.) *A Companion to Linguistic Anthropology* (pp. 496–517). Oxford: Blackwell Publishing.

Kubota, R. (1999) Japanese culture constructed by discourses: Implications for applied linguistic research and English language teaching. *TESOL Quarterly* 33 (1), 9–35.

Kubota, R. (2003) Unfinished knowledge: The story of Barbara. *College ESL* 10 (1&2), 11–21.

Kumaravadivelu, B. (2006) Dangerous liaison: Globalization, empire, and TESOL. In J. Edge (ed.) *(Re)Locating TESOL in an Age of Empire* (pp. 1–26). Houndmills: Palgrave Macmillan.

Kumaravadivelu, B. (2008) *Cultural Globalization and Language Education*. New Haven, CT: Yale University Press.

Lazaraton, A. (2003) Incidental displays of cultural knowledge in the nonnative-English speaking teacher's classroom. *TESOL Quarterly* 37 (2), 213–245.

Leeman, J. and Martinez, G. (2010) From identity to commodity: Ideologies of Spanish heritage language textbooks. *Critical Inquiry in Language Studies* 4 (1), 35–65.

Liaw, M.L. (2006) E-learning and the development of intercultural competence. *Language Learning and Technology* 10 (3), 49–64.

Lin, A. (1999) Doing-English-lessons in the reproduction or transformation of social worlds? *TESOL Quarterly* 33 (3), 393–412.

Loveman, B. (2001) *Chile: The Legacy of Hispanic Capitalism* (3rd edn). Oxford: Oxford University Press.

Luke, A. (2004) Teaching after the market: From commodity to cosmopolitan. *Teachers College Record* 106 (7), 1422–1443.

McKay, S.L. (2002) *Teaching English as an International Language: Rethinking Goals and Approaches*. Oxford: Oxford University Press.

McKay, S.L. (2003) Teaching English as an international language: The Chilean context. *English Language Teaching Journal* 57 (2), 139–148.

Mahler, D. (2012) Learning to listen: Student conceptualizations of culture within the English second language classroom. Unpublished paper, University of California Davis.

Mar-Molinero, C. (2000) *The Politics of Language in the Spanish-Speaking World*. New York: Routledge.

Markee, N. (2000) Some thoughts on globalization: A response to Warschauer. *TESOL Quarterly* 34 (3), 569–574.

Martelly, S. and Poujol Oriol, P. (2005) Marie-Thérèse Colimon Hall. www.lehman.cuny.edu/ile.en.ile/paroles/colimon-hall.html (accessed 18 April 2012).

Matejka, L. and Titunik, I.R. (1986) Translators' preface. *Marxism and the Philosophy of Language* (pp. vii–xii). Cambridge, MA: Harvard University Press.

Maybin, J. (1996) Story voices: The use of reported speech in 10–12-year-olds' spontaneous narratives. *Current Issues in Language and Society* 3 (1), 36–48.

Menard-Warwick, J. (2004) Identity and learning in the narratives of Latina/o immigrants: Contextualizing classroom practices in adult ESL. Unpublished PhD dissertation, Graduate School of Education, University of California, Berkeley.

Menard-Warwick, J. (2005) Transgression narratives, dialogic voicing and cultural change. *Journal of Sociolinguistics* 9 (4), 534–557.

Menard-Warwick, J. (2007) 'My little sister had a disaster, she had a baby': Gendered performance, relational identities, and dialogic voicing. *Narrative Inquiry* 17 (2), 279–297.

Menard-Warwick, J. (2008) The cultural and intercultural identities of transnational English teachers: Two case studies from the Americas. *TESOL Quarterly* 42 (4), 617–640.

Menard-Warwick, J. (2009a) *Gendered Identities and Immigrant Language Learning*. Clevedon: Multilingual Matters (Critical Language and Literacy series) www.multilingual-matters.com

Menard-Warwick, J. (2009b) Comparing protest movements in Chile and California: Interculturality in an Internet chat exchange. *Journal of Language and Intercultural Communication* 9 (2), 105–119.

Menard-Warwick, J. (2009c) Co-constructing representations of culture in ESL and EFL classrooms: Discursive faultlines in Chile and California. *The Modern Language Journal* 93 (1), 30–45.

Menard-Warwick, J. (2009d) The dad in the Che Guevara t-shirt: Narratives of Chilean English teachers. *Critical Inquiry in Language Studies* 5 (4), 243–264.
Menard-Warwick, J. (2011a) Chilean English teacher identity and popular culture: Three generations. *International Journal of Bilingual Education and Bilingualism* 14 (3), 261–277.
Menard-Warwick, J. (2011b) A methodological reflection on the process of narrative analysis: Alienation and identity in the life histories of English language teachers. *TESOL Quarterly* 45 (3), 564–574.
Menard-Warwick, J. (2013) 'The world doesn't end at the corner of their street': Language ideologies of Chilean English teachers. In V. Ramanathan (ed.) *Language Policy and (Dis)Citizenship: Rights, Access, Pedagogies* (pp. 73–91). Bristol: Multilingual Matters.
Menard-Warwick, J., Heredia-Herrera, A. and Soares Palmer, D. (in press) Local and global identities in an EFL Internet chat exchange. *Modern Language Journal*.
Milroy, J. (2001a) Language ideologies and the consequences of standardization. *Journal of Sociolinguistics* 5 (4), 530–555.
Milroy, L. (2001b) Britain and the United States: Two nations divided by the same language (and different language ideologies. *Journal of Linguistic Anthropology* 10 (1), 56–89.
Monzó, L.D. and Rueda, R. (2003) Shaping education through diverse funds of knowledge: A look at one Latina paraeducator's lived experiences, beliefs, and teaching practice. *Anthropology and Education Quarterly* 34 (1), 72–95.
Moonwomon-Baird, B. (2000) What do lesbians do in the daytime? Recover. *Journal of Sociolinguistics* 4, 348–378.
Moore, M. (2002) *Bowling for Columbine* (film). Dog Eat Dog Productions.
Morgan, B. (2004) Teacher identity as pedagogy: Towards a field-internal conceptualisation in bilingual and second language education. *International Journal of Bilingual Education and Bilingualism* 7 (2–3), 172–188.
Moulián, T. (1997) *Chile Actual: Anatomía de un mito*. Santiago de Chile: Editorial LOM Universidad ARCIS.
Nemtchinova, E. (2005) Host teachers' evaluations of nonnative-English-speaking teacher trainees – A perspective from the classroom. *TESOL Quarterly* 39 (2), 235–261.
Niño-Murcia, M. (2003) English is like the dollar: Hard currency ideology and the status of English in Peru. *World Englishes*, 22 (2), 121–142.
Norton, B. (2000) *Identity and Language Learning: Gender, Ethnicity and Educational Change*. Harlow: Pearson Education Limited.
Ochs, E. (1993) Constructing social identity: A language socialization perspective. *Research on Language & Social Interaction* 26 (3), 287–306.
Ochs, E. and Capps, L. (1996) Narrating the self. *Annual Review of Anthropology* 25, 19–43.
O'Dowd, R. (2003) Understanding the 'other side': Intercultural learning in a Spanish-English e-mail exchange. *Language Learning and Technology* 7 (2), 118–144.
Olivo, W. (2003) 'Quit talking and learn English!': Conflicting language ideologies in an ESL classroom. *Anthropology and Education Quarterly* 34 (1), 50–71.
Paige, R.M, Jorstad, H.L., Siaya, L., Klein, F. and Colby, J. (2003) Culture learning in language education: A review of the literature. In D.L. Lange and R.M. Paige (eds) *Culture as the Core: Perspectives on Culture in Second Language Learning* (pp. 173–236). Greenwich, CT: Information Age Publishing.
Park, J.S.Y. and Bae, S. (2009) Language ideologies in educational migration: Korean jogi yuhak families in Singapore. *Linguistics and Education* 20, 366–377.
Pavlenko, A. and Lantolf, J. (2000) Second language learning as participation and the (re) construction of selves. In J.P. Lantolf (ed.) *Sociocultural Theory and Second Language Learning* (pp. 155–177). Oxford: Oxford University Press.

Pennycook, A. (1994) *The Cultural Politics of English as an International Language*. London and New York: Longman.

Pennycook, A. (2010) Rethinking origins and localization in global Englishes. In M. Saxena and T. Omoniyi (eds) *Contending with Globalization in World Englishes* (pp. 196–210). Bristol: Multilingual Matters.

Phan, L.H. (2008) *Teaching English as an International Language: Identity, Resistance and Negotiation*. Clevedon: Multilingual Matters.

Phillips, J.K. (2003) National standards for foreign language learning. In D.L. Lange and R.M. Paige (eds) *Culture as the Core: Perspectives on Culture in Second Language Learning* (pp. 161–171). Greenwich, CT: Information Age Publishing.

Phillipson, R. (1992) *Linguistic Imperialism*. Oxford: Oxford University Press.

Pomerantz, A. (2002) Language ideologies and the production of identities: Spanish as a resource for participation in a multilingual marketplace. *Multilingua* 21 (2–3), 275–302.

PROChile (2007) Estadísticas de comercio exterior. www.prochile.cl/index.php (accessed 30 April 2007).

Qureshi, L.Z. (2009) *Nixon, Kissinger, and Allende: US Involvement in the 1973 Coup in Chile*. Plymouth: Lexington Books.

Ramanathan, V. (2005) *The English-Vernacular Divide: Postcolonial English Politics and Practice*. Clevedon: Multilingual Matters.

Rice, R.B., Bullough, W.A. and Orsi, R.J. (2002) *The Elusive Eden: A New History of California* (3rd edn). Boston: McGraw-Hill.

Riessman, C. (2008) *Narrative Methods for the Human Sciences*. Thousand Oaks, CA: Sage Publications.

Risager, K. (2007) *Language and Culture Pedagogy: From a National to a Transnational Paradigm*. Clevedon: Multilingual Matters.

Rivera, C. (2012) Santa Monica College to offer two-tier course pricing. *Los Angeles Times*, March 14, 2012. www.latimes.com/news/local/la-me-college-classes-20120314, 0,5085401.story (accessed 19 April 2012).

Rohter, L. (2004) Learn English, says Chile, thinking upwardly global. *New York Times*, December 29.

Ros i Solé, C. (2003) Culture for beginners: A subjective and realistic approach for adult language learners. *Language and Intercultural Communication* 3 (2), 141–150.

Ryan, P.M. (1998) Cultural knowledge and foreign language teachers: A case study of a native speaker of English and a native speaker of Spanish. *Language, Culture, and Curriculum* 11 (2), 135–153.

Ryan, P.M. (2003) Foreign language teachers and their role as mediators of language-and-culture: A study in Mexico. *Estudios de Lingüística Aplicada* 37, 99–118.

Savignon, S. (1983) *Communicative Competence*. Reading, MA: Addison Wesley Publishing.

Savignon, S.J. and Sysoyev, P.V. (2002) Sociocultural strategies for a dialogue of cultures. *The Modern Language Journal* 86 (4), 508–524.

Seargeant, P. (2008) Language, ideology, and 'English within a globalized context. *World Englishes* 27 (2), 217–232.

Sellami, A. (2006) Slaves of sex, money, and alcohol: (Re-)locating the target culture of TESOL. In J. Edge (ed.) *(Re-)Locating TESOL in an Age of Empire* (pp. 171–194). Houndmills: Palgrave Macmillan.

Sercu, L. (2006) The foreign language and intercultural competence teacher: The acquisition of a new professional identity. *Intercultural Education* 17 (1), 55–72.

Starr, K. (2004) *Coast of Dreams: California on the Edge, 1990–2003*. New York: Alfred A. Knopf.

Statistical Abstract of the United States (2012) Languages spoken at home by state, 2009. www.census.gov/compendia/statab/2012/tables/12s0054.pdf (accessed 25 September 2012).

Tallman, A.M. (2005) Written testimony regarding the nomination of John G. Roberts, Jr. as Chief Justice of the United States of America. www.judiciary.senate.gov/hearings/testimony.cfm?id = e655f9e2809e5476862f735da10a61d3&wit_id = e655f9 e2809e5476862f735da10a61d3-3-4 (accessed 5 October 2012).

Talmy, S. (2004) Forever FOB: The cultural production of ESL in a high school. *Pragmatics* 14 (2), 149–172.

TESOL (2007) Vision statement. www.tesol.org/s_tesol/sec_document.asp?CID=218& DID=220 (accessed 30 May 2007).

TESOL (2012) TESOL's mission. www.tesol.org/s_tesol/sec_document.asp?CID=218& DID=220 (accessed 10 April2012).

Turiel, E. (1999) Conflict, social development, and cultural change. In E. Turiel (ed.) *Development and Cultural Change: Reciprocal Processes* (pp. 77–92). San Francisco: Jossey Bass.

United States Trade Representative (2003) US and Chile sign historic free trade agreement. www.ustr.gov/archive/Document_Library/Press_Releases/2003/June/ United_States_Chile_Sign_Historic_FreeTrade_Agreement.html (accessed 5 October 2012).

Urciuoli, B. (2008) Whose Spanish? The tension between linguistic correctness and cultural identity. In M. Niño-Murcia and J. Rothman (eds) *Bilingualism and Identity: Spanish at the Crossroads with Other Languages* (pp. 257–278). Amsterdam and Philadelphia: John Benjamins Publishing Company.

Valdés, G., González, S.V., López García, D. and Márquez, P. (2003) Language ideology: The case of Spanish in departments of foreign languages. *Anthropology and Education Quarterly* 34 (1), 3–26.

van Dijk, T.A. (1998) *Ideology: A Multidisciplinary Approach*. London, England: Sage Publications.

Varghese, M., Morgan, B., Johnston, B., and Johnson, K. (2005) *Journal of Language, Identity, and Education* 4 (1), 21–44.

Vitanova, G. (2005) Authoring the self in a non-native language: A dialogic approach to agency and subjectivity. In J.K. Hall, G. Vitanova and L. Marchenkova (eds) *Dialogue with Bakhtin on Second and Foreign Language Learning* (pp. 149–169). Mahwah, NJ: Lawrence Erlbaum.

Vitanova, G. (2010) *Authoring the Dialogic Self: Gender, Agency and Language Practices*. Amsterdam and Philadelphia: John Benjamins.

Vogt, K. (2006) Can you measure attitudinal factors in intercultural communication? Tracing the development of attitudes in e-mail projects. *ReCALL* 18 (2), 153–173.

Voloshinov, V.N. (1986) *Marxism and the Philosophy of Language*. Cambridge, MA: Harvard University Press.

Wallerstein, N. (1983) *Language and Culture in Conflict*. Menlo Park, CA: Addison Wesley.

Ware, P.D. and Kramsch, C. (2005) Toward an intercultural stance: Teaching German and English through telecollaboration. *The Modern Language Journal* 89 (2), 190–205.

Warriner, D.S. (2007) Language learning and the politics of belonging: Sudanese women refugees Becoming and Being 'American'. *Anthropology & Education Quarterly* 38 (4), 343–359.

Watson-Gegeo, K.A. (1988) Ethnography in ESL: Defining the essentials. *TESOL Quarterly,* 22 (4), 575–592.

Weisman, E.M. (2001) Bicultural identity and language attitudes: Perspectives of four Latina teachers. *Urban Education* 36 (2), 203–225.

Wenger, E. (1998) *Communities of Practice: Learning, Meaning & Identity.* Cambridge: Cambridge University Press.

Wesche, M. (2004) Teaching languages and cultures in a post-9/11 world. *Modern Language Journal* 88 (2), 278–285.

White, P.R.R. (2003) Beyond modality and hedging: A dialogic view of the language of intersubjective stance. *Text* 23 (2), 259–284.

Whitener, W. (2012) A situated inquiry into English and globalization in Santiago, Chile: Linguistic landscapes and language policies. Unpublished paper, University of California Davis.

Wiley, T.G. and Lukes, M. (1996) English-Only and Standard English ideologies in the U.S. *TESOL Quarterly* 30 (3), 511–535.

Williams, S. (2012) I say 'I do': Performing and positioning the self in discourse on wedding vows. Unpublished paper, University of California Davis.

Woolard, K. (1989) Sentences in the language prison: The rhetorical structuring of an American language policy debate. *American Ethnologist* 16 (2), 268–278.

Woolard, K.A. (1998) Introduction: Language ideology as a field of inquiry. In B. Schieffelin, K.A. Woolard and P.V. Kroskrity (eds) *Language Ideologies: Practice and Theories* (pp. 3–47). Oxford: Oxford University Press.

Wortham, S. (2001) Language ideology and educational research. *Linguistics and Education* 12 (3), 253–259.

Zarate, G. (1997) Introduction. In M. Byram and G. Zarate (eds) *The Sociocultural and Intercultural Dimension of Language Learning and Teaching* (pp. 7–14). Strasbourg: Council of Europe Publishing.

Zentella, A.C. (2008) Preface. In M. Niño-Murcia and J. Rothman (eds) *Bilingualism and Identity: Spanish at the Crossroads with Other Languages* (pp. 3–10). Amsterdam and Philadelphia: John Benjamins Publishing Company.

Author Index

Topic Index